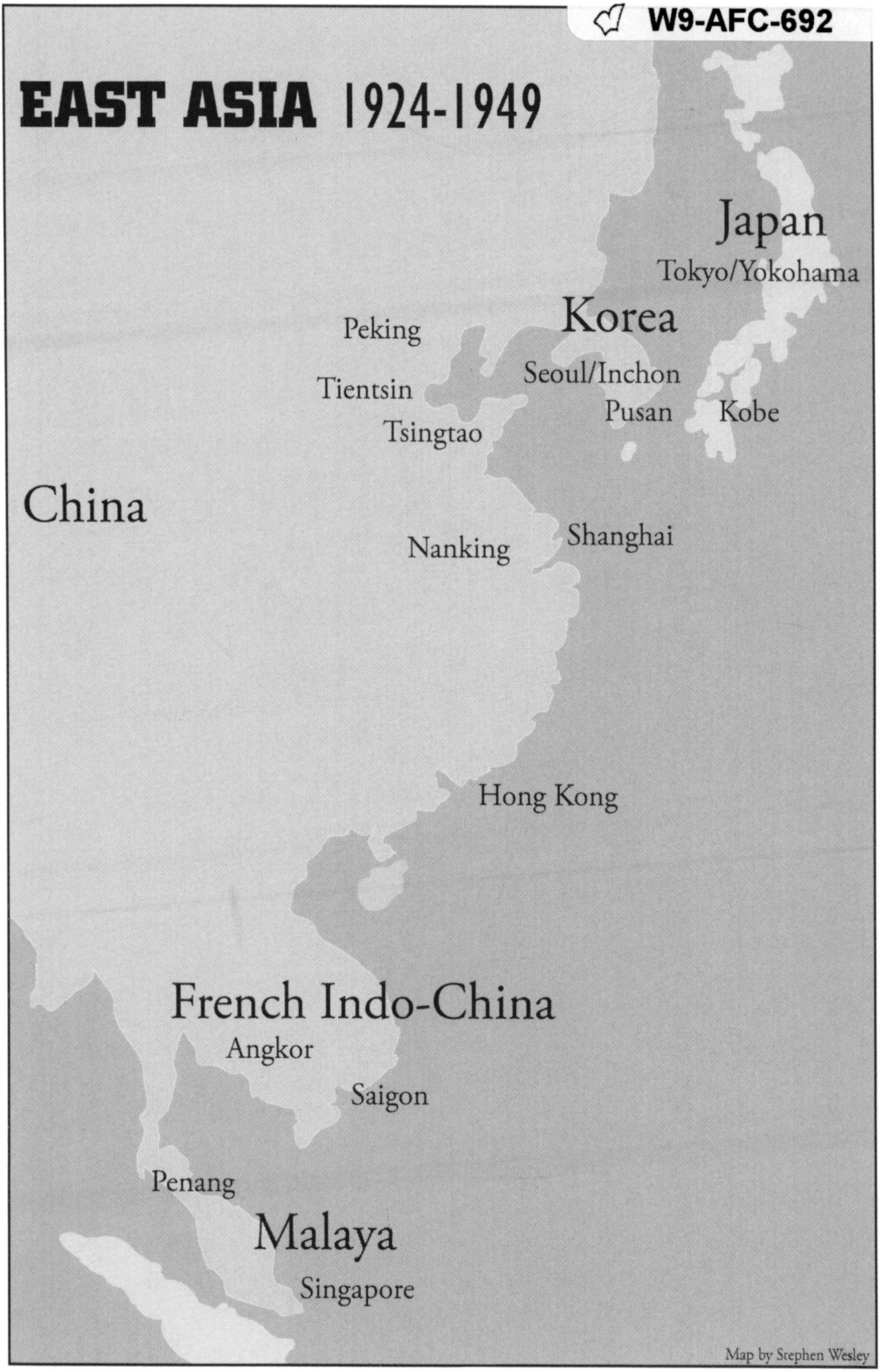

EAST ASIA 1924-1949

Japan

Tokyo/Yokohama

Korea

Peking

Seoul/Inchon

Tientsin

Pusan

Kobe

Tsingtao

China

Shanghai

Nanking

Hong Kong

French Indo-China

Angkor

Saigon

Penang

Malaya

Singapore

Map by Stephen Wesley

I explain to the captain of the President Taft *how to steer the ship.*

MY *FIRST* NINE LIVES

Full Value Received

John Stauffer Potter

2012

BY JOHN STAUFFER POTTER

The Treasure Diver's Guide

The Treasure Divers of Vigo Bay

ISBN-13: 978-1480016699 · ISBN-10: 1480016691

jspotterjr@yahoo.com · P.O. Box 1475, Oak Bluffs, MA 02557

Contact: www.patricialucechapman.com

Maps © 2012 Stephen Wesley

Designed by Janet Holladay, Tisbury Printer

Martha's Vineyard, Massachusetts, USA

Table of Contents – *Highlights*

Dedicated to those rare and restless few who, responding to the call of adventure, jettison the humdrum lifestyle of the pollywog to reach out and taste the excitement of new challenges!

See pollywog story on 236...

Preface

WILLEM VAN BEVEREN WAS A CHARACTER from another era let loose in the British Crown Colony of Hong Kong in the early 1950s. He was medium height, with graying hair and a slightly dissolute appearance that some women find fascinating. His English was fluent, spoken with a cultured European accent. As the charming, debonair managing director of a prominent American shipping and trading firm, he should have been welcomed at all the official and social functions. But he wasn't. In fact, he was ostracized by many of Hong Kong's English elite. It didn't take me long to learn why.

Wimpy, as he was called, loved to drink Dutch gin. If this were not available, he would drink English gin, Russian vodka, Chinese *pai gar* or anything else that came in a bottle with a seal. A few years earlier he was a popular fixture in Hong Kong Then, one afternoon, he had found the gin excellent at the annual Queen's birthday party to which the Governor invited the cream of Hong Hong's government officials and business taipans, with their wives, to toast Her Majesty. Just as His Excellency raised his glass "To the Queen!" Wimpy–who had been surveying the ladies around him–pronounced loudly that the shortage of house maids in England was because they were all in Hong Kong married to government officials and taipans.

I start my story with this introduction to Wimpy because, during the half year before I fell from his good graces, he helped define my goal for a full life. He was then my boss in Hong Kong. He was also the shrewdest and most devious businessman I have ever learned from. And learn I did, about all sorts of machinations they don't teach you at business school–but also to tread cautiously when evaluating any financial dealings with him.

Despite this I, like many others whom he called friends, had a real fondness for Wimpy. And his initial guarded welcome for me grew to genuine affection after I was lucky enough to nail a business deal that netted him a fat personal commission on the company's profits.

Every Thursday Wimpy took me to lunch at the Parisian Grill, probably the finest restaurant in Asia at that time. We would start with a double martini. Then Wimpy would have another double martini while I sampled an *hors d'oeuvre.* As I dug into my steak *au poivre*, he would continue his liquid diet. About that time the conversation became one-sided, as Wimpy repeated well-worn tales of a turbulent life that would have bewildered even Somerset Maugham.

Twice, he had made a multi-million dollar fortune as a sugar broker in Indonesia–or Yaava, as he pronounced Java. After accumulating each fortune, he would repair to Monte Carlo, where he succeeded in going broke during a blissful year or two of drink, gambling and women.

His adventures challenged my credulity, but were probably true. These were crowned by his finest achievement of all: "John," he would boast. "I caught the clap four times when I was in Batavia. And each time I had to take the *verdomde* cure." He then described in detail the excruciating treatment for gonorrhea before penicillin–too horrible to repeat here.

Along about coffee time, Wimpy would sadden and moan that he was dying of cancer (he died years later of alcohol-related causes). Then, suddenly, he brightened and leaned toward me. "But I am ready to go!" he would announce. "When I meet Saint Peter and he hands me a pen and paper, I will write 'Full value received' and sign Willem van Beveren!" He emphasized this with a majestic sweep of his arm across the table to underline his name, scattering glasses, plates and everything else as waiters came scurrying and other diners stared in awe.

I am often reminded of Wimpy's words, "full value received," as my own life path leads me into one exciting adventure after another. I hope you will enjoy sharing these as you travel the world with me in the following pages and meet a galaxy of people I have known. Most are introduced with their correct names; others by pseudonyms. Whether famous, or infamous, all are stimulating and help to bring the satisfaction of full value into my own life.

The title's reference to "My Nine Lives" derives from a period, years after this story, when I was selling Eveready batteries overseas. Our then-famous logo was a cat jumping through the number nine, to relate the long-lasting quality of our product with the nine lives of a cat.

John S. Potter
Martha's Vineyard
2012

PROLOGUE

The Train

1950

THE THREE UNIFORMED MEN had been waiting for me the previous afternoon when I was marched into the guardhouse and shoved rudely against their table. Red stars on their caps identified them as communists, probably officers. They leaned forward, eyeing me curiously. Their first demand, in Mandarin Chinese, came like a rifle shot: "Who were you spying for in Tsingtao?"

Spying? I was stunned. While I struggled to make a safe reply the second interrogator angrily slapped the wood table. "Answer the question!"

Could they actually think I was an enemy spy? I felt stirrings of anger. Then, as the reality of my situation took over, I knew that they really *did* look on me as an enemy spy! Or, more frightening, they could be setting me up to be accused of espionage. I must be very careful in my response. Thinking hard, I replied slowly in Mandarin, "I have been working with your port officers in Tsingtao unloading cargo from our damaged ship. I was the only–"

"Lie! You lie! You are America Navy spy!"

Another shock. American Navy? Where the hell did they get this, out here in the middle of China? Who were they? My mind raced for answers. True, my trip had been publicized before I left Shanghai three weeks earlier, in early January, 1950, but only in connection with my assignment.

Struggling to control rising fear, I protested, "You know I am not a spy. I am a businessman. I work with the Pattison Company in Shanghai. We represent the damaged *Flying Arrow* freight ship, which ran to Tsingtao port when the Kuo Min Tang Nationalist Navy set it on fire. We are working with you!"

"That is lie! You are the American dog that runs all over China digging for secrets. You went to Tsingtao to meet your spy agents there. You learned Chinese to talk with them. We know everything. Confess!"

A dog digging for secrets? How could I reason with that? In desperation, I exclaimed, "But your government gave me permission to make this trip. You have my travel documents to prove this!"

And I no longer had them. These precious documents, covered with Chinese characters and seals, had been taken from me with my briefcase when my train was halted near this country village. I had been shaken awake from my exhausted sleep by a platoon of armed soldiers and–protesting angrily–handed my coat and nudged firmly down the carriage steps. Then marched, block by block, along a narrow cobblestone road into the village.

Despite my exhaustion from many days of hard negotiations with the hostile Communists controlling Tsingtao, the icy January weather snapped me wide awake. Over and over the same question raced through my mind: what was so urgent to the Communist military that they would stop the important Tsingtao-to-Shanghai express train in the middle of China to pull me off?

I became aware of sounds from my military guard close behind. As they marched, the soldiers were chanting in cadence: "*Mei Guo, di guo, Mei Guo, di guo.*" I recognized this as: "American imperialist, American imperialist" and wondered what this meant. Then, in a sobering revelation, I realized they were referring to me! With a touch of gallows humor I thought how little I felt like an imperialist–American or otherwise. Then I noticed the local villagers, and even their mangy dogs, scampering away, terrified, as I approached. Any lingering vestige of humor, which I had clung to, was quickly swept away.

I nearly tripped over the uneven cobblestones and remembered that my marching guards were carrying tommy guns. I glanced back. Just a few yards behind me, chanting soldiers were cradling their weapons, barrels swinging loosely around, pointed more or less in my direction. If one stumbled and pulled the trigger on a chambered gun…

Our march had ended at the door of the guardhouse, and I was guided into the plain wooden structure. The walls were plastered with glamorized pictures of Chairman Mao and happy communist soldiers leering down at me.

There was no furniture except one table and a few wood chairs. Three, across the table, were occupied by soldiers. Their questions kept hammering me all afternoon. At some point the interrogators were replaced by a new team. Night fell and a single dim light bulb flickered on. Still they came at me, hour after hour, repeating accusations, demanding answers, always more threatening. I was startled to hear one suddenly demand: "What secret papers did you give the captain on your spy boat in Tsingtao?"

I could think of no way to answer and remained silent. My legs began to shake as I struggled to stand. Time and again I started to fold, but was rudely prodded back to my feet with a rifle butt. After an eternity the darkness outside the window turned to winter gray. Dawn had come and now they were shouting at me. How long had my inquisition been going on? I couldn't concentrate. My accusers had long ago morphed into faceless blurs in padded jackets and those damn red stars, jabbing questions at me, more and more demanding. They had given me one cup of water and a bowl of rice, and a soldier had escorted me to a hole-in-the-floor urinal.

As more light filtered in, I could make out faces and saw rising anger. I realized that my responses–still polite but passive–might soon bring this interrogation to a new stage. Prison? Or worse? There were rumors in Shanghai about bamboo splints being hammered under fingernails, and I remembered Dad's old friend General Henry Chow, still crazed years after the Japanese had extracted his fingernails. With a sick feeling, I wondered how I would react.

Or would I join the missing American I had heard about, rumored to be in solitary confinement? Since all diplomatic relations were severed, no one had been able to learn where he might be. An awful thought crept in: would my family ever find out what had happened to me?

Clearly my inquisitors were trying to coerce me into admitting some form of espionage, and they were in a hurry. Before my interrogation reached a new stage, I had to make an all out effort to save myself.

It was then that I made my decision. My best hope would be to give them a broad statement covering all of my activities that might interest them. While avoiding anything confidential, everything I said must be plausible, without seeming to leave out anything. My hope was that somewhere in this "confession" I would hit upon something they wanted me to disclose where I could prove my innocence. From their statements and questions I had to assume they knew more about me than I had thought–perhaps even information taken from records in our former naval attaché's office in Shanghai. After their next angry accusation, I took several deep breaths, forced myself out of my stupor, and launched my strategy. I spoke in slow, measured Mandarin:

"You have mentioned Navy intelligence and you are correct." Their heads popped forward with surprise. "Yes, in our war with Japan, I was indeed in American naval intelligence. My rank was lieutenant. During the war I studied Mandarin at a language school in America. The purpose was not to spy. It was to prepare me to come to China and be able to communicate with soldiers in your eighth route army, who also speak Mandarin, as we worked together as allies and fought arm-in-arm to destroy our common enemy, the imperialist Japanese military who had done so much harm to both our countries and people.

"I could not come because my orders to join your forces were cancelled as soon as our countries won our war against the imperialist Japanese. I was quickly released from the Navy and returned to finish Harvard school. I can use my Mandarin now where this dialect is spoken for business, like in Tsingtao.

"When our cargo vessel, *Flying Arrow*, was set on fire by the Kuo Min Tang Nationalist Navy and took refuge there, my Shanghai office was told that anyone sent to help unload the cargo must speak the local dialect, Mandarin. The other shipping managers in our office are Shanghai people and speak only Shanghai dialect, so because I speak Mandarin, I was sent. I supervised the unloading of thousands of tons of badly needed cargo into China.

"I have worked very hard for two weeks, with no rest, doing this job. I am very tired. But I will try to answer any other questions you have for me, and I will answer them truthfully. I believe you are convinced now that I am sincere and that my efforts have been helpful to your country. I hope you will let me go to my home in Shanghai. You have my passport and can always get me there if you wish."

They listened impassively. I leaned against the table to steady myself, pleading silently for a favorable reply. Then one of them responded: "Name your contact in our army."

The bastard! I wanted to kill him. Taking a deep breath, I tried to explain that I had no contact because the war ended before I reached China. He ignored this. "You lie! You went to Tsingtao to spy on our troops and send information on your boat."

My God! Could they still believe this? I had run out of options and did the only thing I could think of doing: "I was indeed in American Navy intelligence. My rank was lieutenant…" and repeated my "confession" until angrily shouted down.

They tried again. No longer able to think, I could only cling to my strategy and repeat, "Yes. In our war with Japan, I was indeed in Navy intelligence…" By then I was so exhausted that I no longer cared what happened. I was probably babbling incoherently most of the time.

Somewhere in the blur I saw my interrogators walk away, silently. Then the platoon leader–if that was his title–helped me to my feet and into a waiting rickshaw. I recalled bouncing over the cobblestones as he accompanied me back to the train.

The train? The ancient first-class *wagon-lit* carriage was still there! I studied my watch dial but could not concentrate. My minder helped me: "Your train has waited here 15 hours." Then he helped me up to my old seat, still empty, returned my briefcase and left. As the train started, the other passengers, who had studiously kept their faces turned away, looked at me with expressions of relief and sympathy. Several offered me cakes, which I accepted gratefully.

I slipped away into a deep sleep, overwhelmed with relief, scarcely believing that this was really happening. My last thoughts were of these other poor passengers waiting all those hours on their wooden seats without knowing when their train would leave, and afraid to ask.

At some point on the trip I came awake as we roared through a tunnel. Despite the windows being closed against the winter cold, wisps of soot from the coal burning locomotive had swept back into my face. The charcoal smell evoked memories of happy times, well before I had reached my teens. On many summers I had traveled on this train, perhaps in this same carriage, while Mother brought my little sister Patty and me back from our beach resort near Tsingtao to our home in Shanghai. It amused us kids to watch her muttering in frustration as she opened and closed our compartment window, searching for the right balance between fresh air and dirty soot.

In those days the ride had been quite different. Our carriage was new and tastefully decorated, with comfortable beds in our compartment and European meals served in the adjacent dining car. Our baby amah, Chau Queh, came with us. She had been an inseparable part of our family since 1924, when Mother brought me back on a Dollar Line passenger ship after my birth in California. A slender woman less than five feet tall, her round, pock-marked face featuring a brilliant gold tooth shining through a perpetual smile, Chau Queh was truly a second mother.

Our home–although across the Pacific–was still very American. It was located in China because my parents were explorers. Dad, born near Pittsburgh, Pennsylvania, traveled to the Philippines in 1903 at the age of 19 to join the Thomasite teaching organization. After a dozen years educating the Luzon Filipinos, he moved to Shanghai to become an officer of an American development company. Later, he added directorships in other companies and became a popular member of many clubs.

Mother took up journalism as a young lady in California and had become "the girl reporter" on the *Los Angelos Herald,* when, at age 22, she jumped at the chance to go overseas with the International News Service as their first American lady war correspondent. She soon became popular with Chinese and foreigners alike and was invited to the city's exclusive clubs. It was at a Casino Night in one of the clubs that she met Dad. They were married in 1922. I was born two years later, followed by Patricia in 1924.

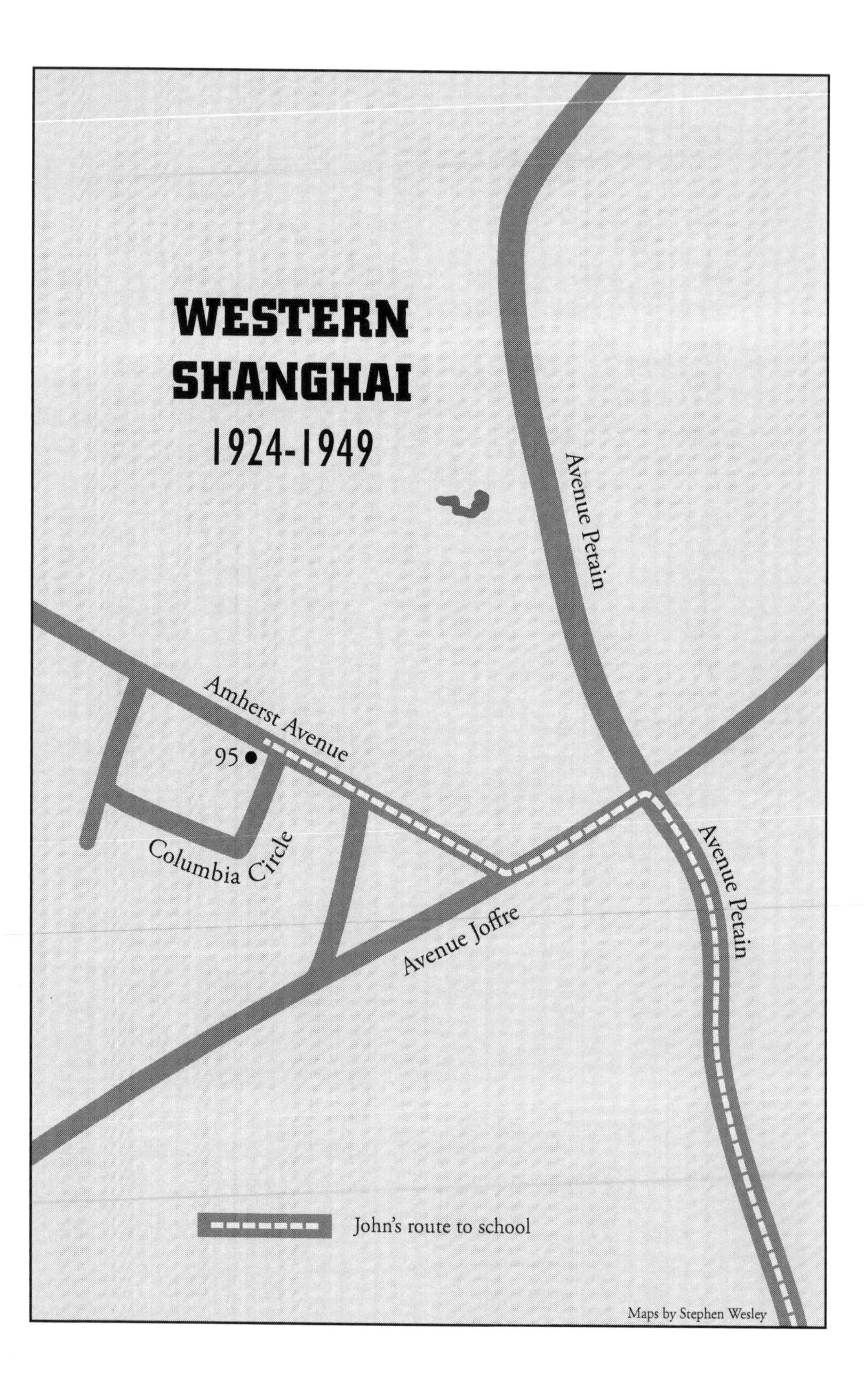

WESTERN
SHANGHAI
1924-1949
Avenue Petain
Amherst Avenue
95
Columbia Circle
Avenue Joffre
Avenue Petain
John's route to school
Maps by Stephen Wesley

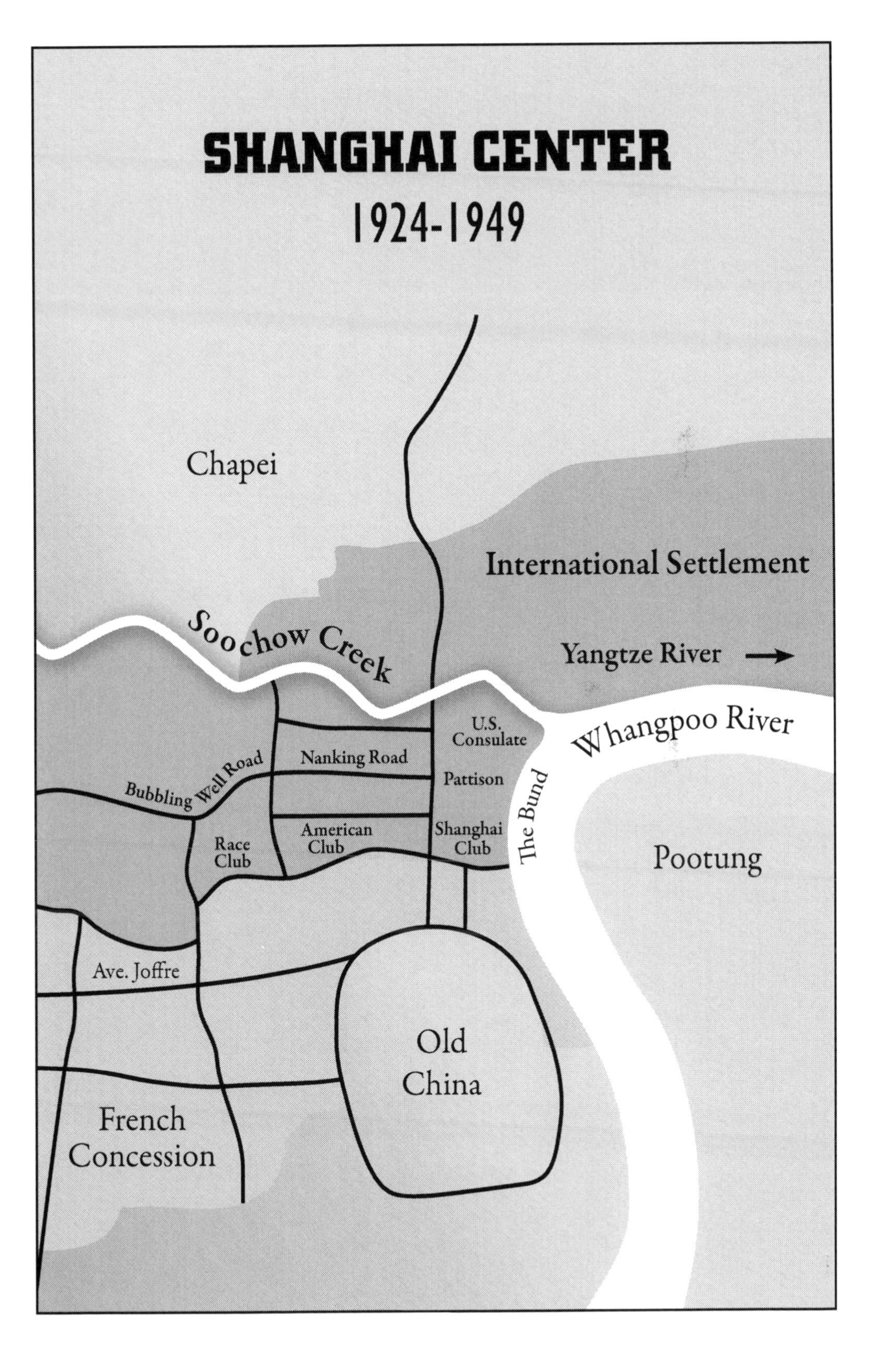
SHANGHAI CENTER
1924-1949
Chapei
International Settlement
Soochow Creek
Yangtze River
Whangpoo River
U.S.
Consulate
Nanking Road
Bubbling Well Road
Pattison
The Bund
Race
Club
American
Club
Shanghai
Club
Pootung
Ave. Joffre
Old
China
French
Concession

Life One: The Boy

PART ONE

Early Childhood

1924-1929

My Happy World as a Young Child

Some 16 hours after boarding the train at Tsingtao, we would arrive at Shanghai's North Station. Here, shouting "Daddy, Daddy," Patty and I would dash off to be the first to hug Dad. He would always have with him Ah Ching, our driver, and several other household servants to carry our bags and steamer trunk into the 1922 Studebaker.

I loved Ah Ching. My first memory as a child was screaming in excitement as he bounced me on his shoulders, and he had been my friend ever since. Dad had selected him because he was an excellent chauffeur. But more important, he was a dependable and formidable bodyguard with the build of a WWF pro wrestler and years of experience as a police officer. In the turbulent, unpredictable Shanghai of the late 1920s no one could tell when his martial skill and police connections might be needed.

Ah Ching ranked second in the hierarchy of Dad's servants, just below number one houseboy, Ah Kung. In addition to them and Chau Queh, the staff included two assistant house boys, one "learn pidgin" apprentice coolie, two cooks–their chief being responsible for insuring that all our fresh foods were disinfected in potassium permanganate–a second amah for Mother, and a "washie-sewie" who laundered, ironed and sewed in her basement room.

We lived in a three-storied red brick house designed a few years earlier by Dad and Shanghai's leading architect, Laszlo Hudec. It was situated in Columbia Circle, a development of some forty homes near the west side of the city built by their real estate company. Ours had a fenced-in garden tended by two gardeners under Mother's supervision. She loved bright flowers, so the lawn flowed on all sides into explosions of color from roses, snap dragons, azaleas, hollyhocks, and other flowers. Behind the flower beds, rows of weeping willows hid a bamboo fence, while near the center was a pavilion sheltered by willows and a pond where our English setters waded, snapping at goldfish.

When I was very young, this was my entire world. It was a happy, secure place. Dad and Mother, when they were home, enveloped me with love; when they were away, my gentle, patient baby amah, Chau Queh, was always with me, caring. Wherever I wandered I was greeted with deference. To our servants I was "young master"–the first son, worthy of special respect. My sister Patty was treated kindly, too, but like all girls she was considered not quite so important.

The dedication to my welfare was stunningly demonstrated when I nearly succumbed to double pneumonia. There were no anti-bacterial weapons like penicillin then, and the best efforts of our family doctor, Bloomenstock, were not producing results. I was bedded down in my third floor room with steam inhalers and painfully hot mustard plasters one afternoon, when an ear-shattering cacophony crashed in from the back.

Mother, who had been with me, dashed out in alarm. A few minutes later she returned. "It's all right, darling," she shouted over the noise. "Chau Queh and your other nice friends are helping to get you well."

Years later she told me that our servants had hired a troop of Buddhist priests to frighten away my demons. They performed this exorcism in our open courtyard with a powerful array of gongs, drums, musical pipes and noisy singsong chants. This went on hour after hour without a break. Mother was still fielding phone calls, some angry, others amused or curious, from neighbors as far as two blocks away when the troop finally departed. Dad had returned from his office by then.

He and Mother were discussing the best way to prevent a recurrence when, to their horror, another group of priests, brightly garbed in red and gold costumes, marched in and the din started up again.

Dad learned that each servant had paid heavily to buy eight days of this exorcism considered necessary to save my life. His challenge was to stop, or at least minimize, the noise without hurting their feelings. He talked this over with Ah Kung, who quickly agreed to shorten sessions to only two hours each day. The reason was evident to Dad. Ah Kung and the staff, who lived in the servants' quarters next to the courtyard, were probably suffering from headaches even worse than his own.

The servants were delighted with the results they perceived from their action. Only two days into the exorcism my fever had dropped and by the end of a week I was scampering around their legs. Dad showed his appreciation the next February by doubling their Chinese New Year bonuses.

Not much later my first best friend came into my life. He was waiting for me under our Christmas tree with a big red bow around his neck. Jim was a handsome pedigreed English setter that Dad had brought home–a loving companion and protector, quietly tolerating all sorts of abuse that kids heap on pets such as tail pulling, back riding and being fought over. His sole fault–for a hunting dog–was that he was desperately gun shy. At the first rumble of thunder he bolted into his hidey-hole under my bed and cowered.

Being a setter, Jim loved the water. Each summer a group of our mothers took us young kids to Wei Hai village in northern China where they rented cottages along its sheltered Half Moon Bay. Here Jim would race down the white sand beach, plunge into the water, and swim forever with his beautiful setter head trailing a wake across the calm surface.

He was my first swimming coach. I waded in, seized his long tail, and hung on for a thrilling ride as he towed me out while Chau Queh, jumping and waving frantically from the water's edge, screamed, "John. You bad boy! You come back light now!" The confidence that Jim instilled in me at that tender age helped me through some really dangerous encounters in the sea later.

Patty and I lived happily in our sheltered world until it was brutally shattered by the intrusion of Frau Zeller. She was an ugly witch of Teutonic extraction with a strong, bony face and thin lips. Within minutes we knew that she hated young children. Dad, who could be firm, made it clear to us that she was our governess, charged with training us in good manners and French. Patty and I agreed that the manners thing was bad enough, but French was too much. We revolted. This didn't work. Our parents supported the old Frau and from then on we could do nothing but cringe under her bullying and verbal lashings.

Our conversations, usually sprinkled with little jokes and laughter, died into silence. If we carelessly let something slip out in English she slammed us with "*Parle francais!*" Or she threw at us another bomb directed at our eating habits: "*Il ne faut pas parler avec la bouche pleine!*" After a while Dad and Mother must have realized that this bullying was impairing our development as normal children and the old witch suddenly disappeared.

She was replaced by a pleasant French governess whose most memorable feature was enormous breasts. At my young age it was only a matter of curiosity, but I was still fascinated by them.

Except for those few months with the child-hating witch, my entire world was cheerful and friendly. Whether scampering around our home, riding through the city with Ah Ching, swimming with Jim at Wei Hai, or hiding live frogs in Patty's doll house, I was encased in a protective cocoon provided by Dad and Mother that sheltered me from the discord outside.

The Outside World of Violence

Outside that cocoon there was discord to spare. The death of Dr. Sun Yat-sen in 1925 deprived China of the widely respected leader who had played the key role in ending the ancient Manchu Dynasty and establishing the Republic of China. His ultimate goal had been to unify China into a modern, free and democratic country, which he expressed in his *Three People's Principals: Nationalism, Democracy and People's Livelihood.* As a vehicle to achieve this, Dr. Sun founded the Kuo Min Tang (literally, The People's Party).

He faced immense challenges. The immediate need was to unify the vast country. Since the defeat of the Manchus, much of China had balkanized into states controlled by military governors, many with their own private armies. These warlords were fiercely independent, and often fought neighbors in attempts to expand their spheres of influence. Two of the most powerful–General Wu Pei-fu in the western region and Chang Tso-lin, the "Mukden Tiger"–could each field an army approaching 100,000 soldiers.

As if this wasn't enough, China itself was threatened by two powerful external forces: Russian communism and Japanese military.

Most insidious was a carefully planned Soviet program to high jack control of the Kuo Min Tang and use this to dominate China. This scheme was spearheaded by the veteran Russian agent Michael Borodin, who supervised scores of Russian-trained Chinese organizers active in cities throughout China. Borodin gained the trust of the elderly Dr. Sun, who made the Russian agent his advisor. He also persuaded Dr. Sun to admit the secretly formed China Communist Party into the governing Kuo Min Tang.

With Sun Yat-sun gone, communist agitators in the major cities organized labor into demonstrations against foreigners–especially Japanese and English–and led boycotts against their imported goods. New communist leaders sprang up, including a former peasant from the northwest named Mao Tse-tung.

Suddenly their efforts met a new force: the modern student. This burst forth in 1925 when fifteen thousand Chinese students marched down Nanking Road, Shanghai's main artery, in a massive display supporting Dr. Sun's goals. Although peaceful in intent, unintended consequences led to arrests and the killing of nine students by panicking police. Shanghai's Chinese populace went on a rampage, then a general strike that quickly spread to other cities. Communists soon seized control and led mobs that threatened the large cities.

Most attractive was Shanghai, with its prosperous financial, commercial and maritime activity. It was home to about 50,000 foreigners: roughly 5,000 British, 2,500 American, 2,000 French and 20,000 Europeans who had fled the Nazis in Europe. There were also about 20,000 "White Russian" refugees from the Bolsheviks, and a Chinese refugee population which varied depending on the degree of terror in their native villages inland.

Most of the foreign population lived in the "foreign concession"–an enclave of several square miles behind The Bund–a wide, frantically busy wharf area that fronted a full half-mile along the Whangpoo River. The concession consisted of the International Settlement, ceded to Great Britain by the Treaty of Nanking in 1842 and soon joined by the Americans, and the French Concession, ceded to France. This area was managed by the all-foreign Shanghai Municipal Council, which supervised the police and judiciary. The cleanliness and order in the foreign concession contrasted with the squalor of the surrounding "Chinese City", where millions of Chinese were crammed along stinking narrow alleys with open sewers.

Shanghai had developed as a trade entrepot and had no defenses. As the threat of communist-led mob violence grew, barricades were urgently constructed. Barbed wire soon ringed the foreign concession, and concrete pillboxes sprouting machine guns were manned at important intersections. A curfew was declared, enforced by patrols of the Shanghai Volunteer Corps and marines from American, British and French warships moored off The Bund.

Despite this, a communist take-over might have succeeded were it not for Dr. Sun's formidable protégé, Chiang Kai-shek, commander of China's Whangpoa Military Academy near Canton. With a force of thousands of loyal cadets as a core, Chiang moved swiftly, lifting the communist threat to Shanghai and arresting many of its leaders.

Months of infighting followed between Chiang's forces and communist-led labor organizations. By 1927 Chiang had ejected communists from the Kuo Min Tang while still retaining a tenuous working cooperation with Mao. When Chiang led 100,000 soldiers north from Canton in a step to carry out Dr. Sun's goal of unifying the country, his Northern Punitive Expedition was joined by troops led by Mao and Borodin. The combined force killed warlord Chiang Tso-lin and took his base, Peking. From there they moved on, rallying support in city after city. At each, Chiang naïvely turned over the organizing to Borodin's agents.

But the communists did not share Dr. Sun's unification goals. They were too busy recruiting new members into their cause. Their violently anti-foreign faction dominated and led to the destruction of mission churches and schools, sabotaging Dr. Sun's goals. Chiang finally had enough and attacked his former allies. A series of battles shattered the communists and, in 1934, Mao escaped on his "Long March" to northwest China. About 100,000 had started with him; less than 10,000 were reported to have survived the long retreat.

The immediate communist problem had ended, but Chiang was preoccupied with a far greater threat. In 1931 a Japanese amphibious force, supported by Navy ships, arrived and started what was to be called "The Second Sino-Japanese War."

Weeks of naval and air bombardment set much of the Chinese City on fire, killing tens of thousands of civilians.

The timorous League of Nations futilely condemned Japan–even as their military forces landed and attacked Shanghai's large Chapei district. Some of the fighting moved close enough for us to see tall flames and smoke from our third floor while explosions rattled our windows so forcefully that our gun-shy setter Jim vanished, trembling, under my bed. When Dad, wearing an army uniform, returned from military duty with the Shanghai Volunteer Corps, he put on a cheerful face. But we could tell he was worried. When the Japanese finally withdrew, they left behind several square miles of ruins and the stripped bodies of thousands of brave Chinese soldiers. And 250,000 destitute, homeless refugees swarming into Shanghai's foreign concession.

A number of businessmen, including Dad, thought that the attack on Chapei might be a feint–a Japanese tactic to divert world attention to Shanghai while they carried out their real objective of occupying the vast, rich lands of Manchuria and its capital, Mukden. But, still uncertain about Japan's next move, and unable to leave their business commitments, they sent their wives and children away to safety until Shanghai's security was assured. Reluctantly leaving Dad behind, Mother took Patty and me–and of course the essential Chau Queh–to the home of her parents, John and Jesse Booker, in Rialto, California.

By the end of the next summer Dad felt that it would be safe to bring us back to Shanghai. We had all benefited from our months in Rialto. Patty and I learned what it was to be American children in America, and Mother had been able to research and organize her memoir, *News is my Job*, soon to be a best seller for Macmillan.

I (Almost) Shoot a Jap Destroyer from the *U.S.S. Houston*

While we were away, additional naval forces to support the American, European, and even Japanese interests had been stationed along off The Bund. Here was the home base of the American Asiatic Fleet–later the Seventh Fleet. Our flagship, the cruiser *U.S.S. Houston,* was also called "The President's Yacht" because Franklin Roosevelt liked to take trips aboard her.

When her captain, David Bagley, asked Dad whether I would like to tour his ship. I jumped at the chance. Soon afterwards a tall, rugged-looking chief, uniform sleeves laddered with chevrons and hash marks, was showing me around. When we reached the upper level gun deck, the friendly, grizzled veteran peered down. "How would you like to shoot a big gun, kid?"

I gasped, all of nine years old. "Can I?"

"Sure can, kid. When you get older. Just pass the physical and join the Navy. You'll see the world," he added, chuckling softly at his wit. Then, to dodge a barrage of questions, he explained, "You'll have to wait a few years. But today you can practice shooting."

He picked me up and placed me on a bike seat at the back of a gun. "Now, we want to shoot something over there–how about that ugly tin can with that dirty red and white flag? It's a disgusting Jap excuse for a destroyer."

I did not like the Japanese. They were rude. "Yeah. Can I shoot him?"

The chief put my hand on a wheel. "Sure can, kid. Turn it."

It was tough, and I tried harder. The gun moved around a little, and the chief said, "No. Turn it the other way."

The gun barrel swung slowly until it pointed at the Japanese vessel. "*Now* can I shoot?"

"Wish you could, kid. I'd surely like to shoot the bas... stinker myself. But you'll have to wait a few years. But when you get back to school tomorrow you can tell the other kids that you traversed a .30 caliber anti-aircraft gun aboard the biggest American warship on the river."

I left, wildly excited, with the *Houston* and her friendly chief forever enshrined in my memory.

PART TWO

Middle Childhood

1929-1931

Visit to Angkor: Lost Empire in the Cambodian Jungle

Every few years Dad took us on ocean voyages aboard passenger-cargo ships that stopped at destinations off the usual shipping route. Instead of joining mobs of travelers who invaded big tourist spots in organized groups, we went with a handful of explorer-minded international voyagers interested in little known, and usually exciting, destinations.

By far the most exciting was the lost empire of Angkor. Deep in the heavy jungle of French Indo-China, this fabulous city had been discovered only a few decades earlier, and was not yet shown on most maps. Yet, five hundred years earlier, it had been the capital of the huge Khmer empire that dominated much of Southeast Asia. We could make this visit because our ship, the German freighter *Mosel*, would load a full cargo of rice at Saigon. This would take three days, enough time to make the long trip through the Cambodian jungle to and from our destination.

Early in the morning, while it was still dark, we got into four cars that formed our little caravan and drove into the jungle with headlights on. The road was very bumpy, and every few hours we stopped to change a flat tire and for us to go to the bathroom among the banyan trees. These were truly amazing–huge monsters with their branches turning down into the ground, and their roots coming up from below, all mixed up so that we couldn't tell where the real tree trunks were. They were so thick that hardly any light came through.

These shadows nearly caused a serious accident. Mother was trying to take a picture with her Kodak and leaned with one hand against a big branch. Then she jumped back, screaming for Dad. Right near where she had placed her hand was a giant tarantula, as big as her hand, which the guard said was venomous. Mother had very nearly been bitten–and in the jungle there was no way to get medical help. From then on, Mother or Dad escorted us each time we had to go.

Late in the afternoon we came to a little stone bridge in a clearing. We stopped to eat and drink while the drivers checked the cars. Suddenly the ladies–Mother, Patty and other passengers screamed and scrambled into the cars. Dozens of monkeys came hopping around us, screeching like I had never heard. They jumped everywhere, acting like they owned the place and weren't the least afraid of us. The guard threw them some leftovers from lunch and we drove on.

We thought we were near Angkor when we passed big chunks of stone high up in the banyan trees. It was hard to believe, but one of them–a square piece of stone bigger than an icebox–was hanging in the air over our heads. Dad explained, "That stone was once part of a building. The tree started growing underneath it hundreds of years ago. As it grew taller it lifted up the stone."

It was getting late, so we drove a few miles to a town called Siem Reap and checked into a shabby French hotel. The ceiling fans weren't working and the rooms were steaming hot. The only lights were candles. Dad spoke French with a fat woman, and some strange looking skinny boys, wearing only dirty loincloths, carried our bags to our room. It was big, but the only furniture was a cabinet with a washbasin and pitcher of water, and two big beds, each with a mosquito net rolled in a ball hanging over it.

Dad talked again with the fat woman, then told Patty and me, "Be careful and don't drink any water here–only the water we brought from the boat. The same with dinner. We will eat soon with the others in the front dining room, but only the food we brought. We all sleep in this room–Mother and me in one bed and you two in the other. While we are here, be very careful to look everywhere you step. There may be poisonous snakes here, even in the hotel. Also spiders like Mother nearly touched, and scorpions and other bad insects."

Properly scared, we needed no urging to follow his instructions. At bedtime Dad loosened the mosquito nets. We crawled in and he tucked the bottom edge tightly under the mattress around us, warning, "Don't pull the net loose even if you get hot. When you want to get out call me first and I will help you. Remember, always keep the net tucked in. And keep your hands and legs away from the net. The mosquitoes can sting right through and make you sick."

We got through the hot, fitful night. Before we dressed the next morning, Dad banged our shoes on the floor and looked inside. "This is to make sure nothing crawled in during the night," he explained. "Scorpions like to hide in places like this."

In the meeting room many of the others complained about the hotel. But as soon as we entered the realm of the Khmer empire, their objections turned to awe. At first we couldn't believe what we saw, here in the middle of this jungle. Angkor rose before us, grey, gigantic, beyond anything we could have imagined, with towers as tall as the biggest hotels in Shanghai.

Covering all the buildings were stone statues of gods and goddesses, thousands of them. Some were as small as my hand; others taller that a house. All were made of the same gray-white sandstone. Most were weird looking, but the strangest ones, at the top of pillars, had four faces, one looking in each direction. Some also had four arms and three eyes, the extra one on the forehead.

Dad talked with a native guide, then explained to us: "The Khmer people who built Angkor worshipped a religion called Hindu which has many gods. Statues of these gods are all around us. The ones with four faces represent their goddess Shiva. She was supposed to protect the people, but didn't seem to do such a good job here!"

All morning we walked along hallways, under arches and in and out of huge temples. Wherever we looked were pale gray statues of Hindu gods and goddesses, and scenes of battles and people carved in *bas-relief*. There was no law against taking some small objects, so I picked up from the grass a broken off statue of the four-faced Shiva as big as my hand and a piece of a battle scene in *bas-relief* with the grooves cut half an inch deep into the sandstone.

The next day, when I was packing my Angkor souvenirs in my bag, I asked Dad, "Why doesn't anyone know what happened to all the people who made Angkor?"

"Good question, son. Some people think they were driven out by powerful enemies; others say that a terrible sickness killed most of them and the survivors ran away." Dad paused, then added, "Only a very few people from the outside world even know about Angkor yet. Some day, when it is easier to travel through the jungle, historians and archaeologists may come here. Perhaps they will find the answer. Until then, Angkor remains one of the great mysteries of the world–a lost treasure as wonderful as anything built by even the Greeks and Romans."

The 200-Pound Diamond-Encrusted Gold Buddha

That afternoon we drove to Phnom-Penh, the capital city of Cambodia, and went to a good hotel. It was French. We soon learned that so many things here were French because France ran the country. That was fine with me–their food was so delicious that I nearly got sick from eating too much. The rooms were nice and we didn't have to worry about poisonous snakes under our beds.

A tourist guide met us early the next morning. He was French and wore a funny round cap called a *beret*. He only spoke a little English so Dad translated for the group. Someone said he had heard about a gold Buddha, and everyone wanted to see it. There was more room in our car because Patty and I were small, so the guide rode with us. He was happy to speak French, and chattered with Dad while he guided the driver to the Silver Pagoda where the Buddha was displayed.

The inside of the Silver Pagoda was full of guards with guns. After the travel agent spoke with them they let us go into a small room, four of us plus the agent, while the others waited outside. Our agent took off his shoes, and we did, too. The floor was gray and felt cool to our feet. As we progressed, the agent kept talking and Dad translated. "This floor is why we took off our shoes. The agent says it is made of five thousand silver bars. We're walking on a solid silver floor!"

That didn't impress me as much as what followed. It was a brightly sparkling object, a little more than a foot high, squatting on a silver table in the middle of the room. Again Dad translated, "That is the famous gold Buddha. It is supposed to be solid gold, and weigh ninety kilos. This would be about two hundred pounds."

Dad, clearly skeptical, questioned the guide again. "Well, that's what he says."

The guide kept talking, with Dad translating. Now clearly amused, he continued, "According to him it is covered with nine thousand five hundred and eighty four diamonds. Exactly."

After exchanging a few more words with Dad, the guide shrugged and seemed amused. Again Dad translated, "I asked him if he was sure about the number of diamonds, and who counted them. He said he didn't know, but would like to be that person–and take a few for himself!"

"Thousands of People Virtually Pauperized"

I had never heard Dad use bad words until that afternoon. It was in our house right after we came back to Shanghai, when he and some of his friends were downstairs. I heard them cursing and saying bad things about somebody. Naturally, after his friends left I ran downstairs and asked him what was wrong.

"Could you understand what we were talking about?" Dad asked.

"No. Only that you were mad at somebody."

Dad thought a few minutes. Then he said, "When we were on the ship quite a lot of our family assets were stolen. Our house and things like that are safe and we will get along all right. Remember that. But we lost most of our savings–money, and stocks and bonds, which can be bought and sold. We didn't have any warning."

He was not alone. Nearly all his friends and business associates had also suffered. Some, whose assets were leveraged, had lost everything. All were entrusted with a bank called the Raven Trust owned by a respected American investment advisor, Frank Jay Raven. The man turned out to be a swindler, world class. He was convicted in an American court on seven counts of embezzlement, and in 1936 was sentenced to five years in jail at McNeil Island, Washington. News of the Raven Trust calamity was reported in business publications all over the Western world. One headlined it: *Thousands of People Virtually Pauperized!*

Raven's five year punishment may have given satisfaction to some of those he mulched but did nothing to help them recoup their crippling losses. Most tragic of these was the resulting suicide of Dad's close friend and business partner, whose home was nearby. His son Robert, my age, was a member of our Columbia Circle group. He moved in with me the day after we returned.

I was happy that this close friend would share my room. We enjoyed the same kind of games, and music, and after we finished our homework we would tune in to Shanghai's English language channel to hear our favorite songs like *Alexander's Ragtime Band* and *Red Sails in the Sunset.* He talked mostly about his father. They had been close and had a lot of fun together. Then suddenly Robert would blurt out, "I saw Daddy. He was on the bathroom floor with his head–his head was broken all over the bathroom floor." And he burst into tears.

Feeling awkward, I held him in my arms until he stopped sobbing. Then he continued, "On my birthday he gave me that electric train and helped me build the tunnel and depot. You remember. The one we played with. He was always doing things like that with me." He was sobbing again.

After a few days he came in the car with us to school. At first he just sat at his desk and wouldn't talk, but then he played soccer and began going to classes. Everyone wanted to help make Robert forget about seeing his father on the floor, but every now and then he remembered and cried. Robert stayed with me for several weeks until his mother, who was counseled and helped by Dad and her many other friends, took Robert back to her parent's home in America. Years later I heard that he was at Yale, doing just fine.

The wound that Robert's family had incurred was far greater than ours. But each family had suffered. Like so many American businessmen who had established their homes and occupations in the volatile, unstable business world of China–although fully recognizing its high risk/high reward environment–Dad had suffered a major blow. Yet neither he, nor any other foreign businessmen, could have anticipated that two more even more violent blows were still to come.

PART THREE

Late Childhood

1931-1939

The Never-Never Land of *Ying* and *Yang*

My homework was interrupted one afternoon by cars coming into the driveway, then banging noises and Ah Kung's high-pitched voice. Hurrying down, I ran into our number one shouting instructions to a cluster of men, some of whom I recognized as servants from our friends' houses. All were busy opening packages on the living room floor, while our own house servants were setting up tables in the dining room. Surprised, I asked, "What fashion you do, Ah Hung?"

He was extracting packs of monogrammed silver cutlery from a large cardboard box. "Makee dinner. Missy telephone have got too muchee man come dinner this side. Velly soon. Missy catchee Flench Club party." He made an excuse for a giggle, "This side no have got chow sixteen man. I telephone too muchee fliend house, houseboy talkee he master missy come no come chow this side. S'pose he talkee come this side I talkee he bling chow, knife, fork this side, chop, chop."

Familiar with pidgin English, I understood that Dad and Mother had been at a cocktail party at the French Club, where they invited sixteen of the guests home to dinner. Mother alerted Ah Kung by a phone call without telling him who was coming. There was not enough food in the house, so Ah Kung phoned his counterparts at our friends' houses until he learned who had been invited, asked each whether their cook had prepared dinner, and if so to have it delivered to our house, with the family's silver, very quickly.

Of course, some of the guests probably recognized their own dinners, or silver. But they were not fazed. They had seen their own servants perform such legerdemain at their own homes. This was just another example of getting along in Shanghai's never-never land.

By age twelve, I had climbed out of my security cocoon far enough to sense the structure of the world around me. Too young to appreciate anything but the obvious, I realized that I was living in a place of extremes, of contradictions where every *ying* seemed to have an opposite *yang*. Dominating everything else was the overpowering contrast between wealth and poverty, the rich and the poor. Later I learned that this disparity existed nearly everywhere. But nowhere did it dominate so powerfully as in Shanghai, where we lived on the edge of a very lively razor.

Dad's income probably placed us well above average among those tens of thousands of foreigners and Chinese who earned for Shanghai the reputation of being the wealthiest city in Asia. Their social lifestyles included 'round-the-clock parties such as my parents had attended at the French Club, and elegant banquets in the world's finest restaurants. The selection included Chinese, French, Russian, Italian, and Spanish feasts created by the world's finest chefs, and luxurious curry tiffins, prepared by prized Indian cooks from Madhya Pradesh, who featured their own specialty dishes of lamb, chicken and shrimp curry with Major Grey's mango chutney.

Many of their social and business events were conducted at the exclusive Shanghai Club, famous for its "longest bar in the world", where Chinese were excluded and women were nearly never admitted; the American Club for business lunches and Columbia Country Club for recreation and sports; the French *Cercle Sportif*, and national clubs for citizens of many other countries.

Shanghai was a giant magnet for gamblers, who bet on everything from drinks over liar's dice to fortunes wagered on the little Mongolian ponies at the Race Club. Here the directors gave parties in their private boxes, visited by jockeys who had a drink and gave betting tips, and served by waiters who also acted as runners for placing bets.

Heavy gamblers also patronized the Shanghai Auditorium where the world's best Filipino and Basque *jai-alai* players commanded large premiums for winning or losing matches. Several casinos, as elegant as Monte Carlo, attracted those who preferred to bet on roulette or *chemin de fer*, and specialty houses existed for players who bet on more exotic acts involving girls.

In sharp contrast was the world of the desperately poor and dying. Only yards away from the stately doorways of the very rich, many thousands of homeless men, women and children, in the final stage of life, lay sprawled on sidewalks, streets, doorways and even stone window ledges. Some wore rags; others lay naked and shivered when the weather was cold; some still had strength to crawl; others could only lie there, jaws hanging open, watering eyes pleading for help. The stench from their bodies drove people away. They would lie in their filthy plots, waiting for death, until it finally arrived. It could come from lack of nourishment, cholera, smallpox, typhoid, or any of the other epidemic diseases that ravaged the homeless.

Most were refugee farmers or factory laborers driven from their villages into the illusory safety of Shanghai's foreign concession to escape the Japanese soldiers who bayoneted and raped young girls for sport. As many as a thousand refugees died on the streets in a single day.

One thousand bodies to be cleared away. Fleets of trucks, sponsored by the Shanghai Municipal Council and various charities, moved along the streets, stopping briefly as their crews of coolies, breathing through cloth masks to ward off contagion from cholera, picked out the dead and loaded them onto the "death wagons." The city could not provide wood for caskets, let alone space to dig graves, so most were unloaded at open mortuaries and incinerated there. As with the living, there was nothing more that could be done for the huge influx of the dead.

The Rule of the Road

On my thirteenth birthday my dream came true. I became a proud owner of a shiny new American Schwinn Aerocycle, with balloon tires, coaster brakes and a strong bike rack. Only two others in our group–Bill and Bob Moody, whose father owned the Chrysler agency–had the same new model. With Robert's departure our group had shrunk to seven. Six, including me, lived in Columbia Circle, and my best friend, Granny (Granville Vincent)), about a mile further out in Hungjao. He rode in and joined up with the others in Columbia Circle, near my house. Then they rode on in a tight group to the American School.

With my acquisition of the Aerocycle, I joined them. Dad, like the other fathers, allowed me to commute to school on Avenue Petain provided that I rode with a group.

The road inside the French Concession was usually pretty clear because the French officials who lived there maintained plenty of police to keep the refugees away. But a stretch of about a half-mile before getting there was often crowded with refugees, and we had to be careful riding along it.

These refugees were mainly men, but also a few women and children. Not as far gone as the dying, they still had no hope of earning a living. Some wore farmers' clothing; others, only grey rags. Most could still move about, either walking or hobbling on crutches made from tree branches, or–if they had lost their legs–pushing their upper torsos forward along the street balanced on dirty wood or cardboard platforms. Many of them pressed forward as we rode by, reaching out with filthy hands, some no more than leprous stumps, trying to touch us.

All cried out Chinese words that we didn't understand. But Ah Ching did. When I rode with him, the former police officer growled, "You go bicycle velly careful. No go close. He velly hungly."

Riding by in our car was one thing. Riding on a bike only a few yards from those protruding hands was quite different. How I wanted to help them! It broke my heart to resist, but yielding to humanitarian instincts could almost be a death sentence. If they saw one of us give something, they would all rush in, dozens of them, begging desperately, pleading for food and money, reaching out, tearing away our clothes and shoes, grabbing at lunch boxes.

No doubt in anticipation of our humanitarian instincts, our parents repeatedly brainwashed us never to forget our cardinal rule of the road: *Never give beggars anything; don't let them see you looking at them; keep close together; ride past them fast!*

Their admonitions made sense. Just one glance at those smooth lumpy stumps of a leper's arm was enough. But Paul was still curious. "Why aren't we supposed to look at them?" he asked. Granny knew the answer. "My Dad says that if they see someone looking at them, they will think he may give them something and will come to grab."

I came close to breaking the cardinal rule myself–but only once. I was riding alone along a "safe" stretch when I saw a pathetic child, probably younger than I was, standing alone, crying, his little face contorted with the pain of hunger. Although partly inured to such sights, I couldn't force myself to resist and was slowing down, intending to give him some of my lunch, when a wave of adult beggars rushed toward me from the other side of the street. No biker ever took off as fast as I did! But still I felt my rack grabbed until it broke loose.

PART FOUR

The Battles of Shanghai

1934-1939

The Japanese Attack Again

On August 11, 1937 a war fleet of 21 Japanese warships anchored at the mouth of the Whangpoo River near Shanghai. Soon after that, fleets of Japanese Mitsubishi "Nell" bombers from Taiwan and Korea began a systematic attack on Shanghai's unprotected Chinese City. For days they shuttled back and forth, protected by fighters from their carrier *Kaga,* bombing and strafing right up to the edge of the foreign concession. Thousands of factories, houses and other structures went up in fire, eliminating much of Shanghai's industrial capacity and killing tens of thousands.

The Chinese fought back valiantly. On August 12, an elite army unit tried to repulse the stronger Japanese, but were pushed back with high casualties. Their squadrons of ageing Curtis Hawk fighters shot down several Japanese bombers, but were no match for the newer enemy fighters with experienced pilots. Other sections of the Chinese City came under attack.

Immediately an influx of panicky Chinese men, women and children–their homes, savings and livelihoods suddenly wiped away–swarmed into Shanghai's International Settlement and French Concession. They came in trucks, wagons, rickshaws, giant wheelbarrows, on foot and on the backs of stronger relatives, stopping anywhere they could find a few square feet of space to park on. Within a week, over a million homeless, destitute refugees had squeezed themselves into a few square miles–the largest influx to have ever been driven in by the Japanese aggressors.

A fortunate few received support from relatives and charities. But this dwindled in time. With no means of finding shelter or earning money for food and medical help, they stripped themselves of anything they still had that would buy a cup of rice, then joined the remnants of refugees from earlier immigrations, settling down to die.

We in the foreign concessions had been spared the direct impact of the Japanese attack. But our sense of security was rudely shattered.

The Chinese defenders, desperate to fend off the continuing attacks, sent a squadron of Northrop bombers to destroy the control center. This was at the Japanese military headquarters aboard the *Idzumo*, an old, captured Russian cruiser anchored in the Whangpoo River near The Bund. When the planes arrived, their target was concealed under clouds. Rather than abort the attempt, they dropped their bombs through the clouds as close to the *Idzumo* as dead reckoning would permit.

The powerful 550–pound bombs missed their intended target. Instead, several damaged Shanghai's waterfront. One exploded in the worst possible place, near several leading hotels along The Bund. This was seen by Mother, attending a tea party at the Palace Hotel. Reverting to her war correspondent persona, she sent the following dispatch:

> *"The blast and pressure wave were unbelievable. Against a background of incessant anti-aircraft gun fire from Japanese warships, the huge aerial bomb exploded near the center of Nanking Road, Shanghai's most crowded intersection. When the flying debris had come back down, 600 men, women and children lay dead and injured and the road surface was covered with bits of their bloody, shredded bodies."*

A few weeks later, on "Bloody Saturday," errant bombs killed several thousand more people in the foreign concession. Widespread panic erupted. Within hours the banks, food stores, and shops were closed and boarded up. An American Emergency Committee, headed by top American military, diplomatic and business leaders, organized the evacuation of American women and children, and acquired ships to take them to safety in the Philippines. Our family did not leave. Dad had made arrangements for us to be urgently evacuated if he felt it necessary.

Once again Shanghai was fortified, with barricades of sand bags and barbed wire going up around the concession perimeter. Concrete pillboxes, sprouting machine guns, were erected at important intersections. Old French Renault tanks clanked slowly along the main streets, while detachments of troops in foreign uniforms marched on patrols.

Japanese attacks around Shanghai continued through November. Again they bombed Chapei, much closer to our home than before. Their little green soldiers marched through the ruins of Chapei and came right up to the barricades around our concessions. Their diplomats increased pressure on the Americans and Europeans by announcing that the Yangtze was closed to foreign shipping. Nearly all commerce, vital to Shanghai was stopped. Up the Yangtze River the infamous "Rape of Nanking" took place as rabid Japanese soldiers brutally slaughtered two hundred thousand Chinese civilians.

In response to the unprovoked Japanese aggression, American and European leadership waffled. Even after the Japanese committed a cold-blooded act of war on December 12, 1937 by deliberately sinking the American riverboat *U.S.S. Panay,* no strong American reaction ensued. Instead, months later the Japanese paid an insultingly inadequate reparation.

Before the year-end Japanese troops, no doubt encouraged by the apparent cowardice of the western nations, occupied a small part of the International Settlement. In a long overdue demonstration of resolve, they were forced to withdraw without fighting by a united front formed by Dad's Shanghai Volunteer Corps and units of the British, French, and Italian army, built around the formidable U.S. Fourth Marine Regiment under Colonel Joseph C. Fegan.

In the river, those in command of the *U.S.S. Augusta* and warships of half a dozen European nations, waited in frustration for orders to respond. Admiral Harry E. Yarnell, commanding the U.S. Asiatic Fleet, fumed at President Roosevelt's refusal to act more forcefully.

Every morning, before leaving for the office, Dad briefed me on what was going on and gave me advice about staying safe. Occasionally he had me go to school in the car with him instead of riding my bike. I didn't know it until later, but Dad–looking at my future–was also quietly sounding out the possibility of transferring me to one of the prep schools in the Northeast. Two of his best friends, Admiral Yarnell and Marine Colonel Fegan, gave him advice and introductions to several of their headmasters.

We Form the Gunpowder Gang

"You'll never guess," gloated Paul, holding out a clenched fist in the hallway between classes.

I studied his hand. "Give me a hint."

"No. I want you all to guess. I'll show you when we're all together."

The guessing took place during the lunch break. No one came close.

We gave up and Paul opened his hand. I scoffed, "Big deal. So it's a bullet."

"Not a bullet, It's a rifle cartridge."

"So, what?" said Pete Ferguson, losing interest.

"Guess where I found it."

"Nah. I'm tired of guessing."

"OK, I'll tell you. It's a cartridge from a rifle that a Chinese soldier had. I found a whole clip of these right next to him. I think he's been dead a long time, because you can see some of his bones sticking out in the mud. They're sort of brown. I think I saw a gun he was lying on."

We digested this silently. Then Bob Moody asked, "Where? Where was this?"

Paul explained. After the fighting had stopped in Chapei, his father had let him come along on a medical mission to survey the progress of cholera there. They rode with an American doctor. Paul made a face, "I had to gargle with some lousy tasting stuff afterward."

"Were there any guards?" Paul thought a moment. "No guards. I didn't see anything to guard except that dead body. There were Jap soldiers wandering around some wrecked houses, but not near."

One thing led to another, resulting in our plan to go back there and get more ammunition and anything interesting we could find.

Several evenings later, just before it got dark, Paul led our group of would-be ninjas, dressed in dark pants and sweaters, along a path we used going to the Columbia Country Club and across a rickety bridge into Chapei. No one saw us. We walked along some sort of alley, stepping over piles of shattered bricks and garbage until we came to the body. It lay in an open place like Paul had said, and smelled terrible. "Phew!" someone sniffed.

"Dead bodies rotting," explained Paul. "The doctor said don't touch them."

"Who would want to touch that?" Peter grimaced at the rotting corpse. Then he pointed, "Hey. That looks like more clips of cartridges there. Let's get them."

We scooped up a few that didn't look too dirty, then tipped over the body with our feet to see the gun underneath. It was a muddy, rusty pistol, broken in half. No one wanted it. We were leaving when Mike noticed a wooden stick with a muddy lump on one end. He went over to pick it up when Bill Moody said sharply, "Mike. Don't touch it. I think that's a hand grenade."

"Nah. Doesn't look like one. Hand grenades are sort of round like little pineapples."

"That one's different. It's called a potato masher–a hand grenade on the end of a stick. The Chinese use them. I saw pictures in the papers. If you move it, it might go off. Anyway we got what we came for. We better get out before it gets dark. If we have to use my flashlight the Japs might see us. I don't want to get caught by Jap soldiers."

We decided to make guns, using the brass cartridges and gunpowder from our looted clips, and fuses from Chinese firecrackers. Our first test was with the finished product held in a vice. After several tries, we were able to coax out a muted "poof" which gently lobbed a wooden bullet a few yards out. Something rewarding happened with the next try: the gun actually fired, sending the wood plug all the way across the room. For the final touch, we mounted our handgun onto metal prongs that fit our grips and held the cartridge tightly at the top.

We stood around the finished product, quiet but deeply satisfied with our achievement. Finally Paul, who had started the whole project, announced, "Now we have a name. We can call ourselves The Gunpowder Gang."

Family friend: Admiral Harry E. Yarnell, U.S. Navy, Commander of U.S. Asiatic Fleet (later the Seventh Fleet), 1935-1939. The humorous background depicts Shanghai turmoil.

Our home at 95 Amherst Avenue, Columbia Circle, Shanghai, China, with Dad's 1922 Studebaker.

A happy lad am I.

Dad, on guard duty, wearing French uniform, coddles me.

Mother & I play in sandbox on deck of President Taft.

Our baby amah Chau Queh helps Patty down the steps.

Chauffeur-bodyguard Ah Ching plays with Patty & me.

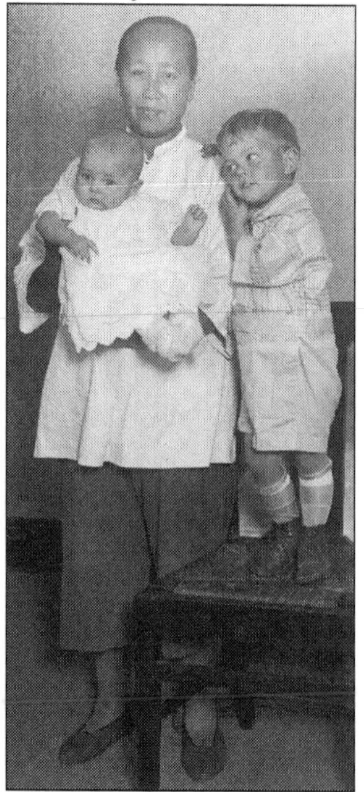

Little sister Patty & I snuggle our baby amah Chau Queh.

DEAR DADDY,

WE SAW THE AQUARIUM AT HONOLULU. THERE VVERE MANY MANY FISHES + I LIKED THE OCTOPUS THE LOBSTER, THE BUTTERFLY FISH, AND STARFISH BEST.

SOME DAY I AM GOING TO BE PRESIDENT.

LOVE FROM PATTY AND ME, JOHN.

For that job, one can't start too early!

Dressed for Sir Victor Sassoon's children's fancy dress party.

On veranda swing with Patty & friend Monkey.

Patty & me in our garden with Mother, English setter Jim, and his son Gibby.

Setting out on a sampan ride with friends at Wei Hai resort.

Our house on Long Island.

Our trip to Angkor wat in Cambodia was memorable.

Ship ahoy!

Dressed for a fancy dress party.

Number One house boy Ah Kung, on right & two junior staff.

Jim and me.

Life Two: Education in America

PART ONE

St. George's School
1939-1942

The New Kid Wore "Peek Pants"

From the far end of the athletic field I looked down the long grassy slope toward Second Beach, watching the breakers roll in from the Atlantic Ocean. I took a deep breath, savoring the tang of the sea. The mid afternoon sun slowly lost its warmth as it set behind me, pushing the shadow of the school's lofty chapel tower past me toward the ocean. For a few minutes the sunset sky silhouetted the magnificent Gothic landmark dominating the school's hilltop compound. Then its light dimmed and I hurried back to my room, again marveling at my good fortune to have been admitted to what must surely be the most beautiful school campus on the East Coast.

It was mid September, 1939, and Mother had taken me to St George's School, overlooking Newport, R.I., early that month. She stayed a few days while I was treated for a bad cold in the school infirmary, then went on to New York for a final review of her book, *News is My Job,* with her editor. After that she returned to Shanghai. From then on, communications with my family were by sea mail across the Pacific, taking one month each way.

My welcome began while still in the infirmary. I was visited there by the school's senior prefects and staff–and particularly the unforgettable headmaster, Mr. Merrick. Time and again he placed his huge frame in a chair facing my bunk, giving me advice and telling humorous stories of St. George's alumni. It was he who told me that Ogden Nash had written some of his humorous verses while a student, and that Admiral Yarnell's home in nearby Newport had a door painted Chinese red. Like every graduate, I always remembered "The Bull" with the greatest respect.

On my discharge from the infirmary I was assigned to the dorm for the fourth form–equivalent to the tenth grade. Then, wearing new clothes made especially for me by our tailor, I was introduced to my future classmates.

My arrival was somewhat of a novelty, since very few students from overseas had yet started to attend East Coast prep schools. "That new kid from China" received welcomes ranging from tentative acceptance to outright curiosity. I sensed that something was wrong, and learned that it was my short pants. Our tailor had patterned them to conform to the current style for boys at England's exclusive "public" schools–Harris tweed jackets and short pants–whereas all the students wore long trousers here. It took only hours for some wag to come up with "peek pants" and that term clung to me for three months—the time it took to communicate instructions, tailoring and shipment of new long trousers. In the process I learned the meaning of "culture shock" long before this buzzword was popularized in foreign job assignments.

My New World

My room contained a bed, bureau, simple closet and chair–adequate furniture, since homework was conducted in a study hall. There was no door, allowing free entry and easy socializing. Classes were conducted by dedicated instructors, many St. George's graduates themselves. One, fondly remembered by every alumnus, inspired his students to superior performance by throwing pitches worthy of a World Series ace. If a student's answer to his question was correct, he smiled. But if wrong, he could hurl a blackboard eraser with uncanny accuracy. The projectile bounced off the student's head, unleashing a cloud of chalk dust that buried his hair and face under a white layer and provoked near-hysterical laughter from the other students. I learned that many defenses had been tried to dodge that eraser. Nearly all failed. Our star Bobby Feller knew every trick and threw knuckle erasers just as accurately as curves.

My curriculum pretty well followed the pattern in Shanghai, featuring English, math, history, French and art. The school's effective learning process motivated me to study and I was able to maintain above–average marks after settling in. Our day usually started with a delicious breakfast and morning prayer in the beautiful chapel, then assembly. After a break came most of the classes lunch, sports and other activities. Evenings were for homework and recreation–which in my case often included an *al muerto* checkers tournament with one of my favorite instructors who insisted on calling me "Chesty."

Too light for football, I took up other sports like swimming, handball, and baseball. My favorite was swimming, and after months of training on the flutter board, I had improved enough to win the 40-yard junior free style race for our school at a Brown Interscholastic swimming meeting in Providence.

Vacation Adventures up the Hudson

My first academic year ended in June 1940. My marks were not spectacular, but good enough to move me up to the fifth form. I now looked forward to three months of vacation in America while my family remained in Shanghai. Fortunately, both parents had many friends on the East Coast with homes where I could stay.

My first summer was spent at Saxon Hall, a beautiful Southern estate at Cornwall-on-the-Hudson, distinguished by a line of white Doric columns marking the perimeter of the front verandah and extending up to the third floor. The owner, Mrs. Peggy Deuell, had been Mother's friend since they were war correspondents in China years earlier. She had recently lost her husband, Harvey Deuell, Editor of the *New York Daily News,* and told me, "It's lonesome here without Harvey, and I am happy to have you stay."

She introduced me to Tom, her gardener who took care of the manicured lawn and a large pond in the center. I liked him immediately–a short, roly-poly southern fellow who wore a perpetual smile. He gestured at the pond, "Don't try to swim in there, or wade around the edge," he warned. "We seem to cultivate water moccasins. Really pit vipers, and they're deadly." Before I left, Tom had taken me out in a leaky rowboat to see a nest of those loathsome snakes on an island. No way would I even go close to that black water.

Within a few days I met Jack, also sixteen, who lived a few miles up river and attended a nearby military academy. We hit it off immediately and my social life started. "I've got a date with my gal tonight who has a good looking friend. How about you coming?" Things went well, and after a promising first session at a movie we continued to go out on double dates. Unfortunately, after only a few more meetings, my date had to leave.

The Giant Waves of Second Beach

After I returned to school, the balmy Indian summer weather continued to draw me outside to read homework on my favorite corner of the campus overlooking Second Beach. I could see a few people in the water, but much as I liked swimming, I stuck with the warmer, more convenient water in our pool. Then a new friend changed all that. This was Sig Olney, also in my class. Towering over me at six feet plus, this slender, highly intelligent and utterly diabolical athlete startled me awake just after dawn one morning. "Come on, John," he bellowed in my ear. "We're going swimming!"

"No," I protested. *You're* going. I'm going back to sleep. The water is too cold."

"Once you start riding those waves you'll get warm right away." He started to pull off my blankets and I reluctantly got to my feet. My swimming shorts were still damp from my flutter board practice but I squeegeed into them. Outside Sig introduced me to several other mentally challenged enthusiasts, all school seniors. One looked at his watch, "Come on. We have to hurry. Can't miss breakfast."

We raced down to the beach, threw off our jackets and made a beeline into the sea. I had never been this close to such big, thundering waves. They towered high over my head when I waded in to my waist. My common sense protested: "What the hell are you doing here? It's dangerous–you should be back in your warm bed."

But I continued wading out until I could barely keep my balance without being battered down. Bucking the impact of the incoming breakers, I watched the others shouting with excitement as they rushed toward me, their heads and arms poking out from walls of foaming blue water.

At that moment I decided that I, too, would be one of those happy shouters. When the next wave came by, I threw myself onto it. After endlessly whirling and somersaulting underwater, I was finally tossed up like a chunk of flotsam, gasping for breath. My eyes, nose, ears and probably every other orifice were clogged by sand.

One of my companions thumped me on the back. "Great work, kid! You're doing fine. Don't give up."

Another added enthusiastically, "Remember the airplane pilot who crashed a plane and wanted to fly another one right away? Quick. Grab a wave!"

I listened, catching my breath, as others stopped off between rides to explain the techniques of body surfing. Then–sure that I had it–I dived forward as the next wave swept by. And once again was whirling and somersaulting underwater and collecting more sand in my orifices.

I tried over and over during the following days, driven by continuing encouragement. Sig made himself my personal trainer. The coaching and encouragement seemed to work, and within a week I was whizzing along, head and arms protruding from the front of the curling waves, shouting my head off and not giving a damn if I *did* collect sand in my orifices.

My High Paying Executive Position

By mid 1941 Dad–increasingly concerned about Japan's aggression–had sent Mother and Patty to America. They were renting a summerhouse in Plymouth when I completed my second year. With nearly three months of holiday ahead, I moved in with them and set about getting a good, high paying executive position in the town.

Three days later, after many visits, I had discovered there were no good, high paying positions for inexperienced boys my age. Not even low paying jobs. Not even *Old Colony Memorial* newspaper delivery jobs. In this end-depression environment nobody was hiring. I finally succeeded in finding employment–scooping up cranberries in a bog near Plymouth, at one dollar per hour.

Early the next morning my new boss received me on the road's edge above the sunken bog. The old, unfriendly, whiskered man took one look at me and spat on the road. "Now they *really* screwed things up," he growled. "Sending me a sweet ass little boy! Jesus Christ, the girls will play with you like a pussycat. They won't work. They'll eat you up alive!"

He shook his head and handed me a scoop and an empty box. "When this is full, take it over to those other boxes under that truck there and grab an empty one. Now get your ass over to the other side of the bog and keep the hell away from my girls!"

A glance told me what he meant. Fifteen or twenty young women, wearing flimsy loose robes, were on their knees below us. They had been pushing wooden scoops, about eighteen inches wide with teeth about an inch apart, through the cranberry shrubs, but stopped to look up at me. Giggling and pointing, they shouted at each other in some foreign language, which I learned was Portuguese. Not a man or boy was in the group.

Thinking "how the hell did I get into this mess?" I carried my scoop and box around to the far end of the bog where the boss had pointed, and clambered down to the bottom. I heard him bantering with the girls in back of me.

The job was boring, entailing hours of crawling over mud and dirt on my knees, pushing the wood scoop into tangles of low plants then pulling out the berries, scoop after scoop. My knees began to ache. But before long I had filled a box and exchanged it for an empty one. By noon I had filled six boxes with cranberries. Then the girls congregated at a wood bench where jugs of water were set out. One called over to me: "Hey, boy. You no work now. *Vem aqui. Comida.*" She pointed to a paper bag she was holding.

The boss had left and I had brought no food, so I welcomed this invitation. Soon I was sitting on the road among the girls, eating squashy buns and receiving a barrage of taunts and jokes I couldn't understand. Then the fun began. One girl–tall, dirty, but not bad looking–slid next to me and squeezed my thigh with a shriek of laughter. The others laughed in appreciation, egging her on. A second girl–the one who had fed me–pressed up against my other side and moved a hand toward my crotch.

I did the only thing I could do to protect my job–if not my virtue. I jumped to my feet and hightailed it over to where I had been working. At the end of the day the boss drove up and checked my work. It apparently pleased him because he drove me home.

The next day I was better prepared, arriving on a borrowed bicycle with my own lunch. Again I spent the morning separated from the girls.

At noon the one who had offered me food walked over. She said, with a sheepish smile, "We sorry. We only make joke yesterday. All day work. We like laugh." I took her at her word, joined the group and learned that their aggressive actions the previous day were simply intended to break up boredom. They were a good-natured group.

A week later the boss told me I was being promoted to a new job. This was to drive the truck delivering the cranberries to town. Hearing that I didn't have a driver's license, he helped me get a temporary one and I started my new job.

The work turned out to be a lot more than just driving a truck. All day long I moved fifty-pound boxes of berries. I lifted each from the floor of the bog, carried it five or six feet up the steep side of the bog, and laid it on the road. Then I lifted the box onto the truck, stacked it and went down for another box. After loading the truck with what must have been several tons of cranberries, I drove to a depot in town, unloaded it, and drove the empty truck back for another load.

By noon, my muscles were hurting so badly I could scarcely carry the weight of a box up the side of the bog. I stretched out the lunch break as much as I could, to rest, but had to resume work in order to deliver the final truckload on time.

My real punishment began after I returned home. Skipping any dinner, I drank several glasses of orange juice and staggered to bed. All that night I lay in agony with burning muscles, unable to sleep. I didn't know how I managed to roll off the bed the next morning to undergo another day of hell. And a third and fourth day. On the fifth day I carried out my job with only insufferable pain. After that, the pain slowly drifted away.

At the end of another week, hardened and having proven myself competent to handle this hard labor, I asked for a raise. The response floored me. It was: "You're fired." I did not back down, as they had expected, since I held a trump card–they would have a hell of a job replacing me on short notice. We agreed on payment commensurate with the greater level of work I produced.

I was now able to comfortably cover my own expenses and start weekly payments on a badly needed family car. This was a used 1937 Ford Tudor costing $285, which I–the only one with a license–used to chauffeur Mother and Patty after work.

Lifelong Friend Paul Brine

That summer I made a new friend, and developed a bond that lasted over 50 years. About six feet tall, Paul had brown hair, a lightly freckled face and a permanent smile that drew people like a magnet. He was a natural charmer–he could prance into a room, smile at everyone, sit at a piano, pound the keys and within minutes have a crowd gathered around laughing and singing at the top of their lungs.

Paul lived in the town of Manomet, a few miles down the road, where he was best known for having built a live-in tree house in his family's backyard. It even had a drawbridge of sorts: a rope ladder that could be lowered through a secret mechanism.

I soon learned that parts of his life also seemed to be cloaked in secrecy. Referring to his past, Paul would describe, in an utterly casual manner, such extraordinary events that after leaving him, people often shook their heads in wonder. A frequent comment would be, "Could that all *really* be true?"

I knew that at least most of it was. At Harvard, Paul teamed up with Jack Lemmon in a successful Hasty Pudding production *Pocahontas*, and after submarine service, went into TV advertising. His commercials were so successful that royalties were still coming in years after he moved on. He was also a successful landlord, owning three apartments on New York's East Side, their walls covered with large glossies of beautiful women in various stages of undress. All were autographed to Paul with inscriptions like "All my love, darling." Many pictured celebrities such as Jacqueline Kennedy, and leading socialites and actresses from Hollywood to Europe.

Paul was rumored to have carried out high-level missions in South America as an "ambassador" for President Eisenhower, which he would neither confirm nor deny. I could confirm myself that he escorted the Panchen Lama–or some one very close to His Highness–to a "secret meeting" in Asia, since they stopped at our Hong Kong home.

Another event that I can attest to be true: he played an important role in my life by introducing me to my wife. This seemed out of character, since Paul–depending on which source you believed–was either married, never married, married but divorced, unmarried with a child, just with a child, or none of the above.

New York City

At the end of summer, before returning to school for my senior year, I drove Mother and Patty to their New York apartment. Old friend Johnny and I continued our visits to Greenwich Village–and especially to Café Society to listen to our idols, Josh White and boogie-woogie players Pete Johnson and Albert Ammons. We also went on double dates, which, in my case, went well enough for me to think about marrying Jaye after college.

The highlight of my New York trip was made possible by my parents' friend Alice McKay Kelly. When Mother told her of my interest in clipper ships, she arranged for me to meet the greatest marine painter of all–Gordon Grant. His classic painting of the *U.S.S. Constitution,* widely known as *Old Ironsides,* is in the White House and copies decorate government offices. The sale of over one million prints in 1927 paid for much of the old frigate's restoration costs.

Scarcely my height, aging but alert, the famous artist welcomed me with bright eyes and a bouncy manner. "Alice tells me you have made several paintings of clipper ships. I would like to see them sometime." He led me to another room and showed me a wall covered with a collection of sailing ships, blue skies and ocean waves. With a twinkle in his eye, he said, "I have painted some, too." Then, for nearly an hour, Gordon Grant described his experiences rounding Cape Horn on square-riggers at the end of the previous century, and the hardships and dangers that the crew faced in those terrible seas.

I left with a gift I have treasured all my life: one of Gordon Grant's favorite lithographs, *The Saucy Brig.* Over his famous signature he had penciled: "With best wishes to John Potter" and the date.

St. George's Goes to War

Right after Pearl Harbor St. George's went to war, with the soaring chapel tower making a significant contribution to the war effort. From its top, nearly 150 feet high, observers had an unobstructed view for ten or more miles, much of it to the east. This made the tower a natural candidate to join the chain of coastal air raid warning posts to detect and identify any enemy planes coming in from the Atlantic.

The location was made even more attractive by the availability of

St. George's students on the premises, day and night. Our briefings explained that we would take shifts in teams of two. Our task was to identify and report any planes observed or heard. After walking up some 130 steps we reached a platform near the very top of the tower. Here was a table, chairs, telephone, binoculars, log book, a huge "ear" that could be swiveled to focus on any suspected sound and a hooded light to help us make log entries.

There was little air traffic to report, but we jotted down and phoned in details of each sight or sound, using the binoculars and "ear" to better identify the number and type of aircraft, speed, direction, altitude, etc. Before long, we students had enough experience to recognize the most common types of planes–mostly civilian and occasionally military. The work was deadly dull, and we felt that any threatening contact was unlikely here. But who could tell? We took our responsibilities very seriously. There would be no replay of Pearl Harbor on *our* watch.

What Happened to Dad?

Right after the Japanese seized Shanghai, they interned the non-Axis country civilians including, of course, Americans and British. We heard that Dad was one of the first to be taken–possibly because he held a power of attorney over the Bank of China's portfolio of properties. After that, despite constant and desperate efforts to learn his fate, we could learn nothing about him.

The consequences of Dad's disappearance brought the question of family finances sharply into focus. Fortunately, Dad–anticipating the worst–had the foresight to build up a reserve in New York that the Japanese could not take. This would provide for Mother and Patty for about two years. To supplement this, Mother arranged for Curtis Brown, Ltd. to book lectures for her in several cities. Later there would be royalties from her book.

In my case, I would work out financing for the fifteen months after graduation until I became old enough to enter active service. My best bet would be a scholarship to college, and I set to work to win this. This effort paid off. At my graduation I received notification that I had been awarded a partial scholarship for 1942-1943, sponsored by a St. George's alumnus. But not just to any college. At first I couldn't believe it, but this was to the most prestigious college of all–Harvard! Revered by leading Chinese as *Ha Fo Da Hsueh*, the name was magic in Asia. Grateful and elated, I planned to earn the balance of the costs for my freshman year from summer jobs and house cleaning work. Then, as soon as I reached enlistment age, I would join the Navy.

The final days passed quickly until the time arrived to say goodbye to friends and instructors. Then, with a diploma and a heart full of gratitude and warm memories, I left for Plymouth.

That summer was pretty much a repeat of the previous one. I was able to meet part of the rent and save more money toward college expenses. Friendship with Paul strengthened, and both Patty and I made new friends. At the bog, my surly boss of last year exposed his dirty, rotten teeth in a horrible grin at me, and even giggled when the girls came up and hugged me.

PART TWO

Harvard: Civilian Freshman

1942-1943

Lessons from a Glass of Urine

In early September a Harvard alumnus friend took me to Cambridge. As he drove along the tree-lined college streets he chatted cheerfully about old college days. I heard not a word. My mind blotted out everything except the overwhelming realization: This is *really* happening to me! I'm going to Harvard!

My old Gunpowder Gang pal, Peter Ferguson, had come one day earlier and met me at the door of our double room in Kirkland House. Taller and heavier than I remembered, Pete still had the same warm Irish grin and disheveled light brown hair as we gave each other a hug. "Johnny! Welcome to our new playground!"

"Yeah. How's our room, Pete?"

"Pretty good. But only one bathroom and I've got first dibs since I beat you here."

"We'll see. What are the guys like around here?"

Peter explained that they seemed fine. One, named Eddie, had a hundred pound dumbbell which we could use. Another, called Big Mac, was tall and fat, and laughed a lot. Our contribution was an open bottle of Scotch that Pete had bought. There were five or six in all, who tended to gather in our room since it was a double.

Pete walked me around while I completed the enrollment process and established my major as chemistry. We then went to a Harvard Square pub for a beer. With Dad on my mind, I asked, "How's your family? Did they all get out OK?"

"Yeah. How about yours?"

"Dad was there when the Japs came in. We don't know what happened after that."

Pete put his drink down and digested this news. Shaking his head, he said gently, "I'm sorry. I really liked your Dad. I tell you, Johnny. As soon as I can join up I'm going in there and kill a million of those bastards."

"That's what I want to do, too."

I started attending classes the next day. Determined to keep my marks high, I included Psychology, reputed to be a snap course, in my curriculum. From the first session it was obvious that in this class we would not listen to boring, heavy lectures. There would be no stereotyped, white beard droning on endlessly. Instead, a young, bright professor walked briskly to a table, lifted a glass of yellow liquid from the top and held it up for all of us to see.

"This is a glass full of urine," he announced.

The reaction was silence with a scattering of nervous laughs. "What the hell?"

He then waved a finger over his head, plunged it into the liquid, and sucked it dry. Our collective gasp must have been audible outside. The professor ignored it.

Sweeping his gaze across his hundred or so stunned students, he said: "Now, I want one of you to come up here and do what you just saw me do."

The silence, as they say, was deafening. The only movement was our heads turning as we looked nervously at each other.

"Come on. It won't hurt." He ran his tongue over his lips. "In fact, it tastes quite good."

Silence.

"I'll make it worthwhile for the first to taste this. You will receive credit in your marks."

At that, one boy from a front row walked briskly forward. The professor held the glass in front of his face.

"Is that urine?"

"Sure smells like piss," said the adventurous lad. Screwing up his face, he cautiously immersed a finger into the glass. Dripping, it was on its way to his open mouth when the professor stopped his hand.

"You have earned an A for courage," he said. "But you failed the test for observation."

He called out to his audience, "How many of you saw me put the urine finger in my mouth? Raise your hands."

To a man, we did.

"You all failed the observation test. Who can tell me why?"

A single voice called out, "You changed fingers."

"My finger was in front of you all the time. Explain."

"You dipped one finger in and put a different one in your mouth!"

And that dazzling opening, I realized, was a taste of what separated Harvard from ordinary colleges.

Skirtlifters

There were things to do besides study. The first was to arrange part time work to supplement my scholarship. The undergraduate employment office handled this efficiently, and by the end of a week I had started housecleaning jobs around the college. The pay was low, but I had control over my hours and the unskilled work was a picnic compared to cranberry bogs. By the end of the year, I was sure I would be able to pay my full expenses–and would know more about the basements and attics in Cambridge that any other living person. The only drawback from this was that the transfer of afternoon time from lab work to housecleaning could impair my Chemistry marks. I hoped not too seriously.

Pete and I formed up with a group of half a dozen other students with common interests. Most immediate was organizing Saturday's football game at Soldiers' Field. The work and costs were divided up and soon we had acquired two rows of good seats–one directly behind the other so drinks could be easily passed to everyone. Just before the game we picked up the liquor, mixes and ice. The critical element–girls–would be provided by the sister of one of our group who was a Radcliffe student.

Big Mac, returning from his shopping expedition, plunked down a box of bottles on our main table. "Here we are," he announced. "Fixings for all the skirtlifters. Everything we need to get the girls drunk and hot and willing."

"Not with you," laughed Pete, who–with several years of hands-on experience with Southern California girls–was clearly ahead of our pack in that department.

"Yeah? Wait 'till you see my skirtlifters in action," Big Mac retorted, with good humor.

Methodically, he filled a row of half-gallon bottles with a deadly mixture of bourbon, gin, vermouth and something soft. He placed the full bottles into the long ice bucket, completely burying each. "*Voila*!" he exclaimed.

We lost the football game, but that didn't seem important. Each of us had paired off with a Radcliffe girl, who sat at his side. Stimulated by the violence of the football game, many of them matched us drink for drink. College regulations prohibited bringing girls in our rooms, so we somehow moved to a large room at Radcliffe and continued there. Things got pretty vague toward the end, and more than one skirt was probably lifted. But, as far as I remembered, not by me. I was relieved to wake up the next morning in my own bed.

The Coconut Grove Nightclub Horror

There had never been such a tragedy in Boston's history. The event caused violent reactions all over the country–especially among the families of the 492 generally young men and women, many college students, who were burned and smothered to death while trapped inside Boston's Coconut Grove flaming nightclub at ten p.m. on November 28, 1942.

Pete and I were stretched out, quietly listening to the radio and reminiscing about Shanghai, when an excited announcer interrupted the program. In a voice alternating between shouting, sobbing and gasping, he begged for medical help of any kind–doctors, nurses, and medicines–to be rushed to the well-known nightclub located between Piedmont and Shawmont streets, and Broadway. The sound of sirens could be heard in the background. Now and then he cautioned anyone offering help to come by foot, since access roads were blocked by fire engines watering down the smoking remains.

Pete and I jumped up. Together we said, "I'm going there to help." We grabbed our coats and dashed out, shouting the news as we ran down the hall.

Doors opened, radios were turned on and several friends came hopping out as they pulled up trousers and threw on jackets. Within minutes four of us were dashing down the stairs. The first suggestion was to take a taxi. Then, remembering that the roads were clogged, we decided that the subway would be faster.

At Harvard Square we jumped into the first Red Line car that came by, getting off at Park Square. Fearing that the Green Line would be mobbed, we set off on foot. And ran right into a huge mob, many obviously relatives, screaming hysterically, pushing, fighting their way toward a scene from Dante's *Inferno* highlighted by red garbed firemen reeling in hoses. Along the sidewalk lay row after row of bodies, placed side by side among rivulets of blackened fire hose water flowing out of the smoking wreckage. Some bodies were still fully clothed and others charred beyond recognition. All were dead.

We looked at each other. "We're too late."

"Well, maybe there's still something we still can do." We advanced, edging along a still standing wall to get closer.

Then it hit us–the overpowering miasma of burnt and still smoking human flesh. Big Mac, who had miraculously made it this far, doubled over and vomited until he was having dry heaves. Pete and I followed, then Eddie.

We were still retching as we hailed a taxi after leaving the scene. I, for one, could not get rid of the horrible taste for days. We all found that the clothes we had worn that night could not be worn to class, since their smell–even after cleaning–sent others backing away from us.

Strangely, we did not have nightmares during the following nights like those frightening dreams my divers and I all had years later, when we were salvaging sailors' dead bodies from under the sea. Still, we were badly affected, and for several days we didn't talk much.

Income from Hourly Work

As the Christmas holiday in New York drew near I tallied up the proceeds from my work cleaning basements and attics. Between days when I could not work, and others when I could fit in two jobs, I earned enough to nearly reach my financial goal. The shortfall was made up by another, more rewarding, job that paid more. This took place early in the morning when rows of trucks, loaded with produce, drove into the Faneuil Hall marketplace to deliver food for the Boston market. Peter and I would arrive just after midnight and spend the next few hours unloading boxes and crates and baskets of vegetables and fruit. After collecting payment, we could usually catch several hours of sleep before our first morning class.

As anticipated, there was a price to pay for the afternoon housecleaning jobs, which sometimes prevented me from participating in chemistry lab experiments. This absence reduced my marks and might have affected my scholarship if not compensated for by good marks in other courses such as English writing.

New York, Christmas

Exactly one year after Pearl Harbor, on December 7, 1942, Johnny Allen and I enlisted together in the U.S. Navy Recruiting Station, New York. We would enter active service as soon as we were old enough to be accepted.

I had taken the train down from Harvard with authorization to leave college a few days early to help my family. Much of this time was spent with Mother and Patty. I was amazed how quickly each had carved out a niche for herself in New York's famously impenetrable social world. Mother, now well respected for her achievements in China, was guest of honor at functions. Patty was not only popular at school and in the social junior set, but also worked part time at *Town and Country* magazine.

More interesting to me was her friendship with Jaye, a playful girl of Patty's age who made her debut with my sister. Slender, a perfect height for me at five feet three, she had short dark hair and large chocolate-colored eyes that really captivated me. After we had gone out a few times, Jaye invited me to her home, where I had spent a fascinating few hours with Mary Roberts Rinehart. Not yet seventy, she was America's leading writer of mysteries, with more than eighty publications to her credit.

Jaye also introduced me to her stepfather, Stanley Rinehart, president of the Farrar & Rinehart publishing company. A Harvard graduate, Stan tossed an iota of college lore my way. I had been attracted by a catchy tune, *Harvard Blues,* popularized by Count Basie. Its chorus went:

> *Rinehart, Rinehart, I'm a most indifferent guy*
> *Rinehart, Rinehart, I'm a most indifferent guy*
> *But I'll love my Vincent baby 'till the moment when I die!*

Curious about the inclusion of his name, I asked Stan whether he had anything to do with this. "Not our family at all," he told me. "I never met that Rinehart. But I was also interested in the use of our name and tracked down the probable source.

"This was an unfortunate person named Rinehart who attended the college a number of years before I did. He was dreadfully unpopular. Being shunned by acquaintances, he set about seeking friends through free advertising. At night he wandered about the campus outside the dorms shouting his name to create the impression that many students were looking for him. Before long, others would open their windows and shout 'Rinehart' right back at him until the campus echoed with the cry 'Rinehart, Rinehart'. Being Harvard students," Stan laughed, "that seems quite plausible."

Over the next two years my friendship with Jaye grew into a form of pre-engagement and we spent many evenings together, often on double dates with Johnny and my sister.

Completing the Freshman Year

After returning from the holidays, I learned that I was to report for active service as an apprentice seaman on July 1–three weeks after I completed my freshman year and the scholarship that had brought me here ran out. My first duty would keep me on at Harvard in a Navy training program called V-12. This struck me a mixed blessing–the emotional part of me, straining to go out and kill Japs, was bitterly disappointed; but the reasoning part was pleased with the chance to first be better prepared. In any case, there was nothing I could do about it.

In February I lost my old friend and roommate, Pete. He had been chafing at the bit to get into action, and suddenly took off for army duty. I would not see him again until we met in Laos during the Vietnam war. He was with a special unit attached to the Foreign Service then, working from a guarded house several miles outside of Vientiane. Right after Pete left, Eddie, still youthful, joined the air force. Several months later I heard that he had been killed while flying a fighter. Later, when his sister Patricia confirmed his loss, I was hit hard emotionally.

I joined the R.O.T.C. unit at Harvard to get at least some action. Wearing a khaki army uniform, I enthusiastically participated in the marching and rifle drills, and practiced handling a WWI French .75 howitzer. Regretfully, we didn't have a chance to carry out my secret wish–to fire the thundering cannon on campus late at night.

All the while, there was still no news about Dad–or any of the other Americans taken by the Japanese in Shanghai.

PART THREE

Navy V-12 at Harvard

1943-1944

Bud Solves the Enigma of the Suspect Eggs

On July 1, 1943 Paul Brine and I entered into active service, joining the Navy V-12 program based in Harvard's centrally located Eliot house. Here we mixed in the open quad with a group of young men, most of whom we had never met, some dressed in "civvies" and others in sailors' white summer uniforms. After completing the registration procedure and picking up our uniforms, we carried our bags to our room, Eliot H-22. This turned out to be a comfortable suite with double bedrooms opening onto a common room. There, waiting for us, were our new roommates, Bud Lane and Sandy Cunningham, also former Harvard freshmen.

Sandy jumped up to welcome us with a wide smile and a slap on the back. "Well, finally you came! We thought you were lost at sea."

Bud, less effusive but just as friendly, got up and shook our hands. "Happy you made it. Now we can finally get some lunch! The mess hall is downstairs–the old cafeteria."

Both my new roommates were medium height, with Bud slimmer and perhaps an inch taller, and they had brown hair. But the resemblance ended here. Bud was more laid back and spoke slowly with a touch of his crisp New England accent. Sandy, in contrast, exuded warmth and enveloped others with his enthusiastic, near-boisterous manner.

We joined a line in the mess hall, picked up tin trays and received splashes of assorted food. Then we settled at a table and got acquainted. We decided that the food was quite good until the next day at breakfast, when Sandy held up a fork full of scrambled eggs.

"This doesn't look like real eggs. It's powdery."

Paul agreed, "That's right. Real scrambled eggs have lumps."

We suspected that these were not scrambled eggs at all, but some imitation. "Like the Nazi *ersatz* coffee," observed Bud. We nodded at his wisdom.

We shared our opinion with other sailors, but received no interest until Bud had asked one of the waitresses. Innocently, she confirmed our suspicion that the yellow food was not fresh eggs. It was powdered, she said, packed in boxes and sent here from somewhere else. Bolstered by this hard fact, we gained immediate support from other sailors, who passed our grievance up the line. Our complaint was acted on right away. Two days later the eggs we were served were clearly the real thing. They were full of bits of eggshell.

We savored our triumph along with our genuine scrambled eggs until Bud thanked the waitress for her help.

"No worry," she assured hum. "Cook fix. Break some real egg and mix up with bucket of powder!"

When Bud passed this on to us, we burst out laughing. I commented, with begrudging admiration, "Really sneaky. We'll have to keep on our toes in this outfit!"

Special: Dad Returns – a Shell of Himself, but Safe!

In early November, 1943, Mother was finally notified that Dad was alive and among the Americans being repatriated on the motor ship *Gripsholm*, scheduled to arrive in New York November 30. Since it was known that the prison camp survivors had been starved for years, I was granted three days compassionate leave to help him.

On December 1, 1943, more than four years since last seeing him, I was able to hold in my arms the frail body of my father. He was barely recognizable with half his weight gone and his skull outlined beneath tightly stretched skin. I wanted desperately to hug him tight, to protect him, but refrained for fear that I might crush this delicate shell.

For the next two days I had priority for his time and we covered, between his frequent naps, many things we needed to talk about. Then I returned to Harvard greatly relieved of my greatest worry, leaving Dad comfortably settled in the apartment that Mother had arranged, in the devoted care of Mother and Patty, while his body slowly healed.

Parties, Games and Sweat in the Navy

Changes in our daily lives soon made us realize that our easygoing days as college civilians were over. Although we continued attending classes and doing homework as before, we felt the cold clamp of discipline inexorably tightening.

It started just before sunrise when we were forced outside to form up for roll call. After the names of absentees were noted for punishment, a muscular chief led us through a regimen of calisthenics, doing push ups, jumping jacks and other exercises nonstop for half an hour to get our red corpuscles rolling and create maximum pain. At this point, with no break, we were sent off on a marathon across the Charles River via Anderson Bridge, down the opposite bank to a distant footbridge, back across, then home. Not one circuit, but two, for total of many miles.

We had known that this physical exercise was designed to toughen us up, and by the end of two weeks this proved true. We were tough enough to do our long run with only moderate suffering and no longer needed to find ways to shortcut the distance.

That is, unless we had been drinking and frolicking at debutante parties until well after midnight. Being among the few men still left in Boston young enough to walk unassisted, with the respectability of being from good schools *and* wearing a Navy war hero's uniform to boot, we became the targets of dozens of little envelope containing invitations to debutante parties.

Who could resist? The one caution was not to be caught outside after midnight, when the Eliot House gate was locked. Since the parties we enjoyed most didn't get going until after that, we became adept at climbing in over Harvard walls in the early morning.

I Stand at Captain's Mast

During weeks of this none of us got caught–except me. This happened one night after the exceptionally strong punch at a deb party helped me convince a nubile brunette in her late 'teens that I should take her safely home. Once inside, it was only a short trip to the living room sofa, far from her parents sleeping upstairs. The ensuing hours were time well spent and only ended when she moaned, "I don't have an ounce of strength left."

After a long walk back in the icy cold, neither did I. In my debilitated condition I found that the wall above our climbing spot seemed higher than usual–dangerously high–and I was wondering how to get in when I spotted an open window right above the sidewalk. Inspired by my discovery of this new entryway, I climbed in.

I tiptoed carefully toward the far wall to find the door. Suddenly the lights went on. I heard the authoritative command, "Halt!" Being a sailor conditioned to obeying direct orders, I did not make a run for the door. Then I saw the commander, in pajamas, climbing from his bed!

The result was that a few days later I became one of the very few V-12 apprentice seamen summoned to a Captain's Mast–which I learned was sort of a junior Court Martial–by our usually genial commander. He was seated comfortably at his desk. A regular Navy yeoman, clutching a manila folder, was at his left. Accompanied by Sandy, who had come to give me support, I stood before them braced in the most extreme attention I could muster.

For a few moments the commander studied me, his expression more puzzled than angry. Finally he said, "At ease, Potter." After consulting briefly with his yeoman, he went on, "As a candidate for naval officer you should by now have learned something about navigating safely. There are dozens of windows around the base of Eliot House. And yet for your unauthorized entry you navigated direct to the window of your commanding officer's quarters." He coughed, covering his mouth. "Can you explain this?"

I knew that keelhauling was no longer in vogue, but being drummed out of the V-12 program was a distinct possibility. Weak with terror, I managed to mouth: "Sir, I didn't know that was your window."

"I see. That stands to reason. Do you know how many infractions you committed, and the nature of their punishments in time of war?"

He seemed to be choking. "No, sir," I stammered. He nodded at the yeoman, who opened his folder and read me a litany of crimes starting with absence without leave. When he had finished the commander said some more words, but they did not register. I remember coming to attention and walking slowly out, overcome with despair. "I guess that's the end for me," I said to Sandy as we walked back to our quarters.

He was silent for a moment. Then he replied, "I don't think so at all. Didn't you hear that he told the yeoman not to take notes? Didn't you see them laughing? The commander was trying so hard to keep a straight face, he nearly choked to death." Sandy paused, then looked at me with an amused expression. "I don't think he'll go too hard on you. You gave him too good a time!"

Sandy was right. I received only token punishment and a firm lecture from this kindly but effective leader. I took his words to heart and followed them because I wanted to.

Punched by the Clubs

My roommates taught me surprising facts about Harvard. One came up when I started receiving handwritten invitations on formal stationery embossed with names like Fly Club and Delphic Club. A typical one read: "You are cordially invited to a punch at seven-thirty on (date) at (house and room number)" and was signed by someone I didn't know. I asked whether anyone knew what this was all about.

They smiled. Then Sandy started, "John, you're being punched. Those are invitations to attend a punch. They're sent by the clubs each year to new sophomores who might fit in with their members. We're all getting them."

"Right," Bud added. "The punch is a recruiting party, with drinks, where members of a club and selected sophomores have a chance to get to know each other. There are about a dozen clubhouses on the campus. They're like fraternities, usually with a butler and maid. Only the members don't live there. They use them to meet and play billiards and have drinks and sandwiches, and sometimes formal dinners."

That night I learned a lot about clubs, and before long we had all been invited to join them. Bud and Sandy chose the Delphic–usually called the Gas–while Paul and I ended up in the D.U.–or Duck–which later merged with the Fly Club. All four of us entered the Hasty Pudding.

The D.U. Club had a distinguished membership. At the top was Harvard President James B. Conant, respected worldwide. He and two other notable alumni gave welcoming speeches at our initiation dinner in the third floor banquet room. Then each of the nine new members was given an unopened bottle of French champagne and challenged to shoot off the cork at a stuffed duck suspended over the center of the table. After most of us had missed, we all drank our full quarts, practically bottoms-up. Things became confusing after we started on the second bottle. All I remember is a lot of shouting and singing, several people rushing to the head to vomit, and Paul and I being helped to our room by unknown benefactors.

I Learn That I Have a Guardian Angel

During Christmas break I discovered how deeply some Americans appreciated the job their military was doing for their country. After one glance at my winter uniform, the white haired train conductor rejected my ticket. "Keep it for some other trip. I can't take it–I owe you too much." The same attitude prevailed in the famously hard-nosed New York City. Wherever I went, I received smiles and words like, "God bless you, sailor."

But not all New Yorkers appreciated their military. I learned this early one evening when Johnny Allen and I, wearing our Navy blues, were walking down 53rd Street after I had seen Jaye home. With no warning, the road ahead was blocked by a group of rough looking men wielding chains and shouting curses at us. We were unarmed and could not outrun them all. Things looked bad when suddenly a taxi backed up the road behind us, honking fiercely.

The cabbie opened his door and shouted, "Come, get in quick. Hurry." We did, followed by the gang's leaders who were clearly attacking. The driver broke away. "You lucky I see you and go back get you. They bastards, hate American sailor, want to hurt you. They catch you, they take everything, maybe kill you."

Obviously sent by my Guardian Angel, our driver had arrived just in time. He turned out to be a very patriotic veteran of the last war, glad to have the chance to help us. He drove us to our apartment and refused any payment.

A few days later we were relieved to read in the newspaper that several

Puerto Rican hoodlums, part of a gang, had been arrested near that area for wounding and robbing a soldier.

Before returning to Harvard, I was treated to an evening with Patty at her official coming out party. Now seventeen and a full-fledged debutante, she radiated young beauty in her debut at the Junior Assembly gala. Johnny, despite their close relationship, had his hands full with competitors–but he still maintained his status as her *numero uno.*

The Second Favorite Investment Corporation

Among the off beat assets acquired during my summer at Mrs. Deuell's estate were the ability to read the racing pages, and a "system" recommended by "Clocker Walker", a handicapper for the *Daily Mirror.* I had never tried his system, and never would have, were it not for the enthusiasm of a fellow V-12 sailor named Eldred.

Eldred was an absolute terror with women. Tall and slender, sporting a big lock of dark hair drooping down across his pale face, he had slow, lazy manner that hypnotized them. They gravitated toward him like bugs to a candle. Time and again I watched normally well-behaved women sidle up to him and "accidentally" slip a hand onto his thigh.

One evening Eldred told me he had been reading about treasure–in particular, a cargo of doubloons and pieces of eight on the pirate ship *Whydah,* which had been wrecked two centuries earlier off Cape Cod. "It's near Wellfleet, not too far from here," he drawled. "Let's go check it out and maybe we'll find some gold."

This seemed reasonable, and on the following Sunday we hitch hiked out to the beach where the wreck was supposed to be. We scooped up wet sand for hours, but the only things we brought home were sore backs and a cold that Eldred caught. We decided to postpone treasure hunting until a more promising opportunity came our way. This would not take place until years later, far across the ocean.

Meanwhile, we decided on an easier way to find treasure: at the racetracks. The *Daily Mirror* handicapper had claimed that his system usually won. It was a martingale–a progression that relied on making increasing bets on successive races until a win: $2 on the first and second races, $4 on the third, then $6, $10, $16 and so on until the twelfth race, when the bet was $260. Playing only second favorite horses in each race, there would nearly always be a winner in twelve consecutive races.

If not, the player was to write off his losses and start a new sequence. This called for $700 in capital but we had only $30. We were looking for something else to venture on when I had an idea. "Why don't we form a company and sell shares?"

"Who the hell would want to buy shares in a crazy scheme to bet on race horses?"

"Let's try it and see." Crazy scheme or not, we soon had $700 from Navy V-12 friends. Each received a share certificate for the Second Favorite Investment Corporation, which we designed, printed and signed. Each afternoon Eldred, I, or both, would place our bets at one of the three racetracks within subway and hitch hiking distance.

On our inaugural day a group of investors in the S.F.I.C. gathered in front of my club to see us off to the subway. We reached the Suffolk Downs track in time for the third race and made our first bet, $2 to win, on the second favorite. Our horse was leading for a while, but folded in the stretch. Eldred shrugged, "Well, it was close."

We won at good odds on the sixth race, and left the track with $17 in winnings. As we rode back, we were thoughtful. It had struck us both that, if it things kept going like this, we could look forward to real profits. Over the following weeks the second favorites kept coming in, and collecting bets became so routine that we no longer worried when we hit a dry stretch between wins. We soon were well enough ahead to repay our investors nearly all of their investments.

At this, overconfidence led us to double our bets, starting with $4 instead of $2. Eldred and I spent money like drunken sailors, draining our capital for expenses like taxis instead of hitch hiking. Our day of reckoning came when we reached twelve losses in a row. We were at the track together and instead of stopping the progression then, we convinced each other that the next horse was sure to win. We lost the remainder of our cash on one final, glorious $400 bet. The next day we sadly announced to our shareholders that their S.F.I.C. had gone broke.

The Hypnotist Gone Wild

About six weeks before our Navy class was to be transferred out, our team in H-22 was split up and assigned to different houses. In my case, I was moved in with a group I had never met before. They had the habit of meeting after dinner in a common room for a smoke and to exchange rumors about the progress of the war and other subjects not related to their studies. One evening we were sitting around talking when a red–haired stranger walked in. Introducing himself as Roger, he looked older than the average V-12 apprentice seamen, and wore a stripe on his uniform that gave him veteran status among us. Within moments he helped himself to a beer, and announced that he had been a professional hypnotist before joining up. Of course, he was immediately asked to demonstrate.

Nodding in agreement, he asked a volunteer. A lazy appearing lad named Oscar came forward. The hypnotist asked him to sit on a chair and, with only a few words and no waving of shiny objects before his eyes, put him under. Oscar kept on sitting, relaxed.

Roger started, "You are a sailor on your destroyer, sitting at the bow. Suddenly you see a torpedo coming in from the starboard side!"

Oscar shouted: "Torpedo! Starboard bow!" and jumped away toward his left. Roger continued: "It hits and your ship is sinking! You're in the water and swimming to get away from the sinking hull!"

I couldn't believe it. Oscar had flopped on his stomach, and was doing a sort of breaststroke across the wood floor. His eyes were open but he did not see us and would have hit our chairs if we hadn't backed away.

Then Roger shouted: "Shark! There's a shark following you!"

Poor Oscar became hysterical, thrashing forward desperately on his elbows and knees as if his life depended on it. He began shouting and crying, "God! God! Please help me. I gotta get back to mama. Help me, God." Churning his elbows, he moved so fast that he was crashing into everybody in his wild maneuvers to save his life.

At that, Roger told him to wake up at the count of three and forget what had happened. Oscar seemed puzzled to find himself on the floor, but returned to his chair and sat down with a small smile. He was skeptical when some of us told him of his swim.

The next volunteer was Sam–a big, tattooed sailor in a T-shirt and white shorts who had obviously been around. Despite his tough appearance, Roger had no trouble putting him under. He asked, "Sam, you are in Hollywood visiting your favorite lady movie stars. Who would you like to see the most?" Sam hesitated only a moment: "Veronica Lake."

"There she is!" Roger exclaimed. "With her blond hair down, waiting for you on that bed right in front of you!"

There was no modesty in what followed. We watched, fascinated and even somewhat embarrassed, as Sam slid forward onto his knees. Reaching greedily, he murmured, "Veronica, baby, I've been wanting you ever since I saw you in *This Gun for Hire.* God, you feel good–all your gorgeous blonde hair!" He pinned her down on the floor and, without removing any clothing got right to work.

For several minutes he pumped the floor, repeatedly saying, "Come on, you hot bitch!" Then he exploded into violent motion, shouting, "Veronica, Veronica!" For few moments he lay still, panting. Then, caressing the air lovingly with his open palm, he whispered, "Damn, that was good! You liked it, didn't you, Veronica?"

Roger had been trying frantically to break in, but could not stop Sam. He clearly felt he had let things get out of control, for he told us urgently, "I didn't think he would move so fast. He was on her before I could stop him. For God's sake, when I wake him up don't let him know what you saw. If any of you tell him, you could hurt him badly and probably make a bad enemy."

That was all well and good until he brought Sam back. As soon as the big sailor was on his feet, he frowned, puzzled, and reached for his crotch. He must have realized in a flash what had happened while he was under Roger's control. With one murderous look at the hypnotist, he shouted, "You frigging bastard! I'll kill you!" and charged. Roger dashed out as if his life depended on it–which might well have been true. I heard later that he escaped Sam's fury and found temporary safety in another Navy unit.

Off to War

My final weeks at Harvard were peaceful, and I spent most of my free time at my clubs to be sure to stay out of trouble. When I moved on, I would have attended college for two full years plus one summer, landing me at some point between sophomore and junior. Depending on my upcoming Navy experience, I might be able to earn a degree in one more year. After spending a few days with my family, I boarded a train heading out to join the real Navy. I would spend the next two and a half years on active duty before returning to Harvard as a civilian in Part Four.

Life Three: The U.S. Navy

PART ONE

The Road To Colorado
1944

Asbury Park – Our Sub-Tropical Not Quite Paradise

In June, 1944 I completed my Navy V-12 training at Harvard and set off to a pre-midshipmen's school in Asbury Park, N.J. This would be temporary duty, pending an opening at a regular midshipmen's school. On the train I met another sailor, a really happy fellow who turned out to be another V-12 graduate. When he heard where I was headed, he whacked me on the back.

"Me, too," he exclaimed. "And are we lucky! I heard we'd be billeted in a luxury hotel right on the beach. With all those sweet broads. Young, in tight bathing suits!"

The jolly sailor was partly right. The Navy had taken not one, but *two* elegant hotels–the Monterey and the Berkeley-Carteret. They were on the beach, all right, but the part about sweet broads or other good things died there. We were billeted in an upper-story double room that required a five-floor climb up a humid stairwell to reach. The window gave us a scenic view–but looking inland, away from the ocean. Finally, a capacity influx of young seamen insured that all our floor space was taken by double-decker bunks, baggage, and sweating sailors.

Our most bitter disappointment was to find that the hotel was enclosed behind a tall, heavy wire fence. Although sweltering in the July heat, our hundreds of frustrated sailors were allowed on the beach only for swimming and calisthenics, under supervision.

This created a situation where every time we could take a break from calisthenics, or k.p. or other duties, we would be pressed against the wire fence trying to make contact with clusters of sadistic girls in bathing suits on the other side, who tantalized us with every trick they knew short of being arrested.

It was bitter irony, indeed, that a popular song at that time was *Don't Fence Me in.*

Despite these mental hardships, our weeks of Navy training at Asbury Park helped us toughen up into good Navy men. And it was here that I learned the most important lesson that every aspiring young sailor should remember:

That if you are a nineteen-year-old apprentice seaman and a senior non-com happens to catch you in a situation where he considers you are being idle, and tells you to get your ass into the galley and peel one hundred potatoes, agree politely, and when you see your first potato crawling with pale weevils, don't throw that potato away or complain about bugs. If you do, the non-com will patiently explain that those weevils are a standard component of the U.S. Navy Potato and, in fact, contain more protein than the potato itself; to convince you, he will pull out one of your bugs and eat it, then suggest that you do likewise, which you will do.

Gaining from such experiences, those of us passing through Asbury Park benefited from those weeks of training–but were not unhappy to transfer out.

With Family in New York

A few days of leave gave me my first real chance to spend relaxed time with my full family. My happiest surprise was Dad's appearance. He had already put on probably twenty pounds since arriving. With our victory over Japan nearly assured, and probably not too far off, he was getting in shape to return to his various businesses in Shanghai after Japan's defeat.

Until then, he and Mother were completing a book covering their adventures before and after the Japanese takeover. It described some of Dad's strategies to survive the privations of his prison camp and detailed some of the Japanese atrocities on the inmates. Like Mother's book, *News Is My Job,* it would be published by Macmillan under the title of *Flight from China.*

This New York visit also gave me a chance to say goodbye to my best friend, Johnny, who had completed his Navy basic training and was expecting orders to ship overseas. We still double-dated, but I spent most of my time alone with Jaye. It was understood that we would postpone completing any plans until I had a better idea of where my immediate future would take me. My priority, unless I remained in the Navy, was to finish my final year and get a Harvard degree.

In the meantime, every day brought me closer to the point where I might finally have the chance to see a Jap through my gun sight.

I Enter Midshipmen's School

Our handsome uniforms were not designed for such activity in the August heat and humidity. Yet here we were, sweating heavily, standing in rows, one behind the other, on Notre Dame's wide parade ground. In front of us unknown officers were standing on the reviewing stand. And off to one side was the military band. The impact of booming drums and powerful brass playing the stirring march, *The Thunderer*, filled me with overwhelming pride. For the first time since signing up, I felt the full excitement of really being a part of our great Navy. A childhood dream had come true.

From parade rest we were ordered to attention and salutes were exchanged. Then we marched, always to the rhythm of that band. Again we lined up in formation, by row and by column, to stand at parade rest. One of the officers on the reviewing stand gave a speech, too distant to understand clearly. Standing motionless, in the blistering heat, I heard a thump to one side. A gap appeared; the midshipman previously standing there was crumpled on the ground, but no one moved to help him. Soon another dropped, then another.

Later the word was passed that several had fainted that afternoon. Before the next drill, salt tablets were distributed to us to prevent a recurrence.

My Amphibious Battleship

Classes were designed to instill in us much of the technical and practical knowledge needed by a line officer. High on the list–in the days before electronics–was celestial navigation, which employed a sextant and Bowditch's essential book of tables. These were both explained carefully by navigation officers, and each trainee was given the opportunity to practice using these aids. Then we were tested in a simulated situation, which required the use of a sextant and Bowditch's tables to fix the position of a battleship at sea. My classmates, with few exceptions, sailed through with flying colors. I thought I had, too, until my result was announced.

"This is the first time," our instructor announced with a straight face. "That one of my navigators has succeeded in creating an amphibious battleship. Here, off our New York coast, is where his thirty thousand ton *U.S.S. Battleship* took off." The granite faced commander held up a chart of the Atlantic coast. "And here is where he landed the heavy ship–oh, we don't seem to have a hydrographic chart of the Rocky Mountains!"

I had to ruefully join in the raucous laughter. Even though I quickly corrected my error–which was caused by a simple adding mistake–I enjoyed a brief moment of dubious fame as the navigator who sailed a battleship into Denver.

The Lovely Blonde from Boston and her Friend

Between classes, drills and homework assignments we still found time for girls. We met several at the U.S.O. socials–which were a huge boost to morale–and really appreciated the effort that the organizers made to arrange these for us. It was here that the magic of our semi–officer's uniforms did its trick. The sailor suit won many hearts and all the rest, but I soon learned that bell-bottoms couldn't compete with a midshipman's irresistible summer uniform.

Within a week I had teamed up with two other cadets of about my age: Tom, who became my best friend there, was a brown haired, perpetually sunburned Texan with a carefree nature that bordered on recklessness, and Jules, a tall, heavy set Conch from Key West whose quick temper and tremendous physical strength discouraged any jokes about his accent. During weekends, aided by the discovery that Tom had access to a car, we surveyed the rewards that South Bend offered. Many of our explorations took place in Tom's comfortable vehicle.

My most exciting surprise occurred when, with little advance notice, I had a visit from the most attractive of the debutantes I had met at Boston's parties. Claire was about my height, beautiful, slender and very graceful. Whenever waltzes had been played, we danced together and I had the pleasure of swinging her around and watching her long blond hair flow out in a golden cascade.

She had driven all the way from Boston in her own car with a petite school friend, who was thoroughly captivated by my rough and tough Conch buddy, Jules. Accustomed to the young gentlemen she met in her circle of friends back home, she gushed. "I've never met anyone quite like your friend. Is he really real?"

It was mutual. Tom, watching them with a big grin, joked, "Boy, this is really a case of opposites attracting. They can't leave each other!" They finally did, but only when Claire had to drive her friend back to Boston. As far as I knew, they communicated for long after that.

Much as I was attracted to Claire, my thoughts kept returning to Jaye, and the life together that we had often talked about. After the war was over.

The Unbeatable Eye Test

About half way through the training program we received word that we faced a final physical to qualify for commissions. My last exam, which I had breezed through during V-12 at Harvard, had accepted lens-corrected vision for near sighted people. This one, I learned, did not. Still, I felt reasonably confident that I would be able to pass by using familiar techniques like squinting to sharpen my vision. To be certain, I reconnoitered the battlefield by questioning fellow cadets. Their answers gave me a rude surprise.

"Sorry, John," said one. "It's just not worth trying. The test is unbeatable. You remember the old chart with the big E on the top? Well, it's gone. They have a box stuck on the wall now with a narrow slit along the front, and in that slit are little black letters–about ten or twelve in a row."

"That doesn't sound bad. I could memorize them."

"It's not that simple. There are many different rows of letters. The corpsman who examines you turns on a light behind them and brings up a row of letters that he tells you to read–maybe forward, maybe backward. Then he pulls up a different row, and so on."

I froze, realizing that, even if I could memorize all the rows, I would have no way of learning which row of letters was being shown since I couldn't see any of them. I felt my confidence drain away, replaced by an icy dread I had not known since my captain's mast at Harvard. My only hope was that, with a week to go before the test, there would be time to find a solution. This would have to be a miracle.

By the time the exams took place, the miracle had materialized. Two of my buddies risked their commissions to help me, and together we devised a method to clue me in with key letters as I was being tested. We agreed that this process would never be disclosed, and to this date I have kept our agreement. I breezed through the "unbeatable" eye test, passing this critical prerequisite for a commission as a line officer.

There was still one more test to take: a Navy I.Q. survey. It resembled those conducted at schools, where we filled in pages of "check one of these" and other questions addressing math, vocabulary, logical thinking, and so on. When I was told the results, I was surprised that I had come in second out of a thousand or more participants. At that time this high score did not seem significant. But only a few weeks later, it turned out to have an important bearing on my future.

The Naval Intelligence Commander

On October 9, 1944 I completed midshipmen's school and was commissioned Ensign, U.S. Naval Reserve. My hopes soared. For the nearly two years since I enlisted, I had been a frustrated spectator as my Navy pounded its way across the Pacific, decimating Japanese forces in battles at Midway, Guadalcanal, and the Pacific atolls. Now, mounting the greatest assembly of naval sea and air power in history, our marine juggernaut was closing in on my enemy!

One by one, my friends Bud Lane, Sandy, Johnny, Paul and others had gone into action, many aboard LSTs and other landing craft. Now it would finally be my turn. I wanted a destroyer–but any ship would do as long as it carried me up against the hated Japanese. It didn't worry me that at this stage of the war a surplus of junior officers was developing, causing many midshipman's school graduates to be held in suspension. I knew I would make it to sea.

Yet, even as I waited for my ship, unknown forces were shaping a different Navy path for me. My China background was certainly a factor. Dad's Navy friends clearly played a major role. In any case, the effect was a summons to meet Albert Hindmarsh, a visiting commander in naval intelligence, who was interviewing candidates for a Navy language school in Boulder, Colorado.

With my mind still focused on my destroyer, I entered his temporary office. Sitting at a wide desk, the dark haired, square faced commander returned my salute. "At ease."

He was flipping through several pages in a folder with the Harvard insignia on its cover and paused to study one. Then he put down the file, removed his glasses and looked hard at me. "Ensign Potter," he asked in a businesslike tone. "How much do you know about my Chinese language program?"

"Nothing, sir."

"Have you ever considered learning the Chinese language?"

"No, sir."

After a pause, he looked up and said, "You are wondering why you were ordered here to meet me. This is because you have been recommended as a candidate for the Navy's program in the Chinese language. I will be forthright with you. This program is extremely challenging. It requires both high intelligence and strong motivation to succeed. For this reason, I have rarely accepted anyone with a college record below the highest level, and even among the best of these there is a high rate of attrition.

"Before you arrived I reviewed your record at Harvard, looking for evidence of consistent performance that supports your recommendations. I was disappointed to find that your marks have been average, at best, consistently falling far below our minimum standards. This should automatically disqualify you.

"However, there can be exceptions for candidates who offer exceptional strengths to offset scholastic weaknesses. Examples in your case are the ability to win a valuable scholarship on short notice when you needed financial assistance, and the very high score in your Navy I.Q. test. Both indicate a latent ability to perform at scholastic levels far higher than your college marks would indicate. Further potential strengths are your China experience, and the recommendations I have received on your behalf from officers I know well and respect.

"This has led to my decision to accept you in my Mandarin language program if you so decide. Throughout your studies there you will be competing with honors scholars, many in the Phi Beta Kappa society.

Your work will call for intense concentration for long periods of time–sometimes referred to as total immersion. Your records, although erratic, indicate that you could manage this if you choose to.

"If you succeed, the Navy can offer you a career with steady promotions, challenging duty including possible combat situations and eventually a distinguished naval or diplomatic career. If, however, you fail to maintain the standards of performance we require, you will be dismissed with no assurance of keeping your rank."

"I would suggest that you think this over carefully. I understand you will be in New York on leave and will keep our offer open for one week. By then you will deliver your reply to the Third Naval District Intelligence Office, 90 Church Street, for onward transmittal. Regardless of your decision, your new orders and travel documents will be cut there."

Sensing a dismissal, I saluted smartly and left. The commander clearly had no wish to prolong our meeting, so I had no chance to express my own feelings that the last damn thing I wanted was to be shackled down in some foreign language school thousands of miles from the Pacific.

Yet, in New York, my thoughts were continuously invaded by the commander's offer. What affected me most was the knowledge that Dad's senior Navy friends were confident enough in my ability to recommend me. This could only mean that they felt I could be a useful asset to our Navy. Dad must have looked on this the same way, and also as an important step in my post-war career. Whether naval or commercial, I realized that fluency in the language could be helpful.

On top of this, I had been learning that new assignments to destroyers were falling off as ship production was cut back. I might even never get sea duty. The Boulder assignment, on the other hand, was real, would certainly be challenging, and might even turn out to be my fastest route to meet the Jap enemy in China.

PART TWO

The U.S. Navy School of Oriental Languages 1944-1946

Into the Halls of Learning

A good omen accompanied me on my train ride to Denver. She was a well-rounded sweetheart named Bonnie with long brown hair and plump lips, and together we found a place to pass the long night far more comfortable than our passenger car seats. This was in the dining car, at one of the comfortable tables with a long, white tablecloth drooping over the sides. Not exactly *at* the dining table, or even *on* the table. *Under* it.

Access to our playground was facilitated by a sympathetic waiter who nourished us with frequent drinks. The gentle old attendant responded soulfully to the scene we painted for him: the brave young naval officer going off to war, accompanied by his newlywed, clinging young bride, who would not let him go until finally, in just hours, he would be torn from her arms and sail away, perhaps never to return. Our patriotic waiter, overwhelmed by emotion, dimmed the car's lights early and left for the night.

Bonnie and I found that the carpet under the table made a serviceable mattress, sheltered by the curtain of the drooping tablecloth. I was soon aware that, despite her fresh, young appearance, she was a veritable cornucopia of sexual experience, with a driving urge and limitless energy to demonstrate this. Now and then people bumped their way through the dimly lit dining car, passing us, but either did not notice the activity under our table or were too well mannered to lift the cloth to peek.

Early in the morning I returned to my seat and slept soundly, missing the sight of the Rocky Mountains as we approached. When we separated at the railway station, Bonnie gave me her address at a Denver women's college for future follow–ups.

I made up for the lost scenery during my two-hour bus ride to Boulder, which took me up another 200 feet from mile-high Denver. A taxi let me off at the University of Colorado.

Standing within sight of the towering sandstone formations called The Flatirons, I surveyed my home-to-be for the next year and a half, called the Men's Dormitory. The brightly colored four-storied building, with facilities and dining hall for several hundred students, was constructed of off-pink sandstone with red tile roofing, in an architectural style which I learned later was whimsically dubbed "Tuscan vernacular."

Most of the rooms were already occupied. I found mine on the second floor, and met my new roommate, a tall, quiet man named Dave Willis. Often during the next months, I was happy to have such a friendly, intelligent roommate. After introductions, he said, "I arrived here two days early and have pretty well learned the ropes. If you like, I can give you a briefing."

"That would be great. I have no idea what's going on."

"Well, our program will last one and a half years with a few days off every few months. Mondays through Fridays we have classes and do homework. On Saturdays there are four 90-minute exams in reading, writing, orals and dictation. We have Sundays off and can play touch football or tennis and other sports. Or just relax. But most students usually study."

I broke in. "Excuse me. What do you know about test Saturdays?"

"Not much. I wouldn't think they're easy. The passing mark is eighty. Anyone who gets a lower grade goes on probation. I've heard that two probations and you're out. But our teachers will try to help us. They want us to succeed. We will be learning only Mandarin, but to pass we have to become fluent. We will have to be able to read and write five thousand characters."

"Five thousand? Read and write?" I looked at him incredulously.

Dave nodded. "I know. It seems impossible, but others have done it. The method is to force feed us in what they call total immersion–as though we were suddenly dumped in the middle of China where no one speaks anything except Chinese. We'll have to be able to communicate in Mandarin quickly. The reason is what they call a two-week cut-off. After that, any of us overheard speaking anything except Chinese goes on probation. If it happens twice, he's out."

I could only shake my head. Things should be pretty quiet around here for a while.

Ne How ma?

This was our welcome into the eight a.m. class and meant: Are you well? Or, Good morning. One by one, all seven of us practiced greeting the slim, young Chinese lady instructress with these words, and receiving her reply: "*How, hsieh hsieh*", meaning good, thank you. Word by word, phrase by phrase, Miss Wong led us gently into the kindergarten stage of Mandarin. But by the end of the hour I felt glimmers of optimism as we trooped, with heads full of strange sounds and binders full of hurried notes, to the next class.

Here we encountered our second instructor, a stout Westerner with white hair and mustache, thick glasses and a strangely melodious tone of speaking. "Good morning. My name is Dr. Jones. I was a missionary in China for thirty years. I lived and taught in four of the central provinces." Looking over our group, he asked, "Has anyone here been to China?"

I was the only person to respond. "Yes. In Shanghai. Our family lived there."

"Good. Shanghai. I will now write for you the Chinese word for Shanghai." He scratched two characters on the black board, one above the other. Pointing to the upper one, which had only three lines, he said, "*Shang*. It means above, or over."

The bottom character was a confusing mass of crisscrossing lines. He explained that, like most Chinese characters, it had two parts: a radical, tending to convey the word's meaning, and the phonetic, usually describing its sound. Marking with his pointer, he explained, "The left side of this character is the radical. It means water, or ocean. And the right side is the phonetic, pronounced *hai*. This gives the character its sound.

"A look at both characters introduces the logic of the Chinese language. Hundreds of years ago, today's city was a fishing village near the delta where the Yangtze River meets the Yellow Sea. The fishermen called the place simply, 'Above the sea'." The professor nodded at me, "Which is still the name you use today."

From here, Dr. Jones took us step by step into the jungle of written Chinese. Careful as he was to explain, we all seemed to be hopelessly entangled before the hour had passed. At the close, our instructor crinkled his thick white mustache in a friendly smile. "Simple, isn't it? Should be no trouble at all to learn five thousand characters!" He then told each of us to pick up his numbered copy of the just-published, many-pound Mathews dictionary, containing about 15,000 entries in its 1,220 pages. "I shouldn't try to memorize it too quickly," he cautioned with a touch of humor.

Only a few minutes after finishing lunch, we went to our next class, orals. Our young Chinese instructor was just as friendly as the previous two, and–like them–wielded an iron fist inside the velvet glove. For an hour we struggled to understand phrases repeated to us over and over, and actually learned to repeat a few ourselves.

The last of our classes, dictation, introduced us to the feature that causes Chinese to be considered the most difficult of all languages to master: the tones. Over and over we repeated after the instructor the four tones, numbered one, two, three and four, used in the Mandarin dialect, until I thought we would all be singing them in our sleep.

Finally someone mildly objected, "Why do they have so many tones?"

He received what was probably the standard answer to a frequently asked question: "Be glad you're not learning Fukienese. They have up to seven tones!"

Some Swim, Some Sink

The next few days were a race to assimilate enough Chinese to communicate basic needs before the cut-off. We were constantly encouraged by our instructors, who gave us pages of useful vocabulary-building aids. David and I drilled each other every opportunity we had, and before long we could actually communicate, if haltingly. Our instructors, understanding our work pressure, rationed our daily vocabulary-building objectives to a challenging, but manageable, number of words. By the time that the two-week deadline arrived, David and I had learned enough to be commended by instructors, and were actually able to converse slowly in Mandarin.

Not so fortunate was another of our group, a Phi Beta Kappa. It became apparent that he had won his key by working at maximum capacity for years, and simply had no reserve that he could draw upon to reach the pace that the program demanded. When he failed to turn up at class Miss Wong, who was crying, gave us the news. She and our other instructors all took his loss as personal failures. We were told later that he had a nervous breakdown.

Good Friends

After surviving my first month on overdrive, I eased up enough to begin associating with other students. Among them were several who became close friends:

SLIM: His name was John Everson, but no one called him anything but Slim–just like his lean shape. A lieutenant (j.g.), he was about five years my senior with a long face topped by curly blond hair. He brought with him a welcome sense of excitement. Unlike most of us with only academic backgrounds, Slim had experienced real war. He had operated for months with Chinese guerillas behind the Japanese lines in China, transmitting information about enemy troop movements. When finally cornered, he escaped to the coast where a submarine picked him up.

Slim was one of very few language students whom the Navy chiefs–the real bosses who ran the place–truly respected. This was evident from the fact that in our dorm, where alcohol was strictly prohibited, half a dozen cases of sherry were openly stacked in his closet. His supply was replenished regularly by the chiefs, who drank with him. It was very good sherry, too.

After months of getting acquainted, Slim brought me into his inner sanctum. To sample his sherry, of course. But more important, to accompany him on travels into dark corners of Arkham and Providence. My warrior friend, incredibly, was hooked on a little known author of horror and fantasy novels, H. P. Lovecraft. By inviting in friends, he had an audience to titillate with his favorite adjectives such as "eldritch" and "miasmal" while we were discussing weird horror tales like *The Call of Cthulhu*, *The Rats in the Walls* and The *Color out of Space*.

Eccentric as this hobby seemed for a naval officer, Slim went far better some weeks later. As I walked into his room he burst out, "I say, Herald. Why do you hold your cloak out from your body? Have you got swellings in your groin?"

"What's wrong, Slim? What cloak?" He jumped up and pointed at my belt buckle. "But you've got an erection! You lewd fellow!"

"Like hell I do!" I protested, annoyed. Then I realized that Slim was trying out one of his whimsical diversions–acting the role of a character in a play. When he got control of his laughter, he explained that this was a scene from the classical Greek comedy, *Lysistrata*, written by Aristophanes over two thousand years earlier. When I read Slim's English translation I found the humor hilarious–every bit as effective as anything I saw in the current media.

Slim had a relatively easy entry into our language world. His months with Mandarin-speaking guerillas had prepared him for our course, giving him time to fully enjoy life's pleasures. Among these was Saturday night sporting occasions at Boulder's jam-packed Timber Tavern. Serving hard liquor without too much concern about age, their bartenders probably helped to deflower more University of Colorado virgins than even the players on their Buffalo football team.

My good omen Bonnie, from Denver, and I met Slim and his WAVE date there one Saturday night. After we polished off a fifth of lethal Southern Comfort–the only whisky available–I was driving a borrowed car up the mountain along a stretch of narrow winding road. Slim and his date were locked together in the back, oblivious of everything except their activities, when Bonnie reached for my zipper. Before I knew it, she was leaning over me and the car had veered right so far that a front tire scraped halfway off the road's edge.

At that moment my Guardian Angel took over. Drawing on every ounce of will power, I shoved the girl away and dragged the wheel back onto the road. Suddenly sober and probably trembling from our narrow escape, I stopped before going on. Slim and his date were still oblivious and Bonnie was resentful, unaware of how close we came to cart wheeling down a steep, rocky slope.

Slim's activities ended abruptly in June, 1946, when he married a tall, beautiful University of Colorado student named Patty Anne, who quickly put him in irons.

My final meeting with Slim took place when I was a civilian working in Hong Kong during the Korean War. Part of the Seventh Fleet had put in, and our naval attaché asked me to contact an officer on the communications ship. This turned out to be Slim, now wearing three stripes as the fleet intelligence officer. His team was working on a matter involving a mysterious Eurasian woman. I knew something about her, and was able to give him a lead.

JIM: A Mandarin student who became a lifelong friend was Jim Wolf. We became close at Boulder, and corresponded for half a century afterward with each letter starting "*Ne how ma*?" Jim was about five foot ten, of average build, with a confident, friendly disposition. What brought us together was the top of our heads–we were both losing hair. Jim led our effort to fight back by finding a clinic in Denver whose "experts" guaranteed full hair restoration if we took a many-week program. So every week Jim drove us to Denver to subject our heads to heavy plastering of stinking goo. There was no growth, and eventually we gave this up in disgust.

Like Slim, Jim was a lieutenant (j.g.) who had experienced real duty as gunnery officer aboard *U.S.S. Enterprise.* His battery was shooting down *kamakazi* planes, when one got through and struck the ship less than fifty yards away. He survived the explosion and was transferred to Boulder, where–with his record–he also won the respect of the chiefs.

I came to know Jim best at the end of 1946, when he invited me to spend the New Year's holiday with him at his ranch in Albion, Nebraska. Stepping from his car under the sign WOLF BROTHERS, I noticed cattle in all directions. A moment later, inside a spacious hall heated by a huge wood fire, I met several members of Jim's family. The men wore western clothing with boots and large belt buckles. They took me in like one of their own.

Warm welcome notwithstanding, I managed to create two incidents during a short visit. The first occurred when we went pheasant hunting. After Jim had bagged a bird I shot at mine, but was too slow raising the shotgun. This sent my shot on a low trajectory right into the flanks of several cattle. The resulting stampede caused a cow to break a leg.

The other incident followed a community dance at which I drank too much. Arriving in our uniforms at a time when most of the other men were away, Jim and I had no trouble meeting girls. One–short, cute, and nicely built–immediately began rubbing herself against me. I pushed her off for a moment to ask Jim where we could go for some privacy.

"Don't do it, John." He warned. "Everybody knows that girl. Molly is very hot, always trying to get a man. She has two big brothers who watch her like hawks, and we don't want trouble." This was all well and good, I thought, but what about basic chivalry? "But, Jim, she needs help. If the poor girl doesn't get laid soon she'll go crazy!"

"You haven't seen her brothers. If they catch you doing anything with that girl, they'll hurt you."

I thought I knew better and led Molly to Jim's car, which was parked quite a way off. We hopped in and she had her skirt up in moments. Molly was on fire. The car radio was playing, "You came to me out of nowhere", which I thought was appropriate, and we were doing just fine when suddenly I heard an angry shout from down the road.

"Damn!" she exclaimed. "My brothers. They'll kill us."

I eased back into the driver's seat, put her in gear, and raced off down some road I'd never seen. "Where do I let you off?"

"I'll show you another place where they won't look. Keep going."

"No!" I exclaimed, suddenly sober. "I'm taking you back."

She grabbed me but I was adamant. And ashamed. I finally dropped her off near the dance hall after she tidied up, and parked Jim's car even further away. Jim heard the next day that she had told her brothers she hated me because I had been a real gentleman and refused to do anything. They couldn't have believed her, but the matter ended there.

Jim and I teamed up again two years later for some good evenings at Harvard, where he was attending law school and I was completing my senior college year. Then, in 1957, he formed the Albion Syndicate, which subscribed to a block of shares in a treasure diving venture off Spain that I organized. Our final meeting was many years later at Harvard, where we were both attending reunions. Our senior status was evinced by the fact that, instead of reminiscing about happy experiences together, we spent most of the time discussing prostates and leg cramps.

Jim had a full life. From the rancher and Navy officer I first knew, he expanded his ranching business into the giant Wagonhammer Cattle Co., owned a bank, and went on to become the Democratic Chairman of the Nebraska State Legislature and sponsored many well-known philanthropic organizations. I have never been able to meet his widow, Elaine, who gave him great support, but we still keep in touch by letter and phone.

BILL: I met my closest lifelong friend one afternoon during a touch football game. I was lying on my back, still clutching the ball, when I looked up at his face. With a worried frown, he was asking, "Are you all right? Sorry I bumped you."

I remembered seeing his powerful form closing in. "I thought this was supposed to be a friendly game of touch!" The trace of a grin formed on his stubbled face. "Yes. But you got in my way."

This was characteristic of Navy lieutenant William Mason Morgenroth. When obstructions got in his way, they usually ended up on their backs. The powerfully built athlete played to win. Behind his deceptively winning smile and soft, almost gentle voice, was a formidable warrior. Although his language course, Malay, lasted only six months, we built in that time a strong friendship. We had an unusual advantage: neither of us was learning the language of the other, so both were released from the ban against speaking English.

Bill had a rich experience in the Navy. At the end of the war, he led a marine detachment to the Andaman Islands to receive the surrender of its Japanese commander. Instead, the commander disobeyed his emperor's orders and made a surprise attack with superior forces, killing several marines before being subdued. Later, Bill personally delivered gifts to President Truman from the Chief of the neighboring Nicobar Islands.

After 27 years' service, he ended his naval career as a senior officer.

Bill's other strong interest was education. Fluent in Latin, Greek, French, German and Malay, he later served as assistant dean of business schools at Michigan, Ohio State, U. of Colorado and other universities. He was a respected educator in business, marketing, mathematics and finance.

It was from Bill, the Senior Officer on Base, that I learned the early history of our language school. It was established with about 150 students at the U. of Colorado in 1942, right after the Battle of Midway, in appreciation that much of our success there could be attributed to naval intelligence for decrypting part of the Japanese naval code. From there, Navy and marine graduates, trained in Japanese, went on to take part in key operations from code breaking to landing with the marines on Pacific atolls. They were so successful that similar programs were set up for other languages.

Bill had nearly completed his Malay language course when, one Saturday before exams, he asked me, "How would you like to go to Flagstaff later? I've been reading its history and think it might be an interesting place to visit."

"You mean that wild west town in Arizona?"

"Yes. We can leave right after the last exam and be back here tomorrow for dinner."

"We can't drive that fast."

"We'll go in the Waco."

"What's a Waco?"

"A plane. You pronounced it wrong. It's not 'way-ko'. That's a town in Texas. It's pronounced 'wah-ko'. A tight two-seater biplane I like to fly. There's one at the airport."

The thought was tantalizing, but I had too much homework to risk it. Anyway, Bill soon returned. "Couldn't do it. Too much weather along the route."

Spontaneous moves like this had made me think that Bill might just make a good match for my sister Patty, who also did impetuous things. Before my plans could hatch, though, they were doused by the radio commentator, Walter Winchell. Every now and then we listened, mildly amused, to a telegraph clicking followed by his urgent staccato: "Good evening, Mr. and Mrs. America, from border to border, coast to coast and all the ships at sea."

I seldom bothered paying attention to his wildly exaggerated news blurbs that followed, until one evening the words "Patricia Potter" brought me to attention. Winchell followed with a tale that my sister had "caught" the handsome, rich Henry Luce III, son of the powerful publisher.

"Hell," I said angrily to Bill, who was sitting with us. "Patty didn't try to catch him. I thought she was getting engaged to a Scot in Nassau, but I guess Hank finally convinced her to marry him. *If* that's true."

News of Winchell's "news flash" had somehow reached my Chinese instructors, along with information that I was Patty's brother. The following day they drew me aside to ask, almost deferentially, if this were true. To them, Henry Luce's father was an important friend, since he and his wife Clare Booth were leaders of the influential "China Lobby" which was effectively promoting support for China among America's leaders.

Even as my idea of a family merger with Bill went out the window, Bill replaced it with a bombshell: "Jeanie and I are getting married and I want you to be stand up with me." I had met Jeanie Hamer only a few times, but knew that she was president of Pi Beta Phi sorority.

I was bowled over. The Senior Officer Present asking a junior ensign to be his best man! Unheard of. "Of course I will. I've never been a best man, but I'll do a good job for you."

Slim knew the procedure and briefed me. When the moment came a few weeks later, I soldiered through, didn't lose the ring, told a few slightly off color jokes and gave my friend what I was told was adequate support.

The married couple moved off campus and I saw very little of Bill until years later, when he visited me in Hong Kong. He and Jeanie were divorced. Over the following years I made sporadic contact with Bill, who had become dean of his business school. We met again in Hong Kong, then Martha's Vineyard, where he met my wife Joanie.

Our last meeting was in 2009, sixty-four years after we had met, in the dining room of his comfortable retirement home in St. Petersburg, Florida. No longer the powerhouse that I remembered, he was standing in a walker wearing a brightly colored checkered jacket. When I approached him, we looked each other up and down and laughed, without saying a word.

Then, for a few moments, we embraced each other with real love. Bill may not have been in full strength, but our friendship was. We had a quiet lunch, knowing that it would be our last.

William P. Hunt

Toward the end of my Boulder training I had an unexpected meeting, which could have shaped my future. It happened in New York, during my end-1945 Christmas break, when Dad suggested that I call on his friend William Hunt, who was interested in talking with me, about a possible job in China. After making an appointment to see him at his office on Pine Street, I asked Dad to for any information that might be helpful.

I received a good briefing. Hunt had a personal interest in China going back to 1926 when he had served as a vice consul in Tientsin. While there, he studied the country and its economy, learning enough to recognize sales opportunities for many American goods, especially engineering products and systems, and railroad equipment.

While making the diplomatic rounds, Bill Hunt was able to develop valuable personal contacts with many of China's future business and government leaders. His preparations came to fruition a few years later when he formed William P. Hunt & Co.

Dad's briefing proved very helpful when I walked into Bill Hunt's office. Big, powerful and dynamic, he received me in a smartly decorated suite. I thought it looked more like a library than office until I recognized that most of the books and magazines seemed to be about China.

Bill rose from his desk and shook my hand firmly. "I have heard some good things about your progress at Boulder, John," he opened. "Sit down. Tell me what you've been doing."

We talked easily, with him asking most of the questions, for a good hour. His questions led to information that he was planning a bold expansion into China right after the war, with headquarters in Shanghai and offices in other cities.

"I believe your Navy training would give you full command of the written language," he said.

"The written language, yes. But as you know, my Mandarin is most useful in the north."

"That would include Peiping and Tientsin and Tsingtao, some places I have in mind.

"And of course the top officials all over the country speak Mandarin."

He switched to other areas, determining that I had no experience with industrial products or commercial sales.

He nodded, "That's quite understandable for someone of your age who is still at college. These qualifications can be developed reasonably quickly with technical training and working experience."

Leaning back, he smiled at me, "Not so easy with Chinese language, eh?"

His final question was, "Have you made any plans for after the war?"

"I'll either stay in the Navy or get my degree from Harvard. After that, no plans."

As we parted company, he said, "Please let me know what you will be doing. My secretary will give you a good book for background. It is a standard primer titled *Village Life in China*. Later you will receive from me other reading material on industrial products."

Although it was never mentioned, Bill Hunt took for granted that I would be interested in joining his company. And of course, at that time, I was.

Hank, Jim and our China Trade & Engineering Co.

Henry Bittner and James Ferrigan were fellow Mandarin students in my class, both a few years older than I was. Soon after we met I learned that they had unique qualities. While most of us came from standard educational backgrounds, these two also had business experience. Hank, a perpetually smiling six-footer, had been a district manager for a major manufacturing company. Jim was a former sales manager. With the common bond of engineering, the two of them teamed up and started doing homework together. They soon learned that some aspects of their business experience were transferable to language study. At the same time, I was discovering ways to simplify my retention of Chinese characters by organizing their shapes and sounds into common groupings.

We learned about each other's progress when our conversation–in relatively good Mandarin–turned to efforts we were making to increase study efficiency. It became clear that we had all arrived at roughly similar objectives and working methods. This resulted in a teamwork through which all three of us were able to learn more, in less time. The success of this cooperation in our language studies led to thoughts about continuing it after the war. "We have such good working relationship together," I ventured. "It would be a waste to throw this away after the war."

Hank agreed, "I've been thinking along those lines, too. I think we could make good partners."

Jimmy agreed. "I have a job waiting for me, but this sounds much more exciting. With a team like ours, we should be able to make a go of it."

"Has anyone thought about exporting to China?" offered Hank. "If we had a company, I bet we could pick up some good agencies for that market."

"I got to know many people at companies that were our customers," Jim added. "Some of them will be good prospects."

We sat silently. Then I ventured, "I haven't any business experience like you do, but my family had plenty of good contacts. I know Dad would be a big help."

Within a few days we agreed on a name: The China Trade and Engineering Company, and an objective: to develop profitable exports of products and services to China.

We would incorporate in Boulder with equal participation in company ownership and bank accounts, and then canvas prospects on impressive letterheads with the address and phone number of a rented premise. If the response were encouraging, we would proceed from there.

Handicapped by the need for study time to maintain the minimum score of 80 on our Saturday tests, we had to ration that which we could spare for our project. Still, after a month we had completed preliminary steps, and started gathering data about companies from commercial magazines and other sources. Two months later, we had fifty names. We arranged for our letters to be typed by a commercial secretary. Since each referred to products specific to one company, its draft needed personal input from Hank or Jim–whoever knew the most about its products.

Then I edited it for typing.

It seemed unbelievable, but only three months after the idea struck us, we had fourteen interested replies from a "Who's Who" of major American companies. They included a new auto company, Kaiser-Fraser, Ingersoll Rand, General Electric, Allis Chalmers and other familiar names. We studied the contents of each letter with growing excitement. Such a strong initial response gave me confidence that we could succeed.

I had made no commitment to Bill Hunt, but as a matter of courtesy I wrote him about our plans and returned his books about China. I received a very friendly note wishing us success.

All three of us, carrying businesslike briefcases, confidently called on the elderly loan officer at our Boulder bank. After his curiosity was satisfied, he gave us pages of forms to fill out, including details of our company assets and liabilities, and previous income tax returns.

We were learning fast. Other surprises followed when we came to recognize that many "interested" responders to our letters were simply curious. The few who seemed really serious asked for information we could not supply, like our company's history and plans when China opened up. One even asked us to "Send details of your engineers' technical training."

Assets, tax returns, technical training history! We had never considered any of these. Let alone financing–with practically no assets to show the bank. The final blow came when we learned that no travel documents postdated to some future time could be issued. With this, our project sank into a deep freeze. We agreed that some day, if opportunity came, the CTEC would be activated.

After we were reassigned to Washington, I saw quite a lot of Hank and his lovely green-eyed wife Shirley, and they met my family in New York. Then I went overseas and we lost contact for 60 years, until I tracked him down. Hank was living happily in Colorado. He had tried repeatedly to contact me, but had finally given up. The only "news" he had received was that I had been captured and executed by the Chinese communists! I assured Hank that this news, like that of Mark Twain, was greatly exaggerated.

Both of us tried to locate Jim, but sadly, without success.

My Rocky Mountain High

As a child I learned to ride horses at Shanghai's Equestrian Academy, perched on an English saddle, and as an early teenager I advanced to where I could post and canter around Shanghai's racetrack, also on an English saddle. All these rides made me a firm believer that the English saddle was the way to go. Until that magic Sunday when I settled into a western saddle and loped lazily into the foothills toward the Rocky Mountains. The feeling of sheer comfort on a horse was something new. I felt I could ride forever without tiring, just like the cowboys on the western range. Wow! No wonder those cowboys sang such happy songs. I was so happy myself that I put my head back and yodeled. Which made my date, Sandy, laugh so hard she nearly fall off her horse.

I owed this unforgettable trip to Sandy, who had extracted me from under a pile of Chinese characters to go riding with her. She was a popular senior, member of a top sorority and exactly my age and height. We had met one evening when I was floored by her combination of blond hair, blue eyes and gorgeous figure squeezed into a tight sweater. As we became better acquainted, I learned that, like many other U. of Colorado girls, she was from Texas. Her family practically owned the state, having settled there at about the time of the Alamo and been amassing property ever since.

About wealth, though, Sandy didn't give a damn. Her life was dedicated to having fun, and her college provided all the goodies to make this happen. Except the most important goodie of all–men. They had nearly all gone off to war. This is where the wisdom of those who selected Colorado for our training venue received such wholehearted appreciation from us. For despite all our hours of exhausting study and painful exams, we were men, and as such we were happy to supply the goodies to fill the unfulfilled needs in the lives of Sandy and her girl friends.

After riding up a trail she knew, Sandy led me into a patch of green grass hidden by pine trees, and threw down a blanket she had packed in her saddle bag. We jumped off, tied our horses and I set about fulfilling her current needs. I seem to have identified these correctly, because it was well over an hour before she broke off. Then, after a rest, Sandy fixed those beautiful blue eyes on me and asked," Who taught you to be so good?"

"You did," I answered truthfully. "You did, by putting me into that comfortable western saddle where I could relax all the way here!"

Many years later I had the pleasure of watching John Denver sing his beautiful signature song, *Rocky Mountain High*. It brought to mind happy memories of comfortable western saddles and the goodies that came with them.

Change of Orders

On August 7, 1945 we were astounded by the news that the Japanese city of Hiroshima had been vaporized by an atomic bomb. On the following days we went through the exciting stages of learning about America's new weapon, realizing that its use could shorten the war and save a huge number of American lives that might otherwise be lost in an invasion of Japan.

The Japanese surrender, that followed, gave us all a night of wild celebration, followed by a period of wondering what would happen to our school. Most likely the Japanese contingent, whose talents would be needed in Japan, would continue studying, as would the Russian class. We were unsure about ourselves until we received orders that the Chinese language students were to continue at Boulder until graduation, then would likely be sent to Honolulu or the Seventh Fleet. Although my shooting war against the Japanese never materialized, I might still be able to participate in other ways. This final hope vanished a few months later when my roommate Dave Willis and I received new orders. Under the caption CHANGE OF DUTY they stated: "On or about 27 April, 1946 you will regard yourself detached from duty...you will proceed to Washington, D.C., and report to the Chief of Naval Operations, Navy Department, for duty..."

PART THREE

My Last Assignment

The Unreal Wartime World of Washington, D.C.

I completed my assignment at Boulder and received a degree in Mandarin Chinese, packed my personal effects and about twenty pounds of training material, and went to New York for ten days of leave. Then, on May 13, with a promotion to lieutenant, j.g., I checked in at the Navy Department in Washington, where I was sent to quarters at the home of a pleasant middle aged couple. I planned to move out as soon as I could because sometimes, when the husband was away, the wife sidled up against me with a dumb remark such as, "Something's coming up between us." Knowing her husband as a decent guy, I felt awkward and backed off.

I was assigned to the Office of Naval Intelligence, where I met, and worked with, several other Boulder graduates as well as many new faces. Special friendships soon developed with three in my unit: American Lieutenant (j.g.) Paul Anspach, who was a rank ahead of me, and two British lieutenants (pronounced "leftenants", I learned). The four of us soon joined forces and took an apartment one block away from the Mayflower Hotel.

In a city where it was nearly impossible to buy a fifth of decent liquor, our place had an irresistible allure: half a wall was stacked several feet high with cases of prized Seagrams VO and Gordon's Gin. These bottles had not been smuggled in; they were legitimate monthly grog rations of our British roommates. Naturally, our home became a very popular congregation point for aficionados of quality booze–mainly junior naval officers from our unit–and good looking girls, who at that time outnumbered men by three to one in Washington, D.C.

Despite heavy consumption at our parties, the stacks of liquor cases brought in by our British friends grew steadily higher. By mid-summer, a crisis point was reached. We had to dispose of the surplus. A happy coincidence took care of the problem. I had been visiting New York on weekends, and on one of these trips was talking with a publisher who complained about the shortage of precisely what we wanted to dispose of. A price was struck, and every weekend several of us took the train to New York carrying boxes for him.

Adventures with girls, facilitated by our handsome uniforms, became almost routine. I did have one bout, however, which was unusual–it was positively terrifying. The girl was a Navy lieutenant, about 24 and a little taller than I was. So attractive was she that whenever she walked by our conversation paused. When it started again, the subject was why the hell no one had been able to score. Cynthia had a domineering roommate, and we agreed that the two had to have something going.

I investigated this rumor one night after she drank enough at one of our parties to let me take her home. We had another drink there, and settled on a sofa. She did not object when I put an arm around her and, to my surprise, responded enthusiastically when I explored under her blouse, then under her skirt. When I went up her thighs, she reciprocated and seemed positively ecstatic when her own hand confirmed that I was interested.

We were working on my trousers when another atomic bomb exploded. It was the door, crashing open. Then followed the shrieking of an enraged harpy as Cynthia's roommate charged at us, waving some sort of stick. I leapt away, pulling up my trousers, and she descended savagely upon the defenseless Cynthia.

With no thought at all of returning to the helpless girl's assistance, I hightailed it out of the apartment, hopping and pulling on clothes, before she could turn on me. The next day when Cynthia walked by she looked tired and didn't give me so much as a friendly nod.

My Final Navy Duty: Operations at Bethesda Naval Hospital

I was preparing to be discharged when I caught tonsillitis. When the infection subsided sufficiently, the doctor arranged for me to have my tonsils out at the Bethesda Naval Hospital. The operation was routine, and I was parked in a ward, minus tonsils, to sip liquids and chew Aspergum until ready to be discharged. The person in the next bunk, a Marine Colonel Powers, had been wounded when led a landing in the Pacific. He had become addicted to poker out there, and brought the game into our ward. It was low stakes–the nickel and dime variety–that allowed me to participate.

All went well until after midnight, when I felt a warmth in my throat. The duty doctor looked, and within minutes had me leaning back in a chair while he and some assistants cauterized my hemorrhage.

Again I was placed in recovery, this time under strict instructions to avoid any strenuous activity. And again, after nearly a week, I was declared ready for discharge the next day. I had played no poker, and was walking quietly down a hall, when a pretty little corps WAVE asked me whether I would like to see the beautiful hospital grounds in the moonlight. Thinking that there could be nothing dangerous about this, I joined her in a slow walk to some hills at the far end.

It had now been over two weeks since I had a woman and the silvery moon brought out curves in her body that were irresistible. For a fatal moment I forgot the doctor's admonition and let myself slip into the strenuous activity that he had warned against. Things went well at first. Then, with no warning, I felt the familiar flowing of warm blood.

Fortunately, my partner was an experienced nurse. She took my arm and carefully steered me across the lawn directly to the emergency room. The patching up took longer this time, and afterwards I was propped upright and told to stay that way under observation for a long time. There were no more hemorrhages, and after another week or so under strict supervision, I was finally released. Someone told me I had established some sort of undesirable record for the longest tonsillectomy.

I had a few days of free time, which I used looking around Silver Springs, MD, for a home that Slim had asked me to rent for him and his new wife. I was able to find a house with garden that made them very happy.

On September 29, 1946 I became a civilian again and returned to Harvard to complete my senior year. Like many other officers, I cut the gold stars and stripes from my blue jacket so that I could continue wearing it. Then I boarded the train north, carrying with me a heart full of warm, never-to-be-forgotten memories covering three and a half years in our U.S. Navy Reserve, serving in five locations as I rose through the ranks from apprentice seaman to Lieutenant (j.g.) in Naval Intelligence.

PART FOUR

Education in America Concluded

1946-1947

Harvard Senior as a Civilian (1946-1947)

I was very touched by the appreciation my country had for veterans like me. This was expressed in free education, including textbooks, at an institute of our choice, and a $20 check every week for one year, leading to the phrase "52/20 Club." There were also other benefits such as the welcome I received when I returned to Harvard in October, 1944. The receiving dean for veterans took the trouble to guide me into a curriculum that–combined with credits from my war service–should satisfy the requirements for a college degree in one busy semester.

My new room was located conveniently close to my D.U. club, which I frequented nearly daily, and the Hasty Pudding Club, with its good meals. Thanks to such similar things, my re-entry went so easily that I soon felt like I had never left. The only real difference was that most of my old friends had not yet returned. Still, invitations to debutante parties continued arriving, and this time there was no forced exercising at dawn or fence climbing to get back in.

The *Lampoon* Light and Other College Tales

The most exciting development was receiving visiting privileges at the *Harvard Lampoon*, oldest and best known of all college humor magazines with a who's who of famous satirists and humorists in its long and rich history. I was brought into the famous Lampoon building, with its round "castle," by my old friend Eldred, and introduced to a group of about ten members who were drinking and laughing at a table in the dining hall. They were easy to meet, and invited me to sit down.

Most exciting of the members was the Lampoon editor, Bill Gaddis. Slightly under six feet tall, noticeably thin, with light brown hair above high cheekbones, his salient feature was deeply sunken eyes with dark bags under them. It was the kind of face that would be hard to forget. A few meetings later Gaddis brought up the possibility of my joining.

"Big John," he said suddenly. "We're always on the alert for new members who can make people laugh: write short, witty stories, parodies, satire, mockery, ridicule, irony – that sort of thing. We have a reputation to maintain, you know, can't subsist on Bob Benchley's name forever." Eldred says you write and you're funny when you're not too drunk. So let me have a sample – one or two pages. If the committee passes it, we'll publish it." He looked around at the others. "Then we can see whether the members want you in."

Everybody laughed. Then Bill Middendorf–tall and heavy with a prominent nose on his clean-cut face–made a surprising offer. "I have a short piece which I don't need which I've titled *One Golden Day*. 'Poon quality, if I say so myself." He swung around to face me. "You can put your name on it and submit it for our consideration."

I was taken somewhat aback. Thanking them profusely, I asked for a few days before replying.

The reason was money. The initiation fee, while modest, was more than I could handle without my Navy income. Dad was still suffering from the theft of his savings in the Raven Trust swindle and the loss of three years' salary during the war. My support helped pay for repair of the damage the Japanese had done to our property in Shanghai, on top of some of the family expenses in America. I explained this to Eldred, who passed it on to the committee. Almost immediately I was told that I would be offered visiting rights–a rare privilege to use the building and some of its facilities. I could not be issued a key, but someone would usually let me in.

I accepted this generous offer with enthusiasm. Soon I was sitting in on wildly humorous interplay, accented by jokes and explosive laughter, as some of America's brightest new wits threw gobs of humor–subtle and raucous–at each other. It seemed inevitable that this group would produce many more great talents like Benchley.

Friendship with Bill Middendorf led to a double date with a pair of respectable Boston girls that nearly ended with serious trouble. It started when one overheard a remark I made about clubs.

"Oh, your clubs!" She exclaimed. "I've always been curious about what you do inside."

"So have I," echoed her friend. And you have such funny names. The Hoot, The Pork."

"The Gas," giggled the other. "Take us to a club. Just a peek inside."

Bill tried to derail this. "Sorry, but women are not allowed in."

But, after more cajoling we yielded. As Bill's Owl Club was right there, he carefully let us in.

A guard unexpectedly turned up and caught us inside with the girls. Fortunately, Bill was not penalized and there was no publicity. I wouldn't ask how he did it, but it must have taken all the clout of our future Secretary of the Navy to pull it off.

The Lampoon activity didn't deter me from enjoying the company of friends at my D.U. Club. One was an accomplished sailor named George O'Day, who later produced the family of popular O'Day sailing boats. Other club members also became good friends. They included Lenny Wright, Bill Olney and Charlie Wadsworth who–with old friend Paul Brine–would all be ushers at my wedding. They were good billiards players, but I could never seem to pocket the balls.

Apart from club activity there were the usual parties. One memorable evening with an adventurous sophomore from a nearby college was instigated by Eldred, who had told me that the top floor of the Lampoon had a bedroom with a light switch near the bed. This turned on a light on the roof, informing members that the room was occupied. I told this to the sophomore. She was skeptical, but willing to be convinced. We went upstairs, I turned on the light, she received proof, and became a believer. I suspected that, after telling this tale to close friends back at college, she gained brief fame as "The co-ed who got laid in the Lampoon."

Adventures with Gaddis continued to fascinate me. The longer I knew this remarkable man, the more unpredictable he became. I learned this late one night when I joined a group who were helping him complete a project that had been fermenting in his brain. The details would not be believable by normal people, but the conclusion might. This took place before dawn.

There, at the center of Anderson Bridge, Bill led his coterie to a railing overlooking the Charles River. He solemnly read from a book what we were told was a burial prayer. Then he toppled a slightly bloody package over the edge and made various pseudo religious gestures. Puzzled, I watched it splash below. Back in my room I didn't bother wondering what was in that package, but instead why I had been crazy enough to go with Bill in the first place. Learning from this experience, I did not stay for the *finale* of another event featuring Bill. He and Eldred had been playing with a starting gun they had somehow acquired with several blank bullets. Bill asked Eldred whether being shot by a blank from the gun could be dangerous. They didn't think so, but Gaddis had to find out. Since neither wanted to provide the proof, and I had bailed out, they went to the room of a sleeping friend, pulled down his covers and–from a "safe" distance–shot him in the chest.

Later Eldred told me that Gaddis had his answer: it *was* dangerous–more or less. Bill's ex-friend awakened with a terrible howl when a few grains of burning black powder from the cartridge reached his chest. He had staggered toward the bathroom, shouting: "Cold water! Cold water!" His attackers sobered up enough to realize that they had committed a crime, and helped him wash off the powder scratch marks. It soon became evident that the victim's howling was mostly from fright. This called for drinks, and the whole episode was forgotten.

My Graduation and Later Meeting with President Pusey

In June, 1947, with credit for my years of naval service factored in, I received a B.S. (War Service Sciences) degree from Harvard. It would be years before I made contact again with my alma mater–in this case, in Hong Kong, with President Nathan Pusey. He and his wife were accompanying the Harvard Glee Club and Radcliffe Choral Society on an international tour, which for three days delighted Hong Kong audiences with joint performances–and in turn thoroughly enjoyed the appreciation with which they were treated.

I was then President of the Harvard Club of Hong Kong–a rapidly growing organization of nearly a hundred members who included many graduates from the business, medical, law and other graduate schools, as well as the college. Our main luncheon was held at the Foreign Correspondents' Club with a guest list including Hong Kong's government, business and community dignitaries.

After my introductory address, Dr. Pusey gave us an update on developments at Harvard. This was followed by questions and answers–normally routine–but not so this time. Early reports of student protests at

Berkeley were discussed and led to Dr. Pusey's assurance that it could not happen at Harvard. He was right until a few years later, when it *did* happen. Several hundred representatives of a radical group did exactly that, occupying Harvard's main administration hall until they were thrown out.

Patty's Wedding

On June 27th Patty married Henry Luce III, the eldest son of the publisher. Hank–as he was familiarly called–had been discharged from the Navy the same time as I was, with the same rank. He was tall–over six feet–and wore his dark hair in a crew cut.

The wedding was held on a clear day on the lawn of the spectacular Luce mansion, Lu Shan, in New Jersey. Patty's maid of honor and bridesmaids were friends from the New York area and Henry was supported by fellow Yale students, and me. Guests included friends of both families, Chinese and European as well as American, many of whom were internationally known. Dad, Mother and I returned to New York soon after the festivities ended, and I did not see the married couple again until I visited them at their home near Yale, where Henry was completing his education.

Bill Gaddis, Billie Holliday and the Rude Shepherd

From Harvard, I moved to my parents' apartment at 960 Park Avenue in New York City while preparing to find a job. I had expected to be taken into Bill Hunt's organization, but had closed that door when I wrote him from Boulder that I was going into my own business. Still, I was fortunate and was hired by Granny's father for a job with a big international insurance company, of which he was a senior officer. This would start in a few weeks when I went on the payroll as a trainee in New York to prepare me for my first post, in Shanghai. Until then, as I had come off a long stretch of fairly intense work, I felt I could use some relaxation. Both Johnny and Jaye were away, so every now and then I spent a few days with Bill Gaddis and Eldred.

Bill had left Harvard early and lived in a cold water flat on Horatio Street in the Village, which he shared with Eldred. Their home consisted of a square room, two closets and a bathroom. It was furnished with simple cots, some folding tables and chairs borrowed from nearby sidewalk cafes. The central decoration was a giant steel blue cockroach pinned onto the wall over a non-functioning fireplace. A small refrigerator and one-plate heater served for food. The entry was a narrow flight of steps leading up to the sidewalk. During evenings I sometimes joined Bill and Eldred on prowls through the Village, which sometimes ended with one or more of us breaking off with a girl. On one such walk, over a beer and sandwich, Gaddis announced, "Billie Holiday is here tonight. I'm going to see her. Coming?"

The immortal singer was performing at a cheap little jazz club on west side. As we entered, Gaddis shook his head slowly. "What a hell of a place to end up. The greatest of them all, once the most beautiful, not old yet but dying of drugs and alcohol. And no one cares, no one even remembers her any more."

Wearing a simple low cut blouse and her trademark white gardenia in her hair, she staggered onto a raised platform before us and clung to the mike stand for support. Then, accompanied by a badly played honky-tonk piano, the great Billie Holiday moaned her classic, "Strange fruit hangin' from the poplar tree."

Looking up at her from only a few feet away, spellbound, we watched her struggle through her familiar songs, weaving from to side to side, barely able to stand, missing words and even phrases. But always the great Billie Holiday. Although only a derelict of her former self, she still sent shivers through me. Gaddis and Eldred sat frozen. When she left, the only applause came from us. We sat quietly with our own thoughts until the lights came on. Finally Gaddis shook himself and muttered, "I feel like I just screwed her."

My future contacts with Gaddis continued to lead to unexpected events. They became less frequent, as I was starting my job training and could only come on occasional weekends. I was there on one of my visits when Gaddis left early Sunday morning, promising to return with a surprise. Soon afterwards he did just that, announcing his arrival with a thundering roar outside our door.

"What the hell?" said Eldred. "Is that him?"

It was. Bill was sitting in the driver's seat of the most incredible car I had ever seen. It was a low white convertible coupe, top down, with huge shiny chrome-plated exhaust pipes running down each side of the wrap-around hood into the fenders below. He turned down the noise and stepped out. "Who's first?" he invited, grinning madly. "Only one at a time."

After he had driven each of us around the neighborhood–no doubt frightening many people headed for church–we sat down for a beer. I asked first, "What the hell is it?"

"Ah-ha! I thought you would ask. That car is the last of the greatest. A 1937 V-8 Cord, model 812. Supercharged. Fastest on the road. Only a few in existence, and I have one."

He drained his beer from the bottle. "I'm driving it to Texas to find a gold mine."

After we recovered, Eldred asked, "How do you know there's gold in Texas?"

Don't. If there's any, I'll bring it back."

Eldred and I exchanged glances. "When do you plan to leave?" we asked together.

"In a few minutes."

We sat, mute with amazement. Then he announced, "There's only room for one passenger. You'll have to fight for it, but I can't wait."

We waved him off. No one heard anything until he returned about two weeks later. By coincidence, this was during my final visit before going overseas. Bill's arrival was again announced by the car's thundering exhaust. He leapt from his car, talking excitedly about the trip. When I finally had the chance to slip in a word, I asked, "Where's the gold?"

He looked startled. "What gold?" Then continued, "He was a loony old man, that shepherd, nutty as hell, jumping up and down and waving me back to stop scaring his sheep. 'You keep that damn noisy contraption away from my Petunia!' he was screaming. Well, after a while things quieted down and he began talking, still about his sheep, very possessively, pointing them out one by one. You know the first thing he asked me? 'Say, Willie. Y'ever screw a sheep?' The way he was acting, he must have screwed every one of them."

We parted company soon after that. I never saw Gaddis again, although I learned that he wrote six novels and received honors as America's most proficient satirist and considerable fame as a "master of satire and black comedy."

It was different with Eldred, who joined me some years later on a treasure diving adventure far across the Atlantic Ocean.

Dad, a prominent American businessman in Shanghai.

Mother, a war correspondent, rides a sedan chair en route to interview a Chinese war lord.

Double room shared with Sig Olney.

St. George's School; Second Beach beyond is where I first body surfed.

After my long trousers arrived from Shanghai, no more "peek pants" for me.

Apprentice seaman at V-12 program at Harvard University.

Claire visits me at Notre Dame Midshipmen's School.

Bringing back liquor for "skirt-lifters" to warm up our Radcliffe dates at post-game party.

Trying out my new Navy uniform.

With roommates Sandy Cunningham, Paul Brine & Bud Lane at reunions.

Granny from the Shanghai Gunpowder Gang visits me.

With my sister Patty in New York.

With Claire at a Boston debutante party.

With Jaye in New York.

Am commissioned Ensign, U.S. N.R.

With Jim Wolf at Boulder in 1945.

Jim Wolf and Culver Gleysteen with two very supportive Chinese instructors.

My last meeting with Jim 60 years later.

Senior Officer Bill Morgenroth at Boulder.

Meeting Bill in Florida, 2003.

Slim Everson at language shcool in Boulder.

Lt. Paul Anspach and I strengthen Anglo-American friendships in Washington, D.C. with British roommate Ronnie.

Life Four: Nationalist Shanghai 1947-1949

PART ONE

Getting There

The OSS Veteran and the Stamp Lickers

It was through Granny, my childhood Gunpowder Gang friend, that I was introduced to my first international employer. His father, a senior officer of the American Foreign Insurance Association, had learned of my Chinese language training and arranged for me to be interviewed for an opening in his company's Shanghai branch. Soon afterwards I joined several other trainees at AFIA's world headquarters in Maiden Lane, New York.

During the following months I learned the principles of general insurance and its three legs: fire, casualty and marine. I studied the centuries-old clauses in insurance policies, and listened to veterans describe their experiences in foreign countries. After listening to their successes, I knew that I was cut out for their kind of work: active marketing and selling. This conviction came sharply to mind whenever I passed the rows of office clerks performing routine jobs like sticking endorsements onto policies. Feeling sorry for them, I thought of them as pitiful stamp lickers.

A fellow trainee, Johnny, shared my yearning for activity and challenges. Big, boisterous and handsome, this cheerful veteran of the OSS often carried the tools of his former trade with him. He had no hesitation in cracking a table top with a sudden swing of his coiled-spring, sharp-edged steel cosh or jolting us to our feet by firing a blank in a .22 cal. disappearing assassination gun—which worked like a miniature recoilless rifle—under our table. We did much of our homework together in Greenwich Village pubs like Julius, where adventurous girls strayed.

Johnny's send–off party in a Brooklyn hotel room featured a virtuoso performance by a whore perched on the side of the bathroom tub. I did not avail myself of her services, but did follow up on Johnny's goodbye present—an introduction to a remarkable young secretary right in our building. Demure in appearance, she turned out to be a wildcat who had to be held face down, ripping sheets with her sharp nails, to prevent her from shredding the back and shoulders.

Johnny and I kept in touch after he went overseas–in his case to Calcutta, where liquor was banned, and available young women only a memory. His first letter described his welcome: "I have been feted by the locals in their own lovable way of riot, assault and other affectionate manifestations of their esteem." His final letter, sent several months later, was a heart-rending description of his suffering with the self-deprecating signature "Office boy with good pay."

Across the Pacific

Right after Patty's wedding in late June, Mother and I boarded the *President Monroe* in San Francisco, sharing one of the twelve cabins on this passenger-freighter. Most of our fellow voyagers were young and interesting. We had no floor shows or casino gambling—just a small pool with canvas sides, a four-seat bar in the dining room, and fairly new movies with the projector mounted between chairs.

Mother spent her time by the pool reading and talking with the captain and fellow passengers. I swam and reviewed my insurance notes during the day and played bridge after dinner. One of the players was a divorcee in her mid-twenties who helped educate me with the bidding. After our game the second night we were having a drink at the bar when she expressed interest in continuing my learning. I was happy to oblige. Since both of our cabins were occupied by roommates, we looked for another venue. Surprisingly, the purser's office was empty, and the door unlocked. And there, right in the middle, was a big flat desk. All went well until the following morning when the purser entered to go to work.

The commotion he stirred up eventually subsided, but from then on the door to our playground was tightly locked.

Toward the end of December the *President Monroe* slipped into Tokyo Bay and docked at Yokohama. The doctor gave us the last of three shots for tetanus and typhoid required for going ashore, Then, after a light lunch, the other passengers were herded off by M.P.s on a rigidly controlled bus tour.

Mother and I wanted no part of regimented travel. We had applied for permission to go ashore unescorted, but without much hope for approval since the process was tangled in red tape and permits were usually restricted to military personnel.

Carl and Shelly Mydans

We were fortunate. Right after the bus left we had two visitors. They turned out to be the internationally respected correspondent Carl Mydans and his wife Shelly, who had been asked to look us up. "We've arranged for you to go ashore with us today," Carl announced. Soon afterwards we were riding with them in a luxurious new Studebaker toward Tokyo.

As the head of TIME's Japan Bureau, Carl knew everyone and had entrée to everything in Japan. He had arranged our permits. He was as likeable a person as I ever met—short, stocky with a quick smile and a pleasant wit. Shelly was slender, with a sharp, pretty face and bright, intelligent eyes. Both were alert and seemed quite happy to answer the torrent of questions Mother and I threw at them.

The driver steered off the wet, cold dock area, past some patched up buildings and onto the eighteen mile rebuilt road that connected Tokyo with Yokohama. When I had last been here in 1939, on the way to St. George's School, this was a jammed highway bordered along its entire length by rows of shops and factories, teeming with masses of colorful people and vehicles. Now all I saw was stark, cold, dreary desolation—the aftermath of what Carl called, "The most devastating job of destruction ever done by man."

Where had once been a great industrial center, all I could see was an endless expanse of gray mud and gray puddles, pock marked here and there with jerry-built shacks and tiny patches of vegetables. Across everything stretched a net of gray cement lines, like a giant checkerboard—all that was left of what had once been the foundations of a thousand homes and factories. Everything around us was obliterated except for these and occasional piles of twisted, rusted girders and scattered bricks.

For many minutes I watched in silence. I remembered the horrors inflicted by the Japanese military on the innocent Chinese and so many other people–and particularly how close to death Dad had been after those many months they stole from his life. I felt no guilt, or remorse. Nor did I feel any satisfaction. There was only a feeling of stunned awe.

Carl interrupted my thoughts, pointing, "Out there is where the jellied gasoline bomb proved itself to be the most horrible weapon of war. Worse than the atom bomb, even." He shook his head slowly, then continued, "In just four hours one afternoon a hundred thousand people were burned and smothered to death in those acres. Whole families destroyed so that there were no relatives left to look for them."

Carl had been at the Marianas island base where our bombers took off and saw this destruction being planned. "A section of buildings was marked off on the map. Then fleets of bombers ringed that area with firebombs, and explosives to discourage fire fighting. Those that didn't burn suffocated, for the fires consumed all the oxygen in the vicinity. The next day, back at the base, the destroyed area was colored on the map."

Carl concluded, "I couldn't believe that this whole region was burned out until I came here after the war and saw it myself."

Strangely spared in this mass destruction were the American and British consulate buildings, which stood alone in the gray rubble. "But of course you can't tell a Japanese that this was pure luck," Carl said. "They believe to a man that the American bombing was so accurate it left them standing."

At this point Mother entered the conversation. "It is hard to believe this really happened. Horrible–like the Kanto earthquake."

Curious, both Mydans turned to her. "You know about that?"

"Yes," Mother answered. "I was here."

Astonished, we stared at her. She had never told me this. Mother then explained that she was living in Shanghai, married to Dad and retired from the Hearst news organization, when Tokyo was flattened by what was still remembered as "The great Kanto earthquake of 1923."

Her former employers had urgently requested her to cover the story and she responded like the proverbial warhorse. She managed to enter Japan without permission, take photos—strictly forbidden by the Japanese military—have them carried out by someone with diplomatic immunity, and return safely, giving Hearst one of the great news scoops of the year. We looked at my little mother—only five feet tail—with new respect. Then Carl said quietly, "You're Edna Lee Booker. I should have recognized you."

"I used my maiden name for my byline."

Carl persisted, "You covered the battles between the war lords in China. I read many of your accounts."

"Yes. You could say we're both war correspondents."

I listened, fascinated, as the two veterans described events they had covered in countries all over the world. Then suddenly my eye was drawn to a strange cloud of black smoke coming down the road toward us. Without thinking, I interrupted, "My God! What's that?"

Shelly laughed. "That's the latest style in modern transportation—a wood gas car." I watched in fascination as the unworldly thing approached and passed us, leaving a trail of dark soot for us to drive through. For a moment we could see the form of a car with a huge lump hanging off its back and a tall chimney belching smoke. It looked like the early locomotives with high funnels pictured in Currier and Ives lithographs.

The Mydans explained. Gasoline was in tight supply to everyone except the privileged occupation personnel. To offset this shortage, many Japanese had converted their pre-war vehicles into charcoal burners by altering their carburetors so that the engine could run on wood gas. This was supplied by an amazing Rube Goldberg contraption resembling a steam engine that filled the trunk and hung over the back fender. Small blocks of wood and twigs were broiled here, generating wood gas, which was piped into the engine.

Starting the thing, or "getting up the smoke", required frantic fanning and puffing and fiddling with levers. A load of wood lasted for about two hours, after which the complicated process was started all over again—if wood could be found. These vehicles seemed to spend half the time stopped by the roadside while the drivers reloaded and restarted—or tried to repair—them.

Not much later we reached an area that had not been bombed and pulled up before the gate to a walled compound. Carl stepped out and helped Mother from the car. Behind the gate we were surprised to see a large luxurious villa with a perfectly maintained Japanese garden. Several servants appeared and bowed.

Carl motioned, "Come into our home. Sorry, it's not much but there's a shortage of housing and it's all we have." Then he laughed, "Not bad, is it?

"This was the home of the finance minister. It was requisitioned for us. Press correspondents are classified as military occupation personnel and entitled to all the privileges accorded to army officers. In my case, a colonel. We are authorized four servants."

After a tour of the premises we sat down for a drink and some delicious *sushi*. Soon after that we were joined by Lt. General Robert Eichelberger, commander of the Eighth Army and charged by General MacArthur with the enormous task of rebuilding Japan.

Right after introductions they began to discuss the war trials that were going on in Tokyo. Tojo, the despised former Japanese prime minister, was being tried for war crimes. He had earlier attempted *hara-kiri*, but the bullet missed his heart and his suicide bid had failed. "Failing to complete *seppuku* is the most ignominious thing that can happen to a *bushido* warrior," Carl told us. "Tojo did not succeed in his suicide attempt. His name is shamed forever."

Tojo had been given blood transfusions and nursed back to health by American doctors, completing his disgrace. General Eichelberger snorted, "Should have let the bastard die. Would have saved us from all this bad publicity." The general was referring to Tojo's defense at the trial. The text of his defense had been given to the tribunal. "It is a compact presentation of all the Japanese war propaganda," Carl explained. "A clever defense blaming American and British economic aggression, and hostile acts of Chinese soldiers, for provoking Japan to attack Pearl as a self-defense measure."

"Exactly," continued Shelly. "Tojo will lose his life, but as a result of this he has already won the trials. Every newspaper has pages one and two plastered solidly with the text. They are censored, but cannot be prevented from printing this for it is directly from the tribunal and therefore official. The rebuttal, and truth, won't come for two weeks and will get only a small display. As Hitler said, the big lie is never totally washed away."

After the general left, the Mydans accompanied us back to the ship, driving through the darkened ghost of a city. Electric power was shut off to everyone except occupation personnel because of the coal shortage.

Our unforgettable visit ended back on the ship. Mother invited the Mydans for cocktails, and we thanked them for having made our visit so memorable. After they left we had dinner and turned in. Early the next morning the *President Monroe* sailed for Shanghai.

For long afterwards I sifted through the amazing events that I had seen and heard that day. I would probably never have believed that they all actually happened if I had not experienced them myself.

PART TWO

Working with AFIA

Return to Shanghai

We were finishing breakfast two days later when the second officer announced, "We are approaching the estuary of the Yangtze River. In a few minutes the ship will enter the Yellow Sea. We will go through a line across the ocean where the muddy Yangtze River meets the Pacific. Blue water on this side, yellow water on the other. Anyone interested in seeing this can come up forward."

Mother and I joined the other passengers along the railing and watched the muddy water approach. Presently the ship's bow cut through, and the ocean around us was muddy. We had entered China's Yellow Sea.

I didn't need my eyes to tell me this. The nose did the job, immediately recognizing the whiff of China in the air. It brought back childhood memories of farmers unloading wooden buckets of brown liquid onto vegetable beds. The liquid was human manure used to fertilize crops throughout China. It was euphemistically called night soil, or even honey. Its odor lightly permeated the air, and from now on there would be no escaping it.

Later, a small boat pulled alongside and motored off, leaving a uniformed officer climbing the Jacob's ladder thrown over the side. Our captain, on his way to greet him, stopped to tell us, "He's a Yangtze River pilot—we couldn't continue without him. Once we get to the river estuary we will cross sand bars and mud flats. They are always shifting and the river pilots are the only people who know which passages are safe to use each day."

By mid afternoon we had navigated some fifty miles up the broad expanse of the Yangtze, past the Woosung fort, and south into the quarter-mile-wide Whangpoo River. An hour later the *President Monroe* berthed off Shanghai's Bund—the long dock interface linking the swarming marine traffic of the river with the noisy, chaotic activity of Shanghai's commercial world.

A well-dressed Chinese businessman, one of the first to come aboard, was escorted to us. "Mrs. Potter," he said, "My name is Jimmy Chan. Mr. Potter sent me to assist you. I work in his office. There are formalities, and it helps to have someone who knows the ropes." Mr. Chan had obviously been educated in America. "May I please have your passports?"

Mother and I handed them over and she explained that her steamer trunk and our bags were locked in our cabin. Mr. Chan walked away and soon returned with several baggage carriers and a uniformed officer. "This is Captain Liu of the Customs Investigation Department. He will examine your luggage for contraband and the coolies will carry them ashore. He spoke some words in Chinese with the captain, but to my chagrin I couldn't understand them. Then I realized that they were speaking Shanghai dialect—incomprehensible to a Mandarin scholar like me.

Our guide and the customs official apparently knew each other, for the "examination" took only a minute without a single bag being opened. Then they led us down the gangway onto the dock, into a mass of Chinese blocking the way. The officer spoke sharply, and a passage quickly opened for us. Then he shook hands and left.

Mr. Chan returned our passports. "You have been granted residence in Shanghai for an indefinite period. This is unusual—probably because of Mr. Potter's senior position in the Bank of China."

A moment later I heard a cry from Mother, who ran forward and threw herself into Dad's arms, sobbing, "John, oh John." I put my arms around him and squeezed, feeling his arm across my back. What a beautiful way to return to our old home!

Dad had not fully recovered from those three years in the concentration camp, but his period of rehabilitation in America plus the joy of seeing us gave him the appearance of strength and confidence. I held his frail body tight for a long time without saying a word.

A young uniformed man walked over from a black sedan and Dad introduced our driver, Wong. Then he thanked Jimmy Chan, who made sure the coolies had loaded all our baggage.

I sat in the front with Wong while Mother and Dad took the back seat, holding hands. While they talked quietly, I began to recognize landmarks from ten years earlier. We butted our way through the impossible traffic of The Bund onto Nanking Road—Shanghai's wide commercial thoroughfare—past the Race Course, into Bubbling Well Road. From here on I was lost. I knew we were headed to a new home, since the Japanese had wrecked our Columbia Circle house, but where? Not wishing to interrupt my parents, I asked the driver, "You savvy what side we go?"

He nodded. "Me savvy. Go Da Ma Lu." Subconsciously I knew this meant Big Horse Road. From somewhere in my memory I dredged up the fact that this was the local name for our Great Western Road, leading to the Columbia Country Club where as children we used to swim and bowl and eat delicious hamburgers soaked in catsup.

We pulled up in front of a nine-storied apartment building as modern as anything on Madison Avenue. A door opened into a large, clean garage, and several servants wearing traditional black and white uniforms rushed out. One woman shouted, sobbing, "Missy, missy!" and clung to Mother.

Our new home occupied the entire ground floor of this luxury fifteen-apartment building, with our own private garden and fountain just outside the wide verandah. The high ceiling living and dining rooms were lined with mahogany. Bookshelves contained much of Mother's famous collection of Asian first editions, many inscribed to her, with original signed scrolls hanging between them. One wing was dedicated to my parents, with spacious bedrooms and bathrooms. The other, where Dad installed me, had a comfortable bedroom, en suite bathroom and private porch. In the back were quarters for the houseboy, cook, amah, coolie, gardener and driver.

I Join the AFIA Staff

By eight the next morning Dad and I had eaten breakfast and Wong was driving us toward our respective offices, both near The Bund. Passing the racetrack on Nanking Road, I remembered that my parents and their friends had often come here to elaborate racing parties. I asked Dad, "Will you and Mother be going to the races like you used to?"

He shook his head. "No more races here, son." He smiled, "Probably just as well for you. Racing and all public gambling was banned by Chiang Kai-shek. The race course is used for sports and exercising horses now."

"But this is in the Foreign Concession," I protested. "Isn't it still run by the Americans and Europeans?"

"No longer. Many of us wish it were, but our extra-territorial rights under the Treaty of Nanking were abrogated during the war, in 1943. We are now subject to Chinese law. Fortunately," he added, "Our countries continue the excellent relations we had during the war. Many of China's leaders are Mother's and my personal friends."

The car jerked to a halt and Wong muttered a Shanghai curse. Angry sounds around us increased to a wild cacophony. We were trapped in a huge traffic jam of cars, buses, trucks, pedicabs and carts all honking and screaming and cursing at once. The cause was a stalled tramcar. Its electric connection had slipped off the overhead power cable and the conductor was running back and forth alongside struggling to reconnect it. Again and again the wires touched, emitting showers of sparks.

Finally they locked in place. The tram started, traffic moved, the din subsided to Nanking Road's normal million-decibel level, and we continued on our way.

Dad's office was the first stop. Before getting out, he handed me an envelope containing a page of phone numbers and addresses and a wad of Chinese paper currency. He explained, "Don't get excited about all this money. It is worth only about two dollars. Wong will drop you off at your office. Your boss, Buster Brown, will take you to lunch and may want to keep you after work. In any case phone my secretary, Phoebe, to tell her when you will need the car. Her number is in the envelope."

I realized that Dad was cutting the umbilical cord. He wanted to make it clear that I was now working for Buster Brown.

At the AFIA office a polite Chinese receptionist said, "Mr. Brown had been expecting you." She ushered me directly into a corner office and left.

My new boss walked over from a neat desk and gripped my hand. "Welcome back to Shanghai, John. I've been hearing good things about you from New York. And of course, your father and I are friends." He motioned me to a sofa and we sat down. A middle aged European lady came in to take our coffee orders, and Buster introduced his secretary, Olga.

Instinctively I liked him. A little less than medium height, he gave the impression of competence and authority. He had the ruddy appearance of a sportsman. His gray hair was neatly combed and his shirt and tie perfectly matched the brown tweed suit.

While we sipped coffee we exchanged the usual introductory phrases. Then he came right to business: "The insurance market of Shanghai is quite different from any other place in the world—especially New York. You will soon realize that many practices you were taught back there simply do not apply here. For instance, the structure of discounts. Instead of the usual two or three stages, the Shanghai market has six or eight, some of them outright kickbacks, which of course we cannot give. This complicates our ability to compete.

"You will need time to familiarize yourself. My senior manager, Winston Chen, can take you in hand and be your guide. You will report to him. Later, when you are ready, we can discuss your progress and I will assign you to a position." No question about it—Buster had my full interest. The more he continued his introduction, the more I realized what a lot I had to learn. My new employment world was clearly quite different from the easygoing ways of New York.

Winston's Briefing

Buster led me into a smaller office next to his. A slim, youngish-appearing Chinese in a dark blue suit stood up. "Morning, Boss," he said easily. Then, shaking my hand, he said, "And you must be Mr. Potter."

Buster walked to the door. "I'll leave you now. Have John in my office by lunchtime. If you're free, join us at the American Club."

I sat with Winston at his desk. His first words were, "God, I hate these familiarizing jobs. Buster always dumps them on me." Then he laughed, "But we'll get through it and have a good time. Understand you have a chemistry degree from Harvard. I wonder how well that prepares a guy for insurance?"

"Guess I'll find out. And how about you?"

Within a few minutes I knew that he was American, a Stanford graduate, married to a Chinese-American wife whom he met at college, loved the insurance business in China and his job with Buster. Then he began the familiarizing job that he said he hated.

"First, office hours are from eight to twelve, then three to six. Also Saturday mornings. Buster likes us to be on time. The long lunch break makes for a great *siesta* after a late night, which explains the number of easy chairs you'll see in the club library. Now–the local money. The government finances itself mostly through the printing press, by pouring large quantities of new bills into the market. This obviously creates inflation, which is completely out of control.

"When they took over in '44 they set the exchange rate at 20 yuan—their dollar—to one US dollar. This lasted a few months, but soon the currency started devaluing and the value of the yuan dropped. Two years later it took 2,000 yuan—a 100 times more—to buy just one dollar. Today's rate is much higher—somewhere over half a million to a dollar. They may be trying to stop this inflation, but cannot collect enough money from taxes and so on to meet their expenses plus the cost of their huge army. Also the major cost of corruption. So they keep issuing new bills in higher and higher denominations. These are imported by shiploads. I know. We have the insurance."

I looked into Dad's envelope. The top bill on the wad was marked 100,000 YUAN. "My God," I exclaimed. "A 100,000 yuan—and Dad said the whole wad was worth only a couple of US dollars."

"Your Dad called it. No one can keep track of the exchange rate. Sometimes it doubles in a month, which means any money you had lost half its value."

"How do you keep from losing with this currency?"

Winston nodded. "That's the question. Holding Chinese money in any form–whether cash, or in bank accounts, or in lOUs from customers–will cost you. So we treat this money like a hot potato. Try to avoid getting it. And if you can't avoid this, pass it on to someone else quick as you can. If you can't do that, buy something like rice with it or try to exchange it for dollars or gold. In case you wondered, our business is conducted entirely in US dollars, so it's protected from this inflation. Just like our salaries, which are deposited into our bank accounts in the States. Where it becomes a nuisance is keeping enough cash available to cover payments like servants' wages, and food, that must be made in yuan. Everyone wants to use foreign currency, but that's illegal. Any Chinese caught with US dollars is punished. Now. Another subject you must be familiar with is our market structure and the main competition. Did they give you a good briefing in New York?"

"Yes. About AFIA's background, and policies and clauses and so on."

"That could help. Then you know AFIA's main purpose is to act as overseas extensions of our American principals–the biggest insurance companies like Home, Aetna and so on–which saves them from having to set up their own branches all over the world. This means that most of our customers here are tied in with businesses back home that use our insurance companies. Emphasis is on service to them, but we can still go after other prospects provided that our bread and butter principals are taken care of.

"Now, the competition. Most of the foreign business, and much of the Chinese, is controlled by the European insurance groups, mostly British. They set the tariffs. Some have been in business here for over a hundred years and others are owned by the big European *hongs* like Jardines and Swire. American insurance companies try to break in, but haven't had too much luck so far.

"There are two other American companies here: one is the Insurance Company of North America, which is friendly. The other is the American International Underwriters, called the AIU, which represents several companies not in our group. They are rough competitors. They have grown very rapidly and only a few people know how they did it.

"The AIU was started nearly thirty years ago by an American named C. V. Starr who was the first to sell life insurance to people in Shanghai. For years his policies were issued in Chinese currency, often called the dollar Mex because it originated with the silver Mexican peso introduced here for trade. This Chinese dollar was a pretty stable currency then, valued nearly on par with the US dollar.

"Then the Nips attacked and the Chinese dollar began losing value. The amounts shown on Starr's earlier policies were still denominated in dollars Mex, but the dollar Mex value dropped until a policy originally worth, say, a million dollars Mex wasn't worth any more than the wad of money your Dad gave you. So the AIU had to pay out practically nothing. Meanwhile their managers invested the premium income in American and other foreign countries. These assets served as the launching platform for AIU to become the big international player that it is today."

At home that evening I mentioned this to Dad. He commented, "Neil Starr. I know him quite well. A very smart businessman. He wasn't afraid to take risks, and brought in very capable people as managers. If you compete against that company, you can't afford to make any slips because you will be up against the toughest competitors in the business."

The American Club

Winston was still describing the insurance market when he glanced at his watch. "Whoops, it's time for you to meet Buster. Please tell him I'm sorry I can't join you." I met my new boss coming out of his office. "Good," he said. "You're right on time. The club is just a couple of blocks off The Bund, on Foochow Road. I usually walk, but I've arranged for my driver to take us today so we can talk without the street noise."

Once settled in his car, he began, "The American Club is a good place for you to start. Most of the American businessmen, and many Chinese and other nationalities, have lunch there and you will quickly meet people we deal with. We'll get your application and you can fill it in during lunch. I'll propose you and we'll get it seconded today.

"The Club has nearly a thousand members. Almost any nationality can join as long as the membership committee approves. Men only, although ladies can visit once a year on Ladies' Day. This also applies to the residential guest rooms upstairs. If you didn't already have a place to stay with your family, I would have suggested that you park here until you get settled."

The car pulled up in front of a five–storied building with a red brick façade that resembled a university club. We entered a large lobby with doorways to a number of rooms, and up and down stairways flanking two elevators. Buster exchanged greetings with several men, then pointed at a double door. "That's the bar, where you'll find most of the members at this time. These other doors lead to the card room and billiards room. The bowling alley and a small gym and changing room are downstairs, and upstairs is the dining room, library and reading room, where members can take a nap. The residential quarters are on the top floors."

The bar room was cloudy with cigarette smoke and noisy with the sound of rattling dice and excited talking and laughing. It was surprisingly large. A wooden bar lined with stools ran down one side. About forty tables occupied the rest of the room. All the seats at the bar, and many of the tables, had been taken and waiters in white uniforms were busily serving drinks. Buster looked over the tables and spotted the one he wanted. Then he glanced at the bulletin board. Pointing at a posted page, he asked, "Do you still remember your pidgin English?"

Next to the usual notices someone had pinned a few lines in pidgin English:

A lady phones the club receptionist:

Lady: "Me wanchee savvy, me husband have got, no got?"

Recpt: "No missy, husband no got."

Lady: "How fashion you savvy no got, me no talkie name?"

Recpt: "Missy, this side any piecey husband any time no got."

"Standing instructions at some other bars," Buster chuckled. "Supposed to keep a husband out of trouble."

He led me to a table with two empty seats and introduced me to two men who were apparently waiting for us. "This is John Potter's son, same name, who will be working with me. Came over yesterday from the States with his mother. To me he added, "These are good friends of your parents: Charles Singer and Willy O'Brien."

The first, white haired and portly, leaned across the table and took my hand. "Call me Charlie, John. Your Dad has been waiting for your arrival. He will be very happy to have you and Edna Lee here with him. And so will we."

The other, middle aged and portly, said cheerfully, "I'm Willy. You may not remember me, Johnny, but when you were about ten we used to look at your clipper ship drawings and talk about sailing around the world in one."

Our waiter arrived and took our orders for scotch and sodas. Then, as he handed out menus, he addressed Singer with a smile, "Master, today cookie make you beef stroganoff you like."

"Thank you, Lee. I'll have it. Also the chicken soup and vegetables." I also selected stroganoff, an old favorite. The others ordered and continued discussing business while I listened.

A shout and loud laughter from a nearby table attracted my attention. Four men sitting there were shaking leather cups about the size of a coffee mug, with one hand covering the top. They banged them, top down, on the table then peered in with their hands cupped to hide the contents from the others.

"Small straight," a tall, sandy haired man announced to the man on his left, an amused yet challenging expression on his ruddy face.

"Don't believe it," snorted the third. "Ace is lying."

"You call him, if you're so sure."

"No. You call him. It's your turn."

"OK. Let's see your small straight."

"You'll be sorry."

"Up. Show me."

The first player exposed five dice under the cup. "One small straight. As advertised. They don't call me Honest Ace in four countries for nothing." He threw his head back, roaring with laughter.

The second player, apparently the loser, turned over a red scoring cube in front of him and they all shook their dice boxes again.

Looking around, I saw that most of the men at the other tables were also playing dice. "Is this what we do at lunch?" I asked.

Buster and the others exchanged glances. The one named Charlie said, "Just about. It's a good way to put aside other matters."

Buster spoke up, "I'm proposing John for membership. We need a seconder." They both responded eagerly and Buster signaled to our waiter, "Lee, would you please bring me a member proposal form?"

He went off and Buster said, "I'll sign as proposer, John. You can fill it in at the library after lunch and give it to Charles or Willy to second—whoever you can find and wake up. Then drop the form off at the desk. That way you can have a temporary membership right away. I have an appointment after lunch and will send the car back for you."

A few minutes later the waiter handed a membership application form to Buster, saying, "Mr. Brown, you lunch leady." We finished our drinks, Buster signed the chit and we walked upstairs to the dining room. The headwaiter led us to our table, my hosts nodding and exchanging words with other diners along the way.

We had just sat down when someone gripped my shoulder from behind. Looking up, I immediately recognized the wildly grinning face of Mike Britton. Although older, many pounds heavier and minus some hair, this was unmistakably my close friend from our Gunpowder Gang days. We hugged and–for a few moments–ten years vanished and we were buddies again.

Mike knew Buster, who introduced him to the others. Then Mike and I agreed to meet during the *siesta* period after lunch, and he rejoined another group. Buster, who had watched the proceedings with an amused smile, noted, "It seems like you won't be lonesome here. You'll probably meet other friends, as well."

My delicious Russian stroganoff, preceded by a hot borsch, was the perfect meal to pave my entry into the cosmopolitan world of Shanghai. After finishing our meals, we parted company and I found a table in the reading room where I filled in the application. Willy was sunk deep in a padded chair but was still able to co-sign my form.

I dropped it off at the front desk, and met Mike in the bar. Normally such a reunion called for drinks, but I was aware that my behavior in the office would be observed and had a coke instead.

Mike had been in Shanghai for nearly two years, As assistant marketing manager for Standard-Vacuum Oil Company, one of largest oil distributing organizations in China, he enjoyed many privileges provided by his employers. These included a comfortable house with shared car and driver, and household servants. We agreed that I would visit his bachelor home for dinner soon. Then I found Buster's car and returned to the office.

I Become the Most Pitiful of Creatures

Winston continued my briefing with introductions. Apart from Olga, who had her own office, about a dozen clerks and two female secretaries were seated at individual desks in a main room. All Chinese, the clerks were steadily clicking their abacuses and jotting down numbers on printed forms. The secretaries typed documents. Both were Eurasian, fairly young and attractive, dressed in western clothing. As a whole, the group gave the impression of quiet efficiency. The last room we visited contained two metal desks, one with a clean top. Gesturing toward it, Winston said, "Here is your desk. You can have your secretary set up whatever you need."

Winston then took me to the other desk, papered over with notes and other items of daily use. "This is Ken McGee's desk." he explained. "He's out doing a survey now but sits here when he's in. You'll like him. He's a former army sergeant that Buster hired about a year ago, good at estimating the values of properties for fire insurance. Buster says you'll be teamed up with him."

Winston continued my familiarization by showing me some tools of Ken's job: a Rolodex and a small stack of lined cards about six by four inches, on his desk. He handed me the top card. I saw, scribbled on it, a rough sketch of a house and several lines of handwritten words and numbers with some strange symbols.

"They may not have shown you these in New York. This is called a line card, the survey report of a property we may decide to insure. It has the description, location, value, construction date, proximity of fire hydrants, and anything negative like having a crooked owner or a fuel tank up close. Ken usually completes two of these in a day.

"When our brokers submit a property for us to insure, the first thing we do is send Ken to survey the site and make one of these cards. Then we slot it into its place among our insured properties nearby and decide whether to accept the insurance risk. There are a number of things to consider—Ken will explain them—but the main one is to determine if its value, added to that of other properties we insure in the same plot, would exceed our block limit.

"This is a critically important part of our work. Buster thinks you can handle it. Once you get the feel for it, you can set up your own system for keeping track of insured values."

A chill crept up my spine. What I was hearing did not jibe with the plans that Johnny and I had discussed in New York to go out and conquer the insurance world!

Instead, I would likely be anchored to that desk, performing the same boring functions with infinite patience, day after day, broken only by rare explosions of wild exultation when I discovered some flaw that called for a minor correction!

With supreme irony I realized that I was on my way to becoming that most pitiful of creatures—an office stamp licker!

Ken McGee

My dismay was mitigated somewhat when Buster introduced me to Ken the next morning. I liked him instinctively. A few years older and a few inches taller than me, the former army ranger was easy going and friendly. His full head of reddish hair and brown eyes topped a face with a short scar on one cheek.

Ken greeted me with an infectious smile. "Boy, am I glad you're here, John. We're getting more and more requests for insurance, and I'm running several weeks late on surveys. With you here to handle this end, I'll have more time and can catch up."

I forced a smile, "Yeah. Sounds great."

Buster nodded his approval and walked out.

The work was basic and we had set up our working arrangement by noon. Then Ken said, "It's a bit early but Buster won't mind if we have a long lunch to get acquainted today. I'll take you to the Race Club." He added happily, "This one's on expense account."

I had never been to Shanghai's famous racecourse as a child, but from what I overheard from my parents, I imagined the interior to be as palatial as the Louvre. Not so, I discovered moments after Ken and I stepped down from our pedicab. The unheated function rooms upstairs were shabby and dirty, showing years of neglect. Only on the ground floor was there activity. Here Ken led me into what had been a kitchen, now converted into a cheap-looking restaurant with 10 or 12 wooden tables and chairs. About 20 men of different nationalities, wearing an assortment of sweaters and jackets, were seated in groups eating and drinking.

A single Chinese waiter in a US military jacket moved languidly between the tables. Spotting Ken, he brought two tumblers containing ice cubes. Ken asked me, "Whisky?"

"I'd like a scotch and soda if he has it."

The waiter nodded and walked out through a door, then returned with two bottles which he left on our table. I poured myself half an inch of the Johnny Walker Red and soda. Ken half filled his glass with scotch, neat. Touching glasses, he said, "We'll do fine together. Just have to keep the bosses happy and we're home free."

After the second round Ken called to the waiter and ordered our lunches, explaining to me, "There's only one course, but it's damn good." This turned out to be chicken stew with soy sauce and rice, and it *was* damn good.

I stopped drinking after my second, but Ken continued. After a third glass he brought over three older men. "John," he said, "These guys are salt of the earth. Romanoff and Tomikov here were the tsar's best pals until they got booted out of Russia. And Ginsburg escaped from Hitler. He's the best accountant you'll ever need if you're missing numbers on an expense account." They all three looked seedy, but Ginsburg took the prize. Short and fat, he had a shiny yellow scalp with tufts of hair around the edges and a thick graying beard dangling from his cheeks and chin. Every part of him looked sloppy.

At this point I told Ken that I had better get back to the office. "Tell them I'm on a survey," he slurred, and wandered over to his friends' table.

I learned later that Ken, a hard–core bachelor, had eschewed the social world of the American Club set and made his home among the more raffish populations of Eurasians, Russian and German refugees and former ship crews who had jumped ship here. His friends were everywhere and of all sorts. He had a knack for finding the easiest passages through life's problems and opportunities, and although army training made him murderous in a fight, he tried to avoid brawls on his occasional excursions through Shanghai's less hospitable areas like Blood Alley.

A few months later I saw Ginsburg again after a party given by an important Chinese insurance customer. At the close Ken and I agreed to accompany the happy host for a final drink. The destination was a house on Rue Petain, which turned out to be one of Shanghai's most respectable brothels. The front hall led into an elegant parlor with a Steinway grand piano, a well-stocked bar served by a naked blond bartender, a flight of stairs leading to the rooms upstairs and a bevy of eager girls who seemed to include every nationality.

The host insisted that everything, including the girls, was on him. We were warming up at the bar ogling the bartender—who turned out to be from California—when a volley of deafening screams came from upstairs.

With a profane Shanghai exclamation, our host swung around and nearly slipped from his stool. Then the house bouncer thundered past toward the stairway. Half way up he nearly collided with the most astonishing spectacle I had ever witnessed.

An apparition right out of a Hieronymus Bosch painting was prancing down the stairs, naked as a jaybird, his fat round belly jiggling and a long, brilliantly colored peacock feather from a lady's hat protruding from his tail. With each leap, he whooped, "Cock-a-doodle-do! I'm a frigging rooster!"

As I exploded in laughter, I recognized that it was Ken's pal Ginsburg.

My Shanghai Welcome Party

Dad warned me in advance to drink two glasses of milk and eat heavily buttered toast before leaving the house. It didn't help. Dad's fellow officers at the Bank of China were determined to make my welcome an event for me—or more to the point, for them—to cherish. And they did. Their traditional welcoming dinner was held in a private room of a restaurant famous for its Peking duck—my favorite. I didn't know it then, but it was also famous for the quality of its *shao-shing* rice wine used for toasts before the lethal *pai gar* liquor was poured.

Dad did not attend for some traditional reason, so I was seated between Jimmy Chan, who had met Mother and me on arrival, and another of Dad's senior officers. In all, there were nearly a dozen respected bankers there around the big round table. I was told that we would have twelve courses, with the Peking duck toward the end.

The dinner started with introductions. Everyone spoke English fluently so it was not necessary for me to grope with my rusty Chinese. Each introduction called for a bottoms up *gan bei*—literally cup empty–from our jigger-size cups filled with warm Chinese wine. These were miraculously always kept filled to the brim. By the time we completed introductions, each of the hosts had emptied his cup once with me, and I had emptied my cup once with each of them.

I didn't think anything of it then, but soon felt that I seemed to be getting drunker than the others. When I commented on this, the cheerful reply was:

"Don't pay any attention, John. It's just our way to welcome friends. You're not used to this Chinese wine." I was congratulated on my skill with chopsticks when the first round of dishes was served. This called for drinks, with each of the diners walking around to click cups and *gan bei* with me. The same happened with the second course.

As more courses—and drinks—kept coming I found that I was spilling most of my wine. Some one noticed this and suggested I drink only *sui bien*—as you wish. Even with small sips, it wasn't long before I found myself drifting away. The last words I heard were friendly and soothing.

Dad told me the next morning that I did him proud. Before sliding under the table I had consumed something like thirty cups of wine, and even a sip of the deadly *bai gar*. Jimmy Chan reported that I didn't get sick once until they had carried me to the car, establishing something of a record.

That was all well and good for them, but I never had even one bite of that Peking duck.

Liar's Dice

My membership in the American Club was approved quickly, and I joined the liar's dice players in the bar at lunch. The first step was to order my leather dice cup. This was done through Ah Ching, the head bartender, who had the club monopoly. Each box was embossed with the owner's name, in English or Chinese characters, and Ah Ching assured me that Dad's Chinese name *Bao De*–meaning Bundle of Virtue–would be lucky. With these Chinese characters adorning the side in shining gold, my box positively radiated good fortune.

Our boxes came with five dice, their sides marked with the usual one through six spots. There was also a large red die, which the player kept on the table in front. Each time he lost it was turned. When it showed three losses he paid for a round of drinks. If there were six or eight players this could be expensive.

I learned that dice games were played at American clubs all over Asia, each of which had its preferred variation. The version popular at our American Club was poker dice–an offshoot of draw poker. Each player rattled his dice in his box and plunked it top down on the table. Then he peeked under the edge to see what he had, and the round started with players taking turns clockwise.

Each "hand" was played like draw poker, with players taking up to three rolls instead of drawing cards. The biggest hand was five of a kind, aces high, then sixes down to twos, then four of a kind, full houses, straights and so on.

The objective was to avoid losing three times. You did this by bluffing, lying, cheating, convincing, bribing, threatening, peeking under your neighbor's box, ganging up or any other tactic you could think of.

The players flipped their cubes to see who started. This person rolled his dice, carefully hiding them under his cup. He might make his call then, but usually took a second or third roll. He could tell the truth or lie, the object being to avoid getting called if he was lying, or to con someone to call him if he told the truth.

At this point the fascination of the game came into full bloom. Countless variations could ensue, as players drew from experience, human psychology, mathematical odds and all sorts of deceptions. Consistent winners, who seldom paid the drinks bills, had these skills in depth, and the revered Judge Norwood Allman, a white haired, genial elder statesman, was the master *guru* of them all.

I met "The Judge" before lunch as he was delivering one of his famous orations over his covered dice box to some half dozen other players. They–mature businessmen all–were staring at him, as mesmerized as chickens before a cobra.

"So you see," The Judge was saying in his muted Virginia drawl, "There is no percentage whatsoever in calling me. My box is loaded, and I give you this advice in memory of my late dear wife who would have been displeased with me if I did not try to dissuade you from wasting your money. In fact…" and he went on for several minutes while I stood there just as fascinated as the others. I was sure most of the group thought he was bluffing, but no one had the *chutzpah* to challenge him.

Over subsequent meetings at the club, and elsewhere, I learned a lot about Allman's full and rich life. He had come to China as a young vice consul at about the time I was born, worked with General Chennault's Flying Tigers during WWII, was a director of the OSS, editor of a Chinese newspaper, war correspondent, and judge at Shanghai's Municipal Court and U.S. Court for China.

When sovereignty over Shanghai's Foreign Concession was transferred to China, the former American-appointed judges were dismissed and Allman joined the bar as a practicing lawyer. Like Dad, he was one of several Americans who alternated as president of the Club.

As I met more of the club members, I was drawn to the big round table at the back of the room. Here representatives of American companies would play dice over sandwich lunches while discussing developments affecting their businesses. I made a point of joining them whenever I could, and over the months came to know managers in leading American firms: the National City Bank, Chase Bank and Bank of America, American President Lines, the Standard-Vacuum and Caltex oil companies, Pan-American Airlines, trading company Getz Brothers, and others.

Between dice rolls I found myself learning information that was not common knowledge. At one of these lunches, in early 1948, the conversation introduced me to a shadow world of influence and power that I had never known about, yet that strongly affected us all. My education started when a foreign exchange expert from the Chase Bank threw out a question at the others, "What do you think about those new foreign exchange restrictions that they announced yesterday?"

"Another impediment to free commerce," snorted the finance manager of a large manufacturing business. "It will affect all of us. But the people who will get hurt the most are the importers."

"The reason they gave for cutting foreign exchange for imports was to restrain the rate of inflation," persisted the first banker. "Does anyone buy that?"

"Bullshit! I have a bridge for sale to anyone who does! There's only one purpose for that regulation–to make certain people richer. This will just move more imports to H.H. and T.V."

I soon learned that he referred to H.H. Kung and T.V. Soong who–with members of Chiang Kai-shek's family–made up the so-called "five holy families" that controlled much of China's textile, manufacturing, shipping, banking, real estate, gold import and other businesses.

This was emphasized by the manager of an international trading company, who complained angrily that his profit margin would be further squeeze on his most profitable imports, American cigarettes. "They know that we have the leading brand, and for a long time have been trying to take a piece of it. Just like they did with Pattison's sugar imports from Grace Brothers."

A junior lawyer who normally kept quiet chimed in, "I think last week's editorial in *The China Weekly Review* said it quite well. You probably read it–the headline was something like: 'American traders protest against corruption in China.'"

"Yes. I read that article. Right to the point."

The cigarette importer shook his head and muttered angrily, "Roosevelt really screwed us when he gave up our foreign concessions here."

A Cold Wind from the North

We were well aware of the civil war. But most believed that the fighting was far away, around the Great Wall, and the topic was rarely mentioned. It was not until summer, 1948, when Roger Jones joined us at the round table, that we gave it the attention it merited. The respected correspondent had arrived from Tsingtao, a port in the north, where he had been covering the withdrawal of the U. S. Marines who had been stationed there since the end of WWII.

Usually a cheerful sort, he was deeply pessimistic. After gulping down a double Scotch, he said quietly, "The situation is bad, and getting worse every day. You wouldn't believe it. When I was there a year ago, Tsingtao and the eastern portion of Shantung peninsula were controlled by the KMT. Of course, they were propped up by our marines. When the last 10,000 Japs were repatriated, and our guys started transferring out, the commies moved in. Now, suddenly, the province is swarming with red troops. Only Tsingtao port is still controlled by the nationalists."

"But Tsingtao should still be safe as long as some of the marines are there," someone offered.

"Forget that," Jones said. "Right after the last Japs were cleared out, our marines were reduced from battalion strength to only one company. They have been under attack by the commies, who greatly outnumber them. A few weeks ago there was a fire fight outside of Tsingtao. One marine was killed. The company has now been moved onto a Navy ship in the harbor."

He looked at us, frowning. "You don't seem to be getting much news here and I better bring you up to date. First, the commies are no longer the ragged band of stragglers, armed with only a few thousand old guns, that they were at the end of the Jap war. You may remember that the Ruskies arranged for the commie general, Lin Piao, to take the surrender of the half million Jap soldiers in Manchuria. What you didn't hear was that they also got about 2000 Jap artillery pieces, 150,000 machine guns and many, many rifles. And plenty of ammo. That still wouldn't be so serious if the KMT troops fought. Only a year or so ago they outnumbered the commies two to one, and had superior American armaments and millions of dollars, which we provided. But massive corruption took care of that.

"Many generals appropriated most of the money they received for their soldiers' pay. So the troops–many were farmers supporting families before they were conscripted–had to run around begging for food. They sold guns, anything for money. And deserted in masses. Many joined the commies, who fed them and treated them handsomely compared with what they were used to. They took with them guns and ammo, which we provided. Because of this, Mao's strength has increased to nearly a million soldiers, many armed with American weapons. *That*–and their comparatively decent treatment of the Nationalist Chinese who surrendered–is what enabled them take over so much territory in barely two years."

The conversation turned into a Q&A session as we probed for clues that might point to our own futures in Shanghai. I was thinking mostly about Dad. Only a few years earlier he had been suffering brutal assaults on his health by Japanese conquerors. Now, at age eighty, could he tolerate another such attack if a new group of Asian masters treated Americans in the same rough way?

Cindy

The question of Shanghai's future was also on the minds of other experienced old timers who had returned since the war. One of these–Dad's closest friend Cornelius Franklin–was another former judge and now a director of many American and Chinese businesses in Shanghai. A stalwart southerner, the judge had recreated his family's Missouri plantation home on the suburbs of Shanghai. Occasionally, on Sunday mornings, he would ask Dad to join him on the verandah to discuss such matters as possible future developments for Shanghai.

I was surprised when Dad asked me to accompany him on one of these visits. As I sat nursing my mint julep, two magnificent black labs dashed up to greet us, followed by a cluster of puppies struggling to keep up. After receiving ear scratches from the judge the parents came over to Dad and me for more pampering. The puppies, meanwhile, were jumping all over my feet, yapping. The judge watched them with amusement. Then he said, "They seem to like you, John. Have you ever had a Labrador retriever?"

"No. I've had English setters, but that's all."

"Would you like one of these pups?" he asked.

Surprised, I looked at Dad for guidance. He was smiling quietly and I realized they had planned this. He said, "You're being offered the pick of the litter, son."

How to select? A thought struck me. I jumped down onto the broad lawn and clapped my hands. The little hoard tumbled down the stairs and scrambled after me. One, slightly smaller than the others, arrived first. A female. I tied a handkerchief loosely around her and repeated the exercise. Again the pack followed and the same puppy scored. This was clearly my baby.

We registered her at the New York Kennel Club as Shanghai Cinders, named after her grandmother Cinders who had been a champion. The sire, Malvadeer Mustang, had a pedigree just as respected. For all her proud lineage, though, my baby was simply called Cindy.

I started her training when she came of age. Guided by the judge, I took her through such basic commands as "sit", "heel" and "fetch." None of this silly "roll over" nonsense for Cindy–she was a huntress! Next came the fun part, training her to retrieve. The actual fetching, of course, came naturally. She chased enthusiastically after everything from sticks to tennis balls and soon learned to drop them at my feet. Developing a "soft mouth"–learning to carry game without biting–took more time. The training instrument was a short stick through which I drove a dozen nails. The cook produced two freshly butchered pheasant wings, which I tied around the stick so that the nail ends barely protruded. Then I threw the stick. Cindy was unpleasantly surprised when she seized it, and gave me a reproachful look. But after a few trials she obediently–and gingerly–fetched it to receive a reward of juicy meat, an ear scratch and "Good girl!"

Cindy perfected her skills on hunting trips we took with the judge and his retrievers. We would drive thirty miles up the Yangtze River to a marsh where flocks of birds settled during migrations. Before long Cindy was retrieving, on command, with the rest of her clan. Then, one hot summer day, she broke training. We had been tramping through dry shrubs all morning without raising a single fowl when at midday we approached a farmer tending a flock of ducks. Cindy also spotted them. She was clearly feeling sorry for us and took off like a black rocket.

Ignoring the farmer's screams, she snatched up a fat duck from his flock and raced back with her trophy clasped firmly in her jaws. Then she placed it at my feet and looked up with an expression that was amazingly human. It seemed to say, "Daddy, I know I did wrong, but you couldn't find food so I brought this back for you!"

By then the farmer stormed up, bellowing Chinese curses and waving a pitchfork. The judge reached in his pocket to pay for the duck. Suddenly it scrambled to its feet, quacked a few times, and waddled back toward its mates. The farmer let out a surprised squawk and hightailed after it.

I hugged my wonderful Cindy–clearly as much of a champion as her famous grandmother. Even the judge shook his head in wonder and gave her a pat. This was not the time for discipline.

Presently she discovered booze. This happened one evening when someone slopped beer on our tiled verandah deck. Suspiciously she approached the spill, carefully sniffing the liquid. She took a lick and immediately sneezed. Not daunted, she took another lick, and between sneezes soon cleaned up the mess. Then, apparently quite sober, she came over and scratched my leg for more. Having downed a few beers myself, it seemed only fair that she should have another swig so I spilled some. Other friends felt as I did and also shared. Cindy handled her liquor that evening like a perfect lady and didn't show the slightest hangover the next morning.

That was the beginning. During subsequent parties she switched to Scotch whisky–but only quality products like Johnny Walker or Haig. Then, one night she was offered champagne from a girl's cupped hand, I would like to report that from then on Cindy would take nothing short of vintage champagne, but no, she would still accept a Scotch–provided it was a good brand.

Big Louie

Big Louie was the most dangerous man I ever met. Towering nearly a foot over me at six foot four, his 220-pound athletic body topped by a flaming red marine crew cut, he was clearly someone to respect in a fight. Yet despite his formidable appearance, the thirty-year-old was normally a polite gentleman attesting to a respectable family background and Ivy League education.

Unless he was provoked. Then, in a flash, he would revert to the ferocious killer into which years of OSS training and bloody unconventional warfare experience had molded him. When this happened people got hurt and things got smashed.

My first encounter with Big Louie took place at the American Club on a quiet weekday afternoon with few people around. Walking into the bar room, I noticed the entire staff of waiters lined up along the back wall with arms reaching above their heads in the "hands up" position. They were clearly terrified, their eyes fixated on a big man facing them with his back to me.

He turned around, saw me, and lowered what appeared to be a Colt .45 in his hand. In an angry voice, he bellowed, "I told them I wanted a frigging drink and these assholes won't serve me!"

The head waiter, Ah Ching, nervously blurted out, "Master, he dlinkee too muchee. Club lules say no can give master more whisky."

Resisting an inclination to bail out of there, I suggested that the threatening gunman join me for a soft drink at a table. To my surprise, he quietly assented. It took only a minute to remind him that any waiter could lose his job if a club officer caught him serving anyone too many drinks. I then carefully asked, "If you had a family to feed, and couldn't get another job, what would you do?"

We ended a short discussion with him sliding his weapon across the table to me. It was not loaded. Without a word, he walked over to each waiter and apologized. We could all sense that his words were sincere, as were the handshakes that followed and the assurances that the whole matter would be forgotten. At my suggestion he checked his weapon at the desk. The upshot was that the waiters, to a man, adopted Big Louie as their new best friend.

Over the following months Big Louie also became *my* best friend–although I learned that best friendship with Big Louie came at a high risk. My introduction to this took place after a session in the popular Aero Club, where Big Louie had brought me to meet a Chinese officer, General Lee, who had fought with him behind the Japanese lines.

Over a light dinner and copious drinks, I listened, nearly incredulous, as they relived clandestine operations they had conducted against the Japanese, laughing boisterously as they described the most blood curdling events. It was not until 2:00 am that we headed out the door for taxis. None were available. General Lee and I decided to wait for one at the door while Big Louie walked toward some pedicabs parked across the street. Four pedaled out and he started bargaining for a price to the American Club, only a few blocks away. When they couldn't agree, Big Louie told one what he could do to his mother. A quick expletive came back, followed by angry gestures and finally an attack by all four. Within minutes they were all groaning on the pavement.

This set off a full-blown melee. Jumping off their pedicabs, a mob of at least a dozen strong men, swinging sharp-edged bicycle chains, attacked from all sides. Big Louie decked probably half of them, but was being overwhelmed by the numbers when the crack of a gun froze everything.

General Lee, waving a German Mauser, stepped out from the club door and identified himself as a much feared security officer in the KMT carrying special authority from Chiang Kai-shek. He shouted a command, punctuated by another shot. The mob panicked and scattered, leaving the street strewn with unconscious colleagues and overturned pedicabs. We returned into the club to let Big Louie wash the many cuts made by slashing bicycle chains. He was in bad shape, so when a taxi finally arrived I took him home where he slept on a sofa in my bedroom.

One unexpected consequence of this episode was the warm friendship that developed between Big Louie and my little mother. After making sure that his cuts were disinfected, she insisted that he stay at our house for a few days where she coddled him like a naughty but spoiled child. I suspected that this was because, with her own war correspondent background of challenging dangers, she sensed a rapport with my violent big friend.

Black Tamara

The episode that *really* convinced me of my idiocy in associating with Big Louie took place at a gala evening at a leading club. Here, Shanghai's leading Americans and selected international guests assembled for an evening of celebration. Dress was formal, with men wearing dinner jackets, sashes and decorations, and ladies displaying the latest ball gowns from Europe. The event was well attended and most guests arrived before nine p.m., when John Cabot, our tall and dignified new Consul General, would start dinner with his toast and welcoming address. As they came in, the men congregated in the Men's Bar while the ladies went upstairs. Drinking was heavy, reflecting growing concern about the war, deteriorating business, and just about everything else.

Nevertheless, our worries were put aside and soon the bar area was packed with men loudly telling stories and laughing at jokes. The carefree mood was boosted by the arrival of a quartette of popular young Americans, led by radio commentator Bill Crum, who danced in, arm in arm, bellowing the hit song: "Cigareeetes, an' Wusky an′ Wild, Wild Women. They'll drive you crazy, they'll drive you in-sa-a-ane!" We joined in.

A few moments later a strange thing happened: the revelers near the door became oddly quiet. Their silence spread to their neighbors, then right across the room, engulfing everyone included the bartenders. For a long moment the place was absolutely still. Then the silence was shattered by a bloodcurdling shriek in an accent right off the Volga River: "Dah-link!"

Heads swung toward the door and mouths fell open in disbelief. Next to me a consular officer gasped, "My God!" and whispers of "Jesus Christ!" and "Oh – no!" arose around me.

Being short, I couldn't see over the crowd until I stepped up on the bar rail. Then I saw the disheveled red hair of Big Louie–who on an insane impulse I had earlier invited–pushing his way in. This was bad enough, but it paled alongside of the sight next to him.

There, staggering and laughing drunkenly, was the beautiful Black Tamara, the most popular–and expensive–whore in all of Asia, who had probably bedded a quarter of the men present. Eyes flashing under raven black hair, she lurched toward a distinguished European guest decked in red diplomatic sash and medals.

"Dah-link!" she cried out again in her throaty Slavic accent. "Ven you come see me again?"

The result was too much. Most of the men scrambled for the doors in a panicky exodus toward safety in the men's rooms. These were jammed in minutes and refugees fled on to other sanctuaries. Even some who had not experienced the delights of a *séance* with Black Tamara joined the rush in a sort of mob hysteria. I could only stand frozen at the bar. An irrational impulse to laugh was quickly dampened by fear that this might attract attention. Inside I was cringing with shame when Big Louie spotted me. Grinning wildly, he staggered over and demanded, "John! Where the hell are the frigging drinks?"

I would have killed him if I could. No one–certainly not the waiters, who were already cowering before this huge invader–would step forward to boot him and his loud whore out of the club. But Big Louie had a strange respect for me, and eventually I persuaded him to shove Black Tamara into a taxi and follow her away.

Then I returned to the angry shout: "Who the hell let them in?" Well, I didn't get kicked out of the club, obviously because of respect for Dad, a former president. But things were pretty frosty at home for a while and I got used to cold stares during lunch.

The story of Black Tamara's venture into high society gained fame as it made the rounds, and she acquired somewhat of a cult status. Not much later, I heard that she paid $10,000 to American engineer Dave Workman to marry her, and took off with him to Bangkok.

I Ride a Champion

I would never have known the excitement of owning a champion race horse if Mother hadn't introduced me to her friend Billy Liddell. Billy was the epitome of the English grand dame. Tall, elegant and gray haired, she was an international socialite with homes in London, France and Shanghai. Billy's love was racing, and she was much admired for her skill in handling race horses. She and a former partner, also English, had once owned the most successful stable in China which they named We Two. As we sat on our verandah having a drink, Billy said, "Your Mother tells me that you enjoy riding. Are you comfortable on an English saddle?"

"Yes, but I haven't ridden one for years. I prefer the Western saddle."

"Being American, I can understand that. But would you like to try a ride on one of my horses?"

When I hesitated, she added, "It will be like riding a bicycle; once one learns, one never forgets."

A few days later, after an early lunch, I drove with Billy to the Race Course. We walked to the stables, stopping at some old stalls with the faded "WE TWO" sign still visible over the entrance. Billy motioned to some half dozen horses standing inside.

"This is all I have left, John. A few souvenirs of what was once the pride of Shanghai's racing world."

I followed her to a quiet tan horse, who raised his head to nuzzle her. She placed a sugar cube into his mouth, stroking him gently. "My favorite, Cheefoo Castle. He has won every prize in China, including the Shanghai Darby. I ride him whenever I have the opportunity."

I observed that Cheefoo Castle was smaller than the horses I had ridden in Boulder. Billy explained, "The horses raced here are not Arabs. They are a different breed called Mongolian ponies. But what they lack in size, they make up for in endurance, speed and courage. The breed originated in northwest China. Some say that they were ridden by Genghis Khan and his warriors. Probably not true. Who knows?"

An ancient looking Chinese emerged from the back of the stables. They spoke in Shanghai dialect for a few minutes, then Billy introduced him. "This is The Castle's mafoo. He has taken care of the pony since he was foaled, and this continues to be his sole purpose in life. He doesn't seem to have a name–just mafoo, which means horse attendant."

I stroked the horse's flank. The coat was soft, like a sheep. Billy noticed my surprise. "That's another characteristic of the Mongolian pony: a soft coat.

"You may wonder why I brought you here. The reason is because I will be leaving Shanghai in a few weeks, probably for good. I cannot bring The Castle with me and want to assure that he is happy.

"His old stable mates and the mafoo will take care of his basic needs, which are simple. But they cannot give him the one thing that he needs most–his weekly gallop. He loves to circle the track at speed, and I really believe he thinks he is in a real race. A friend and I have been riding him, but she is also leaving and I cannot find anyone else here whom I would trust. I was hoping you would consider doing this."

I was surprised, to put it mildly. But what an opportunity! Without hesitation, I answered, "I'll take a ride and see how it goes."

"Give it a try. Then if you are agreeable, I would like you to have him."

I realized she was giving him to me, but before I could protest she continued, "This would make you no trouble. The pony will stay here.

The mafoo will continue to feed and groom him and take him for walks, and saddle him for you when you want to ride."

A few days later the mafoo led the pony from the stable while Billy walked alongside talking soothingly and stroking his flank. I slipped a foot into a stirrup and mounted. The Castle responded with a nervous whinny and tossed his head, but as Billy continued to provide reassurance, his agitation subsided and I was able to steer him onto the track.

He walked quietly until we reached the spot where, years earlier, the starting gate had been positioned. At that point the quiet little pony turned into a wild stallion. He gave an excited snort and lurched forward.

I nearly fell off. Only by clinging desperately to the reins and gripping until my calves ached could I keep from being left behind. How I missed the security of the Western saddle horn! Using all the skill I remembered from childhood lessons, I gradually gained control. By the four furlong mark I was shouting with excitement, riding the wind aboard this magnificent mount. Cheefoo Castle and I were racing again for the championship!

As we came into the final furlong he really proved his heart. At the head of the stretch, just as I expected him to slow to a canter, his ears flipped back and a new surge of power pulled me forward so violently that I felt I was being shot off on an arrow. Then, his stretch run completed and the race won, the champion–my champion–slowed to a walk and returned to the stable to be greeted by the mafoo and an exuberant Billy.

High on adrenalin, I jumped down and embraced my wonderful steed. Although sweating and still panting, he calmly accepted sugar lumps from Billy and me while the mafoo set about his tasks. Billy and I signed a transfer of ownership for a fee equivalent to nine dollars per month for the mafoo's wages and the pony's food, board and other costs. From then on, I took my champion for a gallop at every opportunity. I soon discovered that these runs gave me, apart from the exercise and excitement, another benefit which seemed important–an escape, for a few heady moments, from the brain-atrophying work of tabulating insurance line cards at my desk.

The exciting runs around the track continued for months, until the bitter day when I arrived to find the mafoo squatting in the stall alone, wailing with grief. His lifelong companion had died during the night and had been carted away. I felt the loss deeply, and it was only partial consolation to learn that the old warrior had passed away peacefully in his sleep. I tried to ease the poor mafoo's pain with a gold bar, but he was still shaking with sobs when I left the WE TWO stables for the last time.

The International Entrepreneur

Early in 1949 the exciting possibility appeared that I might be able to upgrade my boring job to something much more challenging. This came one evening when Big Louie took me for dinner to meet his new boss. I had reservations about anyone actually employing Big Louie, who had the reputation of being a large caliber loose cannon, until I saw a new, quietly competent personality emerge when he introduced us.

His boss, Timothy J. O'Sullivan, was clearly no ordinary businessman. It took only a moment for me to recognize him as the classic international merchant adventurer–a modern incarnation of the old China clipper ship captains. Tall, slender and immaculately dressed, he seemed to have a perpetual gray hue over his face, which suggested sleepless nights planning business coups. This impression was intensified when he spoke. Although his voice was low and emotionless, it commanded immediate respect.

Big Louie spent days closeted with O'Sullivan in a luxurious suite at the Cathay Mansions. Now and then they invited me in briefly to provide information about marine insurance. When I asked Big Louie about this, he replied, "Can't say anything now. Just wait. Tim likes you and will fill you in when he is ready. Until then, don't ask questions and for God's sake don't say anything to anyone."

I learned what was going on at lunch in the hotel's private dining room. With no waiters present, Tim told me, "I've decided to give you an early briefing about a project I am organizing. You are here on Louie's recommendation, because of your father's reputation, and the fact that you were a Navy officer. I would like your assurance now that you will divulge nothing about what you hear today to anyone other than officers in your company with a need to know."

I agreed.

"Good. You may be able to participate in a large marine shipment.

During the war the Japanese stockpiled one million tons of ore–primarily iron with some lead and wolfram–along the south bank of the Yangtze. They intended to ship this to Japan to be refined into steel. However, attacks by our submarines interdicted their plans and the ore remains there now."

As I listened with increasing excitement, he continued, "One of my companies, General Commodities, has contracted to ship this ore to Kobe. The buyer is MITI–the Japanese Ministry of Trade and Industry. The ore will be transported aboard China Steam Navigation Company ships carrying about eight thousand tons apiece, with three or four sailings a week, starting in a few weeks. You can assume a total value of twenty-five million dollars. Allowing delays for floods and other natural obstructions, the entire transfer should be completed within a year.

"Your role would be to arrange marine insurance covering five consecutive contracts of two hundred thousand tons. For each, we will need an open policy covering C.I.F. and war risk, tailored to MITI's specifications, issued by a reputable American or European underwriter."

He paused, watching me closely. "Can you handle this?"

My mind was racing. The reference to the China Steam Navigation Company guaranteed high-level government participation. The value was way beyond anything I could have imagined. Authority to commit AFIA to anything like this would have to come from the very top in New York, and probably be subject to delays.

These could start right in our office. Just a few weeks earlier Buster had been transferred and replaced by an older gentleman named Edgar. The new manager was understandably cautious and I had no idea how he would react to this sudden bombshell. I explained this frankly and asked for time to obtain authorization from New York. Tim thought for a moment before replying. "Delays provide opportunities for unexpected problems. But I understand your situation and will give you three days of exclusivity. After that I may invite competition."

Buster's replacement manager was clearly interested. After the usual questions, he asked me to prepare a proposal for him to telex to the head office. It took only an hour to hand him the draft. I went home excited–not only for this potential new business for my company, but also because by acquiring it, I would surely have a chance to break loose from my "stamp licking" desk work.

Two days later Edgar called me into his office where he and Winston were huddled over a long telex. Looking up, my boss said, "We have approval for an open policy and a rate for the requested F.P.A. and War Risk coverage."

I read the response carefully and said, "Those are the terms Mr. O'Sullivan wants. He asked for a prompt reply, and I will deliver our offer right now."

The Ugly Face of Competition

Tim and Big Louie were studying a document laid out on a table when I entered. My friend's expression was uncharacteristically solemn. As I approached, I saw the top page of a professionally printed offer captioned "Open Policy" and "General Commodities," under the dominant letterhead "AIU."

I froze, recognizing what this was. Winston's caution that the AIU was a rough competitor came sharply to mind. But how could this have happened with Tim's assurance that he would wait three days before alerting competition?

Tim answered my unspoken question. "Your competitor's commercial intelligence is remarkably effective. Their messenger hand-delivered this a few minutes ago. You will see that their offer is so specific that it can have been prepared only with inside knowledge. This means there was a leak at high level. Either in Japan or China. Possibly right in this hotel. Or in your company."

Still numb, I could only shake my head. "No. I'm sure it wasn't us." There was still a chance that we had won the business, so I asked, "Could we see how our quotations compare?"

Tim laid them side-by-side. It was immediately apparent that AIU had underbid us. Not hugely, but enough to knock us out. As I struggled for something to say, Tim reminded me, "You will recall that I made my offer conditional to your obtaining the most competitive rate."

With sinking heart I made a final attempt, "If we can match AIU's quote would you still insure through us?"

"That is asking a lot, John, considering your high offer. But undercut their quotation one percent and I will be justified in selecting your company for this contract. You still have until tomorrow afternoon for your reply."

That night I sat with Edgar in his office while he made the difficult phone call across the twelve-hour time difference to New York. But it was no use. The head office firmly rejected any reduction from their original quote. Our opportunity had died–and with it my hopes for an exciting future as an insurance producer.

I visited Tim and gave him the news in person. He was discussing a trip for Big Louie to China's new capital, Nanking, and asked me to wait. When he finished, he said, "Louie is really pushing for you. I've decided to give you another chance.

"You will recall that this shipment will be accomplished in five contracts of two hundred thousand tons each. Your competitor, AIU, has won the first. The second contract should pick up as soon as it has been completed. I will need another open policy for that, and for each of the other three contracts later. In each case, the insurance will go to the lowest bidder meeting my approval. Because of the work you have done for us, I will see that you have every opportunity–subject to lowest bid."

While I appreciated Tim's words, I knew that my company–like many others–did not engage in a rate-cutting warfare with companies like AIU, who would go to extremes to keep such valuable businesses. Apparently reading my thoughts, Big Louie broke in, "John, you wouldn't be restricted to your company if they won't compete. Maybe you could find another good insurance company and broker the deal yourself!"

A Friendly Parting

The significance of Big Louie's suggestion struck me immediately. The broker's commission for just one of these contracts would exceed several years' of my current salary, and the cost of operating a small insurance office in one of Dad's properties would be minimal. I could tie in with good insurance companies. Even without Tim's shipment, my good relationships with managers at other firms should assure success.

I lay awake for hours that night considering pros and cons, my thoughts going back all the way to Boulder when Jim and Hank and I had started our China Trade and Engineering Co. Next day I woke up feeling that a heavy load had been pulled from my shoulders.

First, I wanted Dad's opinion. In a frank talk, he told me that he understood, having taken the adventurous route himself when younger. But he was concerned with the timing. "You may be setting off into a bog of quicksand, son, without any way to prepare for the risks ahead. Of course I will back you by arranging an office and any other way I can. But I would prefer you stayed where you are until our future here in China is clearer."

I understood Dad's caution, thanked him for his support, and explained that I would have to move immediately if I were to take advantage of this once-in-a-lifetime opportunity. After a moment of silence, Dad, who was a Latin scholar, replied, "You have no real responsibilities yet, and apparently this could be a truly promising opportunity for you to seize. So go ahead, son. *Carpe diem.*"

I then met with Edgar, whom I had come to respect greatly, to arrange my resignation. He recognized that I was, as he put it, a square peg in a round hole at my sedentary desk job. Since the function of our office was primarily to represent the interests of our American principals, there was no other position emphasizing sales where I could fit in.

After he had communicated with the head office, we agreed on the terms. I would refund all of AFIA's expenses in bringing me out from America and refrain from competing for AFIA's established business. For their part, AFIA would continue my salary and allow me use of my office until I was ready to move out, and after that would assist me in any reasonable way, including recommendations to prospects.

With that accomplished, Winston and Ken gave me a lively lunch. Our friendship would continue.

PART THREE

Working with Lloyds of London

Making Arrangements

My experience in Shanghai's insurance arena had hammered home one lesson: other factors being equal, low cost was critical. Low cost had wrenched my business with Tim away from AFIA. I set about to find an even more competitive underwriter to wrench it back to *me.* The famous Lloyd's of London came immediately to mind. I could scarcely believe my good luck when I found out that they were not exclusively represented in Shanghai–or even really active. I set about to acquire representation.

First, I needed credibility as a *bona fide* insurance producer. Dad helped me set up a two-room office in the Continental Bank Building on Kiukiang Road in Shanghai's financial center. A hard-to-get telephone line was already in place. I hired a smart young German secretary, fluent in English and Chinese, and an office boy/runner, printed stationery and calling cards–English on one side, Chinese on the other. Finally I placed a small notice in the American-owned newspaper *The Shanghai Evening Post.*

This done, I airmailed the Lloyd's broker Walround, Scarman & Co., introduced by a friend, for a quotation on Tim's shipment. Ten days later, it arrived:

> We thank you very much for your letter of the 28th inst. in which you inquire into the rate on various ores from China to Japan…In your letter you speak of an amount of $25,000,000; we presume that this is the year's sendings. We have seen Underwriters at Lloyds and they have intimated the rates as follows:
> China Ports to Japan: .125%+.125% C. M. S. + Scale War (at the time of writing .375%).
> As you are well aware of the position in the Inland of China, you will understand that we cannot quote any definite war rate…as it is left entirely to Underwriters discretion. At the moment it would be somewhere in the neighborhood of 2%.

I was relieved to see that the "intimated" quotations were well under AIU's. I had found my competitive underwriter! Following two weeks of telexes and airmailed letters shuttling back and forth, they sent a comprehensive offer that was firm and undercut the AIU quotation, while including a generous commission for me. I passed it on to Tim, who agreed to give me the next contract provided my rate remained the lowest.

I saw a lot of Tim, even though Big Louie was often away, shuttling bulging duffle bags to Nanking where top government officers were stationed. I knew better than to ask what those bags contained.

AIU Makes Me an Offer I Can't Refuse

At about this time I received a surprising invitation to lunch with an AIU veteran, a man about twice my age, whom I had recently met. Curious, I accepted. Instead of the usual American Club, he took me to the Renaissance, a popular Russian restaurant, where he gave me another surprise:

"When you resigned from AFIA," he started, right to the point. "We considered you out of the running. But we were wrong. You have impressed us with your innovative ideas and the speed you moved." I listened to more flattery, waiting for him to explain his purpose for this meeting. Then it came:

"You were clever bringing in that Lloyd's broker. Of course we know them very well–we do considerable reinsurance with Lloyd's. But sometimes their entry can roil up a calm market. In the case of General Commodities, it would be better if they were not introduced."

I must have started in surprise. How the hell did he know all this? And what nerve! But I kept listening.

"Because of this, we have a proposal for you: place the insurance for this business with us at the same rate Lloyd's broker has offered, and we will guarantee your commission, to be paid in full upon the signing of each contract." He was watching me intently, his white hair glistening in the candlelight. He added, "You will have the security of the same commission income, an experienced partner on site here, and freedom from competition."

As I started my rejection, he interrupted, "Otherwise, Mr. Potter, you *will* have competition. We will not allow this business to get away from us. You must know by now how effectively we can compete. However, it would be to our joint advantage–and certainly to *your* advantage–to work together on this."

There was no question that they were dead serious. In a head-to-head fight with the powerful, experienced AIU organization, I realized I would lose. Besides price-cutting, they had too many other ways to win.

The upshot of this and subsequent discussions was agreement all around. I explained the new arrangement to Tim, who was pleased with the reduced insurance premium to AIU on the second contract, thanks to my introduction of Lloyd's.

His ore shipments under the first contract had already started. And in just a few weeks the ore under his second contract would be flowing out to Japan–and my huge commissions would be flowing in to me!

The Loss of Manchuria

My exuberance lasted several blissful weeks. Then, with no warning, Tim stunned me with the news that his shipments had been stopped. The freighter that was loading had been sent away half empty, and no more ships would be arriving. The ship owners had suspended their contract owing to the approach of fighting.

To underscore this, I received a telex from my Lloyd's brokers regretting that their underwriters would no longer cover war risk on the Yangtze River.

This was crazy. There was a war, sure, and I had heard things were going badly. But the fighting was far away in the north and could not possibly threaten Yangtze shipping. Then I realized that I had been so busy setting up my insurance brokerage and prospecting for clients that I had lost touch with current events.

I caught up quickly enough after rejoining the group at the round table. Big changes had taken place. Following a series of victories over KMT forces in distant Manchuria, the Communist armies had greatly increased in size and effectiveness. More and more KMT soldiers were deserting to them as they learned of Mao Tse-deng's promise that his cadres would receive a good meal every day. As Ace Smith observed, "This is probably the only promise ever made to those poor hungry bastards that was actually kept."

I had come to know Ace as the "Honest Ace" dice player at the next table when Buster introduced me to the bar room. After an absence of several weeks, the tall, sandy–haired businessman had started coming to the round table for dice and lunch again. We became better acquainted, and I learned that he owned Shanghai's most popular liquor business. He was also a member of many foreign clubs, on close terms with business and diplomatic leaders.

Although easy going and genial in manner, Ace was so well informed about everything going on that he was widely suspected of being with the CIA. I could not help thinking this at our lunches, as I listened to his briefings on what was being called "China's civil war."

Once, when a new arrival asked how the Communists had been able to dominate the more powerful Nationalists so quickly, Ace explained:

"Superior leadership and quality. Both sides are about equal in numbers now, but that's where it ends. The Communist generals, Lin Piao and Chen Yi, are among the most brilliant and experienced anywhere. Most of their troops are combat veterans with good morale. They are well led and treated, armed with modern American ordnance and supported by most of the Chinese because they behave relatively well. Remember Mao's admonition to move around the people like a fish swimming in the sea?

"On the other side, the Nationalists troops are treated so badly that most will desert if given half a chance. They are poorly led and many are cheated out of pay and even rations by their officers. Morale is poor. It's no secret that their generals–with a few exceptions–are corrupt and incompetent. Nearly all got their jobs through connections or bribes."

Returning to the questioner, Ace concluded, "And that's how Mao's Communists, who had so little only a few years ago, are now able to win their battles against the KMT."

After we broke for a drink and a few rounds of dice, Ace returned to the subject. "A good example is what happened in Manchuria. Just last summer the three big cities there were considered safe, defended by half a million KMT troops. The most important, Changchun, was garrisoned by the elite Seventh Army, which we trained.

"The Communists attacked it first. They isolated and surrounded the city. The KMT planners thought they could keep the garrison supplied by mounting another Berlin airlift, but couldn't send in enough planes with supplies. The soldiers fought well, but finally ran out of ammo and food. The general defected with his soldiers and American ordnance.

"The Communists scored a propaganda coup by giving free food to the starving people and soldiers. After that, the generals of the other two big cities, Chinchow and Mukden, put up only token resistance. They also made deals to save their hides. In just three months the KMT lost half a million of their best soldiers and an arsenal of weapons–mostly American.

"With the takeover of Manchuria," Ace concluded. "The Communists now own one quarter of China."

The Red Juggernaut Approaches

Shanghai's two English-language newspapers, the British-owned *North China Daily News* and American-owned *Shanghai Evening Post,* usually down played the war. But toward the end of the year both headlined news of heavy fighting at a place I had never heard of called Hsuchow. Here, two Communist field armies numbering half a million troops attacked a slightly smaller, but well entrenched, KMT garrison.

No one at the table knew much about Hsuchow except my old friend Mike Britton. "I went there a couple of years ago to check up on our oil distributor," he said. "It's in the middle of China, two, three hundred miles north of here. A real dump. Wrecked buildings still not rebuilt after bombing in the Jap war."

Mike's words "two, three hundred miles" caught my attention. This proximity had obviously attracted the interest of the news editors, also, to merit those headlines.

Day after day we followed the news as the defenders held off the larger attacking force, despite a series of morale-crushing betrayals by superiors. Most damaging was the disappearance of the KMT's powerful air force. Fleets of bombers and fighters had been committed to back up the defenders, but when most urgently needed, not one showed up.

"The reason?" replied Ace to our unspoken questions. "You might not believe it, but I've heard that Chiang ordered those planes reserved to support his future plans." There were frequent reports of defending generals causing chaos by issuing conflicting orders. Ammunition and rations ran out, and even when parachuted, were insufficient. Finally, one division defected.

In face of these problems, the defenders held out for over two months, fighting among their own dead and decaying bodies. When they finally surrendered at end-December, half were dead or wounded. The other 200,000, along with all the American-supplied ordnance, were integrated into the Communist army.

As we entered 1949, we faced the inevitable: war was finally coming to the Yangtze River–and possibly to our homes in Shanghai. This was driven home at the end of January when Tientsin, followed by the former capital, Peking, surrendered with only token resistance, turning over another supply of ordnance and troops.

The fall of Hsuchow brought realization that the Yangtze might not be the barrier to the Communist advance that many had hoped for. Rumors that their units had been seen on the north bank intensified this concern, and Shanghai reacted. Instead of the usual attitude of *mas-kee*–meaning "don't worry, things will turn out all right"– people *did* start worrying.

Our Consul General John Cabot had been warning of the Communist threat for months, but few would listen. The tall, distinguished Brahmin had expressed his feelings a few months earlier at our home when I made a fourth at a bridge game: "They still believe the Communists are only agrarian reformers who can't wait to do business with us," John had said in frustration. "This is so naïve. But I can't get through to them." Now, suddenly, he received plenty of attention when he urged that preparations be made for the evacuation of women and children if this proved necessary.

On the other hand, British Consul General, Robert Urquhart, shared the opinion of most of the British, whose companies had much larger vested interests in city properties, utilities, warehouses and other assets to protect. As one of their *taipans* urged, "Not the time to get your knickers in a twist, old boy. The Communists want to do business with us. They bloody well can't *live* without us!"

At end-January Chiang Kai-chek announced his retirement and returned to his birthplace in south China, leaving Vice-President Li Tsung-jen to take over. This brought a short interval of hope for a peace agreement, and the mood of "peace at any price" prevailed. We quickly learned that the V.P. was only a figurehead with little authority. Chiang was secretly maintaining control as suspicion grew that he planned to move his government and military units to Taiwan.

Caught in a Deadly Riot

Discontent in Shanghai increased. Just months earlier Chiang had made his son Ching-kuo the economic dictator of the city and in a futile attack on inflation, the inexperienced officer ordered gold and silver to be turned in to the state and issued a new paper currency–ironically named the gold yuan–pegged at four to a dollar. Then he froze shop prices and wages and banned money changing. The predictable result was that food and other consumer items instantly disappeared from the shops. Many were closed and shuttered.

Shanghai's residents exploded with anger, giving me the chance to become an authority on what it is like to be caught in a riot.

I was sitting in front with Dad's driver, Wong, when he turned into a street off Nanking Road. He suddenly muttered Shanghai's distress exclamation "*ah-yah!*" and jammed on the brakes. Ahead was an approaching wall of hysterically screaming men, arms flailing.

Wong tried to back out and ran into another threatening roadblock. The two angry masses closed in and we were tightly squeezed in a writhing mass of angry laborers, many stripped to the waist, all screaming at the top of their lungs. Their cries merged into a single vibrating high-pitched din, painfully loud and shrill, so frightening that Wong and I shrank down under the dashboard trying to escape from it.

The car rocked and bounced from heavy pounding on the sides. I caught glimpses of dirty, contorted faces as fists hammered the window glass inches from my head. I was sure they would turn the car over or set it on fire, when columns of club-wielding mounted police charged in. Leaning sidewise from their saddles to slash at the rioters, they cleared a passageway for us. Wong was able to back out past overturned cars with shattered windows and blooded passengers crawling out.

Riots like this occurred more frequently as popular resentment increased. Meanwhile, Ching-kuo's efforts resulted in hundreds of millions of new gold yuan notes being circulated. They lost value rapidly, and after a few months, had devalued to nothing. Someone calculated that these bills actually had become worth less than the paper they were printed on. In the end, Ching-kuo withdrew the controls he had imposed, and resigned with a public apology: "After seventy days I feel I have failed..."

"Damn right he failed," one of our dice players commented. "Best thing that bastard ever did."

The Plunder of China's Treasure

But Chiang Kai-shek's machinations were not yet finished. On the last night of January, coinciding with his resignation, all traffic on The Bund was blocked off from the front of the Bank of China. There was a report that columns of coolies were seen carrying bundles from the bank onto a small freighter docked alongside. By morning the ship had disappeared.

The suspicion that these bags contained treasure gained credibility a few days later when it became known that the financial reserves of China–$300,000,000 in gold, silver and foreign bank notes–had been shipped away to Taiwan, presumable to be joined there later by Chiang and his entourage.

What little faith had remained in the government was wiped away when news got out of this secret plundering of the country's wealth by the country's own leader.

Lessons From My Riot Experience

I could not forget those riot scenes of overturned cars with shattered windows and flames flickering up the sides. The experience started me thinking about the security of our home, and the Chinese antiques and other treasures my parents had collected. Just a few years earlier they had lost their real estate and many other assets to the Japanese. Dad must not, at his age, be faced with such a ruinous blow again. I realized that our household insurance would not cover all the losses if discipline broke down and the ground-floor apartment was ransacked. Even more troubling was what might happen, if the Communists took the city, during the turnover when there might be no law and order at all.

The answer was war risk insurance. I checked with friends at several insurance offices and learned that not one provided this cover in Shanghai because of what they called the Waterborne Agreement. This led me to notes from my AFIA training. Sure enough, in 1937 Lloyd's and the other main insurers had agreed not to extend marine war risk insurance beyond the water's edge. It was great on the Yangtze, but useless in Shanghai.

Digging further into my notes, I came onto "Strikes, Riots and Civil Commotion." This special insurance compensated for all sorts of losses caused by riots. A telex exchange with my Lloyd's brokers confirmed their interest in providing this cover.

It looked good to me, but would it sell? I made a simple survey with Mark Ferguson, a friend who managed a car agency with dozens of vehicles parked in front. He was worried about their exposure in the open. Mark had tried to obtain war risk protection, but his insurer would not provide it. When I offered the cover from Lloyd's, he was immediately interested. An exchange of telexes with my Lloyd's broker resulted in a quotation that he found acceptable, and I had my first big S R & CC client.

I promptly offered this coverage to existing customers and likely prospects. Their reaction amazed me. Typical was, "Johnny, I've been worried what to do with the cargo in my warehouse. My insurance won't pay if a mob breaks in and cleans it out."

I had the solution, and within weeks had arranged S R & CC policies for nearly thirty customers–more than half being new responders to ads that I rushed into the *Daily News* and *Evening Post*. Coat-tailed on these were commitments for fire and auto insurance. Added up, the commissions nearly offset my loss from Tim's cancelled ore shipments.

PART FOUR

Pattison

The Maverick

One of the new customers was Jimmy James, owner of Jimmy's Kitchen on Szechuan Road. In the twenty years since it opened, it had acquired enough popularity to earn the Shanghai dialect nickname, "The white table cloth place", and that is the destination I gave driver Wong when he took me there. Jimmy was an American Navy vet, who either took discharge or jumped ship here, depending on whom you listened to. In any case, Jimmy's served real American hamburgers, hot dogs, baked beans and corned beef hash which crewmen from visiting American ships could not find anywhere else.

I was relishing a perfect burger there while waiting to close a policy with Jimmy, when a smiling waiter handed me a calling card. It was elegantly engraved: a red, white and blue ship's pennant above the name of the sender, Alfred P. Pattison, President, and that of a company bearing his name. Neatly written in ink was the Latin: "*Quo vadis*?"

Looking up, I caught the eye of the amazing man who for years to come would bring into my life unimaginable excitement, danger, and ultimately, fortune.

I had met Pattison only once, at a reception. A brief conversation indicated that he was an American who owned a trading and shipping business with offices in principal ports of Asia–clearly a prospect for insurance, so I put him on my list for a follow up call. Not expecting him to remember me, I was surprised by the "Where are you going?" question on his card and walked over to his table. "Sit down, John," he said in a friendly voice. "Jimmy won't be able to see you for several minutes. Meantime, I'd like to learn something about you. Something other than your business–we can talk about insurance later. You can call me Pat–everyone does."

I was sure I hadn't mentioned insurance when we met and asked him how he knew this.

"You interested me."

Our conversation was pretty well a one-way street: he asked and I answered. It ended when Jimmy walked in and joined us. He and Pat were obviously friends and exchanged opinions about Shanghai's future while I completed Jimmy's policy application. When I returned to my table, I was not surprised that my bill had been paid.

Before keeping an appointment with Pat, I did my usual research and came up with some surprising facts. Although a very successful American businessman, he was not a member of the American business establishment. In fact, he had somewhat of a maverick image. The reason intrigued me.

Pat was the Far East general agent for the Isbrandtsen Steamship Line, an aggressive American company operating passenger-freighters that visited major ports on round-the-world itineraries. The distinguishing feature about his ships was that they were considered a threat by the other big American and European shipping companies.

For years, these international lines had been banded together in price-fixing agreements called "conferences" which established freight rates for shippers and prevented them from negotiating lower prices. One, The Far East Freight Conference, had controlled Shanghai exporters very effectively until a few years earlier, when Pat brought in Isbrandtsen and refused to join the conference cartel.

His Isbrandtsen vessels themselves did not offer the old established lines any serious competition–most were war surplus Victory and C-2 freighters with a few passenger cabins. Nor were they particularly fast or attractive. But Pat's ships had one big competitive strength: price. They diverted certain Shanghai exporters' cargoes, originally destined for conference vessels, onto Isbrandtsen ships by offering freight rates that undercut the conference by ten percent or even more. This "non-conference" offense was exacerbated by the aggressive appearance of the word ISBRANDTSEN emblazoned in giant white letters along their ships' black hulls.

From the viewpoint of conference line managers, Pat was just as much of a maverick himself. When I knew him better I realized that, as a champion of freedom and free choice, he abhorred price fixing and relished the act of sticking it to conference shipping companies.

In appearance Pat made as much of an impression as his flamboyant ships. Only a little over average in height, he projected the image of a giant. The reason stood out in front. Starting near the tip of his chin, his chest slanted forward in a steep slope all the way down his stomach to the large western buckle holding a belt that must have been twice the length of those worn by ordinary cowboys.

Yet although carrying nearly three hundred pounds, much of this out in front, he walked tall and confidently–not at all like an eight-month-pregnant woman. But the Alfred Hitchcock resemblance ended there. Complementing this huge body was an equally outsized head with a deceptively peaceful face and a full head of hair. His blue eyes had two settings: either bright and alert, or half closed and sleepy. Both settings indicated intense mental activity from his brain–the latter when he was concentrating the hardest.

The better I came to know Pat, the more difficult I found it to anticipate his mental process. Time and again his innovative Mensa brain produced decisions I would never have thought rational. But they usually were. He was brilliant, highly educated, imaginative, bold, determined, adventurous–ready to try the untried, and–an anomaly in a business world rampant with corruption–absolutely honest.

He was also a born teacher. If someone suggested, "Could we try.,.", like as not Pat would reply, "Let us consider your idea. Write it down. Then add everything you can think of that might go wrong and we'll look at it together." Suffice it to say, all but a few such proposals were filtered out in this self-education process, leaving only the most promising for Pat for review. In an environment where finding some way to make a profit was very difficult, Pat would say, "I look at one hundred business proposals every month. My problem is winnowing them down to a manageable few, then selecting from these the single one to run with." Of all his admirable qualities, I most respected his unshakable loyalty to friends. Time and again, over the following years, I would see him extend his support to those deserving his help, and–sometimes to his personal cost–also those not deserving it.

Before long Pat asked me for lunch in his office. As I walked in, I looked squarely at a huge floor-to-ceiling mural. Its fourteen-foot width spanned the world, bright blue for the sea and khaki for the land. Major cities–but only port cities–were identified. Linking them across the north Pacific, Atlantic and Indian oceans were irregular chains of half-foot-long model ships with miniature white ISBRANDTSEN letters on their black sides, all heading eastward. Under each was a ship's name. They seemed to be held in place with magnets.

To a person who, as a child, drew pictures and wrote poems about clipper ships, it gave me a strangely excited feeling to see their romantic names like *Flying Cloud.* Another, the *Flying Enterprise*, was sitting right off Shanghai. I stood, fascinated, counting them when Pat explained, "My office staff gave this to me after I took on the agency. Every ship is at its correct location."

"But how do you keep track of them all?"

He smiled, "My secretary handles this. She worked out some communication system with the ships' captains she meets here. I've never checked, but know they're all correctly sited."

All the cities were north of the equator except one on South America's west coast. Pointing toward it, I observed, "That city doesn't seem to belong with the others."

"You're quite right, John. Lima is not in my business universe today. But two years ago, a product from Peru played an important role in building up my company. This was sugar, shipped to us from Lima by Grace Brothers. We represented them in China, starting right after the war ended. At one time we had five Grace ships out there-" he pointed out a picture window toward the Whampoo River–"all discharging our sugar cargoes at the same time."

I was impressed and tried to be witty. "Sounds like enough for all the tea in China."

"There's a lot of tea in China," Pat agreed. Then he chuckled. "But by tonight, not quite so much. Captain Carlson, who you will meet at lunch, is loading four thousand cases of *Chun Mee* green tea aboard the *Flying Enterprise* for Casablanca. She's out there in midstream. Take a look."

I hurried to the picture window. There she was, easy to see, in the middle of the river. A black hull with prominent white letters, surrounded by lighters.

Merchant Marine Hero Kurt Carlson, Captain of the *Flying Enterprise*

While we ate a well-prepared sandwich lunch in Pat's office, we were joined by a third man. He was tall, clean cut, about thirty and wore a beaten up officer's uniform and cap. Pat introduced us casually, adding to me, "Kurt Carlson is captain of the *Flying Enterprise,* the ship you just looked at." Then they discussed the loading and other ships' business while I listened.

At one point Pat showed the captain a telex and said, "For you, from Hans."

Laughing out loud, Captain Carlson asked, "Is it the block buster or the atom bomb?"

"There seems to be some of both in here. He must be in a *real* hurry." Noticing me, Pat explained, "Hans Isbrandtsen, in New York, likes to have his ships turned around quickly. All ship owners do, of course, but Hans makes a ritual of it. So two days before one of his ships reaches port the agent receives a telex asking: "When did the ship sail?" We call this the bomb. Next day we receive the blockbuster, demanding an immediate answer to the first telex. By the third day, when the ship has arrived and is still unloading, the agent receives the atom bomb. You can imagine what that says."

Pat and the captain ignored the telex, reverting to their relaxed discussion about business. It was a joy to watch the warm interplay between them.

Little could we imagine that three years later, right after Christmas, this amiable Kurt Carlson would become the most famous–and most honored–seafarer in the world. For sixteen brutal days and nights the heroic Danish captain refused to abandon the sinking *Flying Enterprise,* her hull cracked by a rogue sea in the Atlantic. Sending his crew to safety, he remained alone on her wildly gyrating deck, deluged by heavy waves, guarding her owners' interests by staying with his ship. Only when the broken freighter had listed to 70 degrees and was sliding under, did Carlson scramble to safety on a tug. For his heroism, Captain Carlson was honored with a ticker tape parade in New York and medals which–characteristically–he would never wear.

I Join A.P. Pattison

After Carlson had left for his ship, Pat kept me back while we arranged insurance for his office and the *godown* where cargoes were stored. Both locations were on The Bund–the office occupying half a floor of the Messageries Maritimes building, overlooking the river, and the warehouse two blocks away opening onto the street. On Pat's instruction, the insurance was in the name of A.P. Pattison & Co., Fed. Inc., U.S.A. I had seen the same Fed. Inc., U.S.A. on O'Sullivan's company stationery and asked Pat what this signified.

"Good observation," he nodded in approval. "It is an abbreviation for Federal Incorporated, U.S.A., identifying it as one of a limited number of American-owned China Trade Act companies doing business exclusively in China and Hong Kong. In 1922 British and European companies paid no taxes on China business profits while American companies did, putting them at a competitive disadvantage. Our government created China Trade Act companies, exempted from taxes, to put them on equal footing."

By mid-afternoon, when I left Pat's office, I knew that I had found my niche. I knew, also, that Pat had already planned where I would fit in his organization. There was no mention of salary or benefits, other than his assurance, "If you ever need your own place to live, we can add on the cost." Dad was clearly relieved when I told him, and accepted my offer to share our living costs and pay all my office expenses. Pat had agreed that I continue my insurance business. It was still producing a good income, although less as Shanghai's commerce dried up under the threat of the approaching communists."

They Cross the Yangtze

Rumors about KMT military losses came to a head in February, when it was confirmed that Nationalist General Pai Chung-hsi had withdrawn his forces to what was scornfully referred to as "The Yangtze Line" along the south bank of the Yangtze River. The foreign community was assured that the Communists would advance no further. What wasn't so well publicized was the progress that the Communists were making.

Even Ace, with his all-knowing sources of information, could only say, "Everyone seems to know what their goals are–to take over China, of course. But how, where, when?" He shrugged. "That is the question."

By mid-April, less than a month later, Ace had a pretty good sense of the answer. The man who joined us at the table was no longer the relaxed, laid back dice player that I knew. In a deadly serious manner, he started, "They have been moving faster than anyone expected. I have it on good authority that Mao will cross soon. He has already positioned four field armies along the other side of the Yangtze, two under General Lin Piao across from Nanking, and the other two, under General Chen Yi between there and Shanghai. Rumors are that their advance agents have been here, bribing KMT generals, as usual."

Ace looked us over and raised his bushy eyebrows, "My guess is that they will move soon, and that they will have a Sunday stroll all the way down to Soochow Creek. After that, anything might happen, but one thing is certain: those of us who stay in Shanghai will be living in a Communist country."

We were impressed at his assured manner. One asked, "What are you planning to do, Ace?"

"I don't intend to live under a Communist regime. There will be plenty of planes and ships leaving the city." Ace left, and we toyed with our dice game, thinking about wives, children at the Shanghai American School, obligations of all sorts–and, in my case, employment for both Dad and me. Given any realistic prospect of continuing to earn income, Dad would no doubt stay, but insist on sending Mother back. I would remain with Dad, and hopefully, with Pattison.

I passed on Ace's information to him. He seemed unconcerned, commenting only that he had anticipated this. Dad had already come to the same conclusion as Ace, and was making plans to send Mother to California.

Less than a month later Ace's scenario came true, almost to the word. On the night of April 21, 1950, over one million Communist soldiers came ashore on the south bank aboard crowded sampans and barges, rafts and just hanging onto floats. Their crossing followed a four-hour bombardment by mainly captured American 75 and 105 millimeter guns, using the classic Soviet tactic of shell-shocking the enemy before attacking. Ace's comment about a Sunday stroll also came true. The general in charge of Nanking surrendered immediately, and the road to Shanghai was open. The changes coming to our environment worried us all, but did not have the shock effect of the news that followed the next day.

The Unprovoked Communist Attack on *H.M.S. Amethyst*

For years small foreign gunboats had enjoyed passage rights to diplomatic stations up the Yangtze, and on April 20 the British frigate was making a routine trip carrying supplies to the British embassy in Nanking. Just over a 100 miles up the river, even as the attack was in full flood, the little ship was battered at nearly point blank range by massive arrays of communist artillery batteries placed to support their river crossing. The shelling finally stopped after *Amethyst* had been hit 53 times and grounded on a sand bar. Of her 183-man crew, 54 had been killed or wounded.

News reached Shanghai and Nanking the same day. A second frigate, the *Consort*, went out to rescue her but was forced back by heavy shelling. Then the 10,000-ton cruiser *London*, and another frigate were sent, but again driven back by enormous concentrations of fire from shore batteries. This brought the incident to a stalemate. The question was: Why did they do it?

In Shanghai, two things were made clear to us: any vestiges of the good old days of the white *raj* had to be jettisoned, and our navies could not be depended on to protect us.

Mother Leaves for America as my Insurance Business Hits a Jackpot

With scattered reports from Tientsin and Peking too vague to mean much, questions were being raised as to whether the communist regime would permit Americans to take out their personal effects. Or, for that matter, whether we would be permitted to leave at all. Consul General

John Cabot reinforced his often-expressed concern in his statement: "I assume that all those who are not prepared to face the dangers of remaining in a war area have already left...if Shanghai should become so hazardous as to make it inadvisable to stay, Americans remaining cannot count on safety through emergency evacuation." To emphasize this, he had sent his wife away.

Most of Shanghai's American businessmen followed suit–some 1,500 wives and children were soon sailing to San Francisco on the passenger ship *General Gordon* and other transports. With them was Mother, making yet another trip across the Pacific. She would soon be in America with Patty, who was preparing to give birth to her first child. I, of course, would remain with Dad.

The departure of so many foreigners meant the transfer of thousands of cases, trunks and cartons of personal effects–many containing valuable antiques–from Shanghai to addresses all over the world. Most of these were handled by one big shipping group. Moving quietly, I arranged a marine insurance cover for these shipments at an all risks premium that brought wide smiles to both their managements and me.

Pat, when I thanked him again for allowing me to keep my sideline active, smiled, "I seem to be not the only one who can seize a good business idea when it floats by."

Lifestyles Change

Me no worry, me no care. Me go marry millionaire.
If he die, me no cry. Me go marry other guy.

With the Communists approaching, the atmosphere in the city reflected a curious mix of nervousness and tempered relief. The relief was felt by most of the foreign business community, nervous about their future but thoroughly fed up with the government corruption and the out-of-control inflation. Their attitude was "anything must be better than what we have now," with the most optimistic promoting the canard that the Communists were only "agrarian reformers" sympathetic to foreign business methods. Even greater enthusiasm was felt by millions of Chinese, mostly hungry and searching for work, who had been assured of a better life by the reams of Communist propaganda flooding the city.

On the other hand, growing apprehension was felt by the "White Russian" refugees, unable to escape for lack of travel documents. About 20,000 men, women and children had found their way to Shanghai after the Russian Revolution, arriving in flotillas of small ships from Vladivostok. Of these, nearly all had moved on to The Philippines, America and other sympathetic nations. But there were still about a thousand waiting for a country to accept them. Most were crammed into old wooden barracks with little heating and other facilities, under the care of reputably corrupt officials of U.N.'s International Refugee Association, widely suspected of appropriating for themselves some of the food allowance provided by their agency.

In our foreign business community the greatest immediate effect was a change in life styles. The mass exodus of wives and children left most of the men living in empty shells. The eager attention of old–time servants, who maintained strong loyalties to their foreign employers, merely served to remind the "master" of how lonely things could be after their families, and often personal effects accumulated over years, had been sent away. The bar of the American Club and other gathering places became noisier as more men stayed later and drank more heavily.

The situation changed in other ways for the bachelors and more than a few married "widowers." After the *General Gordon's* departure, the most attractive Russia girls–not a few claiming blood lines to the Czarist aristocrats–moved out of their miserable refugee barracks into the comfortable premises of bachelors who were no longer under the eyes of their superiors' wives. The bachelors were not alone; even married men succumbed. A strange new, almost fatalistic, atmosphere seemed to be taking over the behavior patterns of these renascent bachelors. With the steadying influence of families removed, and facing an unknown future that could become very dangerous, they found it easy to "live it up while we can, for tomorrow...who knows?"

My old pal Mike Britton was among the bachelors. I enjoyed parties with his group of oil company friends. Many of them lived with girl friends who had moved in with them. Although Dad would not tolerate any live-ins at our home, there were many at my friends' houses.

Ralph's "Stable"

One senior manager, Ralph–who years later became an investor in my treasure diving venture off Spain–was the uncontested champion of the hosts. This tall, handsome friend was Shanghai's chess champion. He also supported the largest group of attractive girls in his house, his primary live-in being a stunningly beautiful and voluptuous young blonde named Galina. One afternoon she was keeping his chess skills honed to a sharp edge by exercising him in their bedroom while he played a game with me–giving me a rook, as usual. I was sitting over our chessboard in the next room and we called our moves back and forth through the open door while I moved the pieces for both of us.

I had just shouted, "King's bishop to the queen's knight five" and Ralph's reply, partly garbled by Galina's screams of "oye, oye, oye," was coming in through the open doorway, when a newcomer walked in. He stopped short, stared in amazement at the open door then beat a fast retreat. I'll never forget the expression of disbelief on his face.

Ralph had our heartfelt gratitude for sharing with us many of his girls. Besides Galina, there were usually four or five other beauties living happily on his premises: Luba, Vera, Sonya, Katrina–better known as Kiss Me All Over, Katie–and one named Tanya whom I always fled from after our first encounter, when her frenzied bites and scratches must have cost me a pint of blood. It would be unnecessary to say that–among the American bachelors and many widowed husbands alike–Ralph was the most popular man in the city.

Martial Law

On April 23, 1949 the KMT government fled south to Canton, followed by a scramble for tickets on trains and any other transport south by junior government and military personnel. At the same time martial law was declared in Shanghai.

I had never realized how inconvenient this was until I experienced it. First, was the curfew that required a special pass for any street travel between 10 p.m. and 6 am. Confident that a small bribe of fifty million or so gold yuan would take care of any problem, several of us left a restaurant about midnight. We were all arrested. Fortunately one of our group was manager of a well-respected Chinese-American company and was able to have us released. We were lucky. Others were jailed overnight.

Just as troubling was the censorship. It affected all radio and press news. Both English-language newspapers were censored with the result that any printed report not favorable to the KMT was ordered to be deleted. This move was immediately challenged by Randall Gould, who became our hero. The respected editor of the *Shanghai Evening Post* kept the space for a censored item blank except for the notice: "Material which occupied this space was deleted by censor."

The infuriated government bureau threatened to close the newspaper. Gould just laughed, and printed that threat in the next issue. The censors persisted; Gould retaliated with notices like: "All the news that's fit to print (passed by censor)." The battle was ended by war developments.

Bill Crum's radio station was so badly harassed that he closed it down, to our regret. From then on Dad and I made good use of a big Halliburton short wave radio I had brought over from America. Careful jiggering of the dial produced clear transmissions from the news services of the Voice of America and British Broadcasting Company. We continued listening to my radio after the Communist takeover, but by then both the set and the long antenna were well hidden.

The Silk Man Wanted Gold

Ever since I could remember our home was visited each year by an ancient Chinese who staggered in carrying a huge bundle wrapped in a colorful Chinese cloth. To my parents, and all of our neighbors, he was known simply as "The Silk Man." Without a word he would place his bundle on the living room rug, and lay out an exciting array of Chinese antiques collected during a long trek across many provinces inland from Shanghai. His treasures included old bronzes. often authentic Sung pieces, Ching, Ming and earlier porcelains and gorgeous scrolls signed by well-known artists of past centuries. His visit in 1949 was no different from others, except that this time he seemed desperate to unload his merchandise and, oddly, would bargain only in "yellow fish."

He had always insisted in American dollar bills, but no longer trusted any paper currency or silver dollars "mex" which were sometimes counterfeit. But why was he suddenly insisting on small gold bars?

Dad summoned number one houseboy, Ah Kung, to investigate. A noisy diatribe in Shanghai dialect produced the news that Silk Man planned to run south dressed as a poor farmer before the Communists took over. He was in the process of converting everything he owned into the lightest high value currency that could be sewn into shabby clothes.

This made sense, and after we had concluded our purchase at a good price, Dad arranged for the agreed number of easily concealed "yellow fish", each weighing about an ounce, to be delivered to him.

The Animal Party

The surprisingly effective curfew at first had a debilitative effect on our parties, but American ingenuity soon adopted our life styles to handle this obstacle. The American Club responded by providing guest rooms to members who overstayed at the bar. And occupants of private homes–especially those of the oil companies–organized all night activities called, of course, "curfew parties."

These typically started late afternoon and continued through dinner, after which the remaining participants split into those continuing downstairs and those continuing upstairs in the bedrooms. All were confined until the curfew lifted at six the next morning, although sometimes these parties lasted for days.

Attendees at curfew parties may not remember them all, but none will ever forget the events at the great granddaddy of them all. This was held at an oil company bachelors' quarters with ample bedrooms upstairs and a spacious living-dining room below.

Twenty or so young men had invited at least as many Russian girls, including those in Ralph's stable, who arrived carrying their finest silk gowns. With them they also brought a feast of savory Russian specialties, prepared in the kitchens of the best Russian restaurants like Kafka's and The Renaissance. The girls, chattering excitedly in Russian, laid out dish after dish in attractive arrays on long, narrow tables near one side of the room. Behind them, comfortable sofas and chairs were placed against the wall.

My nose drew me to a tall, silver samovar, heated by a small flame, on a table. It was emitting a stimulating aroma and I asked a new friend, Olga, what it was.

"This is a Russian hot drink which we call *glintvein,"* she explained. "It has dry red wine and perhaps some brandy, with spices in it: cloves, cinnamon, nutmeg. Sometimes wild honey." Olga poured us a glass, which was irresistibly delicious. We had another.

Then she led me to the center of the room. Here, on a colorful table cloth draped over the house poker table, was the true *piece de resistance*:

a large silver platter piled high with red pearl caviar just a bit smaller than peas, surrounded by mounds of chopped egg, grated onion, lemon slices and miniature pancakes called *blintzes*. Olga placed a spoonful of caviar on a *blintz*, tamped it down with the chopped eggs and onion, then added a squirt of lemon. Handing it to me, she said happily, "Try this. Nowhere in the world will you taste anything so delicious."

Olga was right. Anticipating my question, she said, "This is the best caviar we could get–from a Russian smuggler. It comes from wild salmon in north China. We tried to get Beluga or Ossetra black caviar from the Caspian Sea sturgeon, but could not find enough because import is banned."

That was all right with me. All caviar was delicious, and I actually preferred the taste of these red pearls. Olga continued our tour, leading me past bowls, plates and bubbling cauldrons, each smelling more enticing than the previous one. We finished with another caviar braced with a shot of vodka. "The way it should be eaten," she laughed.

What a girl! In spite of the hard existence I heard that she and most of the other refugees had lived through, she was as buoyant as a New York debutante. When I asked her how she spoke English so well, she answered, "I went to convent school in Tientsin. Then I married an American marine and lived with the military families in Tsingtao. I had a nice home and commissary privileges like all the American dependents until the marines left. Then the U.N. brought me here with some other Russians who were married to Americans. I am waiting now for my American visa so I can join my husband in Oklahoma."

Whoever that marine was, he was a lucky man. Olga was just about the most desirable girl I had ever met. She told me that she had been repeatedly asked out on dates, but refused because she did not want to jeopardize the approval of her American visa.

Her story completely disabused my concept of Olga and her fellow Russian refugees. I no longer thought of the girls as inhabitants of someone's "stable." Indeed, as I came to know them better, thanks to Olga, I would realize that they were in every way just as respectable and talented as our own sisters. Several at the party turned out to be accomplished musicians, one being the violin soloist in the respected Shanghai Municipal Orchestra. When younger, after many violin lessons, I had been accepted there, but only as an unimportant second violinist.

Leaving Olga, I joined a group of older men who were discussing the party. The feature that distinguished it from other curfew parties had been highlighted in the invitations: "This is an animal party. No guest will be admitted unless he brings a live, well-trained animal."

The response was now running, hopping, barking and flapping about us: about a dozen cats and dogs, including my party girl Cindy, rabbits, chickens, turtles, a collection of Chinese birds merrily cackling in bamboo cages, and two horses that were kept out on the verandah. All were ignored, except Cindy, whose drinking habit made her instantly popular.

The girls, who had gone upstairs to change into their finest, returned in an excited, chattering flock. There were blonde, brunette and black haired beauties and even one redhead. Drinking was heavy, with the animals gradually eased out, and we attacked the feast spread across the tables. Drinks began with scotch, bourbon, rye and beer, but as time passed, veered toward vodka.

Most of the partygoers were pretty well along by midnight. A record of Russian dance music was played, and the girls, prancing to the lively music, grabbed us, and each other. I dimly remembered Olga trying to teach me a wild Cossack dance which she called something like *pradjatka.*

At some point someone remembered the horses, and it seemed that the logical thing to do was to have a horse race. The owners, claiming rights to be the jockeys, decided that the best venue for the racetrack was in the dining room, around the table holding the caviar platter. Ace, who of course was there, set up a bookmaking shop at a small booth well back from the track. From its safety, he announced that the race would be three laps around the table and started taking bets at even odds. The official starter and judge were selected.

The two horses, snorting in panic, resisting and minus saddles, were coaxed in and steadied. Then the jockeys, both wobbly, were pushed up onto the bare backs of their mounts by the few men still sober enough to shove. Ace stuffed a hand full of wagered bills and IOUs in a pocket and the starter announced, "They're off!"

The jockeys prodded their clearly terrified mounts down the first lap, between the caviar table and the one containing our half-eaten dishes of beef and chicken stroganoff. Neck to neck, they were snorting in panic, crashing, banging, side swiping, bumping, goaded on by our drunken shouts and waves of Russian screams from the girls. In a moment of reality I knew that there had never been such a scene in the history of racing–or perhaps even in the history of mankind.

Of course, such a tumultuous scramble needed a climax. This started toward the end of the second lap when one of the jockeys, accompanied by our cheers and boos, slid slowly, but with dignity, off his mount onto the tile floor, and lay there. His horse–released from its heavy rider–whinnied and backed up over a place on the sofa occupied by the shiny new white silk dress of a panicking spectator.

And unloaded.

The discharge landed right on the lap of Tanya–the girl who scratched and bit. Leaping up like a released spring with an ear-puncturing shriek, she kicked the poor dumb beast away, exposing the beautiful façade of her white silk dress now sullied by a huge ugly brown stain across her thighs from waist down. As the other girls dived away to avoid getting splattered, she went berserk.

Screaming non-stop at the top of her lungs, Tanya lunged at the food tables. In full attack mode, blond hair flying, she systematically cleaned them off, hurling plate after plate at anyone she could see. We dashed behind the protection of sofas and chairs like soldiers cowering in fox-holes. Only instead of bullets and shrapnel zinging past, we were beset by a storm of flying saucers with *zakuskis*, hot *pirozhki* pastries, tasty *pelmini* meat dumplings, *shashliks* on dangerous sharp skewers, and finally bowls of steaming *borscht* which flew by to splatter onto the walls and floor.

Amazingly, the only person to be hit was the second jockey, too drunk to get off his horse. But he was anesthetized and didn't even feel the samovar splash hot wine over him.

Of all those affected by the events of that night, only the house staff–inured to such goings-on–took things in stride. The animals were produced, dry and well fed, late the next day and low level staff members from the homes of the other party goers turned up to help clear the carnage. There was salvage work to be done to assuage the injured feelings of the girls who had worked so long preparing the partly wasted feast. Also to replace Tanya's new white gown and the shattered tableware. This was taken care of by the considerable wad of our bets. Ace personally converted the IOUs into US dollars and distributed the money to all the girls.

The Admirable White Russians–and Dangerous Olga

The animal party–and particularly Olga's contributions–drew my attention to a remarkable group within Shanghai: the "White Russians." Most were survivors of the czarist nobility who had managed to escape murder by the Bolsheviks during the Russian revolution in 1917. By the thousands, remnants of entire families had struggled, under continuous attack, from Moscow and St. Petersburg, all the way across Russia to Vladivostok, the major port on the east. Here, under the protection of their hastily re-assembled Czarist Pan Eastern White Army, they sought to rebuild their shattered lives.

Olga's parents and grandparents were all part of this enormous hegira. Almost crying, she told me, "The cruel Bolsheviks gave my people no chance. My Daddy said they kept attacking. They captured my uncle–he was a colonel in the Cossacks and insisted on charging at them on his warhorse he brought all the way from Moscow. They shot him before he could even draw his *shashqua* saber."

She shook her head, "Such a brave man. He was still alive and they hung him by the hands in some old dungeon until he died. I learned this later."

"God, I'm so sorry. So what happened to the others?"

"They were being pushed into the sea. So their leader, a hero admiral, organized a fleet of small ships and nearly all sailed off. But they had no place to go. They tried Korea, then Japan, but nobody wanted them. Finally they came to China. My mother and father were allowed to get off in Tientsin and started a restaurant. Later, they came here and I was born. Most of the others on the ships suffered and some died, but nearly twenty thousand got off here, in Shanghai. None spoke any language except Russian, and perhaps French, and had a hard time getting work."

"What could they do?"

"They took any work they could get. Some started restaurants like my family. But most of the men worked as drivers, bank guards, waiters, messengers, and even rickshaw pullers. They were proud and would not beg, so some had to get jobs as street sweepers and garbage collectors. It was easier for the women. Most were educated, and became governesses, teachers, music instructors, and secretaries in businesses. Some started the fancy clothing stores which are still here. The most beautiful girls worked in cabarets and became rich."

I could not help thinking of my childhood governess and the Russian wives of some of my parents' friends. And Black Tamara.

I saw more and more of Olga, but never tried to date her. Once she was with a group of her friends at the Columbia Country Club tea dance and asked me to join her. A well-known Belgian banker saw her, and stopped. They exchanged a few words and he persuaded her to have a dance. A few moments later she returned and sat down, angry. The middle-aged *roué* tried again, and was flatly ignored. Then, shaking his head, he murmured, "*Ma cherie, tu est dangereuse,*" and backed off.

Olga was indeed dangerous. She was stunningly beautiful, but seemed not to be aware of this and did not flaunt that attractiveness. Her pale skin color was set off by the jet black hair that cascaded down her shoulders, and any men's eyes glancing downward was sure to be transfixed by what must certainly be the world's most perfect breasts. About my height, 120 pounds, and a year younger, she would certainly make a perfect partner for me.

I made up my mind that, if her America visa did not come soon, I would try to catch this angel.

Tension Mounts Behind "The Great Wall of Shanghai"

Half a month had passed since the KMT government had fled to Taiwan, leaving their General Chen Liang as token Mayor in charge of Shanghai's defenses. One of his first "morale-building" moves was to announce, with much official ballyhoo and much "squeeze" paid to government officials by the contractor who built it, the construction of a "strong defensive wall" surrounding the city. This incredible, 30-mile-long structure turned out to be built of wood–vertical pieces of American-donated lumber–tied together and propped into the ground!

This event was gleefully seized upon by *Shanghai Evening Post* Editor Randall Gould, who mockingly called it "The Great Wall of Shanghai", commenting that a good rain would wash the whole thing away.

As if this wasn't enough, a few days later–even as the sound of artillery could be heard in the distance–the mayor ordered a big "victory parade" featuring columns of mechanized vehicles and trucks full of soldiers clanking and rumbling down Nanking Road. Clusters of Nationalist flags and pictures of Chiang had sprouted on all sides.

But not even this was enough for the imaginative mayor. He proclaimed "Health Week", promoted by public demonstrations of ways to improve sanitary conditions. Editor Gould learned that on that same day the mayor and his whole family had flown off to Taiwan. His editorial, a classic in journalism, announced, "The mayor was certainly sincere about Health Week. He found out what was best for his own health, and did it!"

Some of the Americans at our American Club table were missing, too. Most notable was Ace. This was noted with the comment, "Well, he said he wouldn't stay under the Communists."

"He flew to Hong Kong few days ago. Moved his main office there."

"The judge left, too. Went to America to retire. *Really* retire this time."""

"Maybe they're the smart ones."

The Moment of Truth

Harbingers of the impending future continued to spring up. The dozen or so American, British and French warships, so familiar at their stations off The Bund, vanished to new moorings downstream off the mouth of the Whangpoo River. Among them were Admiral Oscar Badger's flagship *El Dorado* and the marines' base ship *Chilton*. The blanket of sampans across Soochow Creek disappeared. John Cabot changed his living quarters from Shanghai's outskirts to the better security of The Bund. A feeling of tension seemed to permeate the atmosphere.

By the second week of May sounds of distant battle could be heard over the clatter of dice at the lunch table. Big Louie, who I had brought into our group, perked his ears when he heard the staccato sound of a machine gun. "Damn my soul," he exclaimed. "If that isn't a Browning .30 caliber." When artillery sounded, he would snort in disgust, "Sounds like a 105–probably one we gave the brave defenders to lose when they bugged out."

Pat released me from the office to help Dad prepare for whatever might be coming. Both he and Dad had excellent information sources, but were no better informed about what to expect than anyone else. There was no doubt that our city would be lost. The question was whether Shanghai would be turned over in an "arranged" surrender after a token display of fighting, or defended with all the determination displayed in the battle for Hsuchow a few months earlier.

In either case, Dad and I recognized that any danger we might face would probably be not from the advancing Communists, but from the fleeing Nationalist soldiers, who were already ransacking every place they could enter like swarms of locusts. Many had not been paid or fed for weeks, and were becoming aggressive in their struggle for food.

Working with other apartment owners in the building, we reinforced the defensive walls we had built out of wood boxes at the entrances and along the stairways. The fire hoses were run out and tested, as were fire extinguishers. They might deter marauders, but would not hold back any determined assault. For these, Dad had prepared dozens of bundles of bills to offer as bribes. This cash had been carried home in several carloads prepared for him at his bank. Shaking his head, Dad said, "I ordered fifty billion yuan in the biggest bills they had. There it is–worth no more than fifty cents. But it might hold them off."

During the next days the war closed in. With heavy artillery battles and skirmishes, General Chen Yi's forces fought and infiltrated their way past Granny's now-deserted house in Hungjao, as other units entered the city from all sides. At night parts of the city were lit by burning warehouses and factories. Swarms of red-hot shells which the Chinese called "fire meteors" crisscrossed overhead. Flames from a huge tank farm owned by the Standard Oil Company in Pootung, across the Whampoo River, filled the eastern sky with a hellish glow.

By May 24, 1949 the ring of fire closed in and the sound of shells seemed very close. Dad and I were having lunch with his old friends at the American Club when warnings swept through the room. A deal had been made: Shanghai was to be turned over that night. Groups of Nationalist soldiers tearing off their uniforms as they ran down the street without guns made this more plausible. So did the obvious consternation of our waiters talking nervously in groups.

Dad, deeply respected by them all, asked, "What you think, Wong?"

"Maybe big tlouble tonite, master. Too muchee soldier lookee every side, wanche go home."

That night we carefully checked our "defenses", then waited, listening to the news from America on my radio. By 10 p.m. the city grew quiet. No one dared to challenge the curfew. At midnight someone threw stones at the streetlights along our road, knocking them out. The surroundings of our building were eerily silent. Other tenants drifted into our apartment, and we talked softly, and listened. We had an ominous feeling that something would happen soon.

At about one am the dark streets filled with the sounds of shuffling feet. A flock of shadows crept up Great Western Road past the main door. There was a long rat-tat-tat and a volley of rifle shots from the next block. Then silence.

The world's largest city had changed owners.

Life Four: Communist Shanghai 1949-1951

PART ONE:

The Screw Begins to Turn

Initial Impressions–Are They Really "Agrarian Reformers?"

Early the next morning Dad invited a group of the apartment owners to the roof garden to discuss any potential problems. No one had heard any sounds of trouble during the night. We looked over the ninth floor railing, up and down the length of the road. The only change was the appearance of soldiers wearing green uniforms and tennis shoes, standing in groups and sitting along the curb as if waiting for instructions. We saw no guns.

One of the apartment owners turned to Dad, "Whew. Appears that we've weathered this storm quite well."

"Indeed," agreed another. "Now we'll see whether things remain this way."

Just then we were interrupted by the sound of machine guns. Someone pointed upward, "Look!"

A Mustang P-51 was diving toward our rooftop. The front of its wings speckled with tiny white dots as the sound of machine guns intensified.

"Jesus Christ!" shouted someone. "The bastard's shooting at us! He seemed to be right. As we ran to shelter behind a concrete elevator tower, .50 caliber bullets splattered against the concrete roof, digging little pits as they followed us.

The Chinese Air Force fighter made another pass, this time scattering the soldiers in the street below. I realized that they–not us–were the pilot's targets.

Driver Wong, who lived a few blacks away, arrived to take us to work. I phoned Pat to confirm that the office was open, learning that he was already there, and was expecting me–not to work, but to accompany him on a walk through the business district to observe. We had a sandwich and embarked on foot.

The Chinese in the street–usually loud, boisterous and even rude–were calm and subdued. At intersections Pat and I were greeted politely by soldiers. Many, incredibly, had smiles of welcome on their faces! Signs for the victors were everywhere, some prepared earlier and others hastily drawn. Most common were the professionally printed Chinese language posters which I translated for Pat: WELCOME, PEOPLE'S LIBERATION ARMY! We saw these arranged neatly on every storefront, as if quality control officials had supervised their placement. Just as common were pictures of a benevolent Mao Tse-deng plastered over those of Chiang Kai-shek, which had been ripped off.

The new leaders had put up their own posters, in Chinese, to reassure Shanghai residents. Of more immediate interest to us was one in English. Copies had been carefully arranged on the walls of the post office and other municipal buildings. Pat and I saw that it was a message over the name of General Chen Yi, newly appointed Shanghai's mayor. It was in two parts: first, we were assured that the soldiers' behavior would be polite and fair, and guaranteed complete protection of our lives and property.

The second part described four "rules" which we were required to obey: (1) do not break any Peoples' Government laws; (2) refrain from espionage or politics; (3) refuse help to war criminals; and (4) remain neutral in the struggle of the Chinese people in self-expression.

Pat and I examined this wording. Always alert to latent problems, he said: "The first rule would seem to be straightforward. The other three...so innocent at first reading. We'll have to see. I suggest you prepare by rereading *Alice in Wonderland.* For instance, your interpretation of rule number four. Would a Communist doctrinaire judge define self-expression in the same way you would?"

I didn't read *Alice* again, but understood that Pat was preparing me for the doublethink of the Communist philosophy. It would repeatedly attack my concept of logic during the next months.

Early Warning Signals

Small pockets of resistance were quickly erased. Then General Chen Yi put on a massive parade through the central district, ironically using the same vehicles as his predecessor had employed before fleeing to Taiwan. Stores were reopened with full shelves, and most of the Shanghai population seemed buoyant and optimistic. Communist symbols–red flags, posters of joyful Chinese with clenched fists, more posters in Chinese promising good things–were everywhere. Now and then snatches of Communist motivating songs like *The East is Red* could be heard from tinny speakers newly installed on telephone poles.

Bit by bit the American Club bar returned to normal as members filtered back. The full staff was present, except two missing waiters. When Dad's friend Charlie Singer asked the head bartender, Ah Ching, where they were, he simply looked down and shook his head.

"Strange," Singer commented when reporting this at lunch. "I'm sure Ah Ching knows, but..."

We agreed that the missing men had probably been arrested as Nationalist agents. Whether true or false, there was nothing we could do about it.

It was immediately apparent that an array of stringent new Communist laws was being enforced. One–and only one–was welcomed. This was the introduction of the *jen min piao*–people's money–a national currency that would maintain its value and put an end to the debilitating inflation. All other currencies had to be exchanged for its new bills featuring Chairman Mao's round face.

This spelled doom for the money changers.

"The police call them black marketeers," said Charlie Singer. Several were arrested a few days ago and taken for questioning. They were told to stop. I heard that most did and that the only punishment they got was a warning. But one was caught money changing again yesterday. They refused the usual bribe and took him to the racetrack. He was hoisted to the top of a pole in front of a mob and dropped to the ground. He was still alive, so they repeated it until he was dead."

After a moment, someone murmured, "They sure don't waste time with trials and lawyers." I hesitated, then added my own story. On the way to the office that morning, we had passed a mob of Chinese laborers blocking off a square. Someone was shouting in a voice that sounded like records of Hitler ranting at his wildest, interrupted now and then by angry roars. There would be a pause, followed by the only Shanghai dialect words I understood: "*Sha, sha, sha!*" shrieked hysterically by the crowd at the top of their voices. A moment passed, followed by the crack of a pistol and more hysterical cheering. I knew that the word *sha* meant "kill."

Driver Wong and I had been through enough for him to open up. "He kill some man he say velly bad. Have too muchee house, too muchee money." Wong explained that these landlords were favorite targets. Many who had not fled earlier were dragged out of their homes, forced to squat on their knees with hands tied behind their backs and shot in the back of the neck by young Communist commissars while the mob cheered.

Wong himself was terrified that someone in his own family might be singled out for this treatment. People–especially children–were informing on others, and even on their parents, for revenge or to get even for slights. Innocence was no defense, for seldom was any opportunity given for defense. I thought of the Silk Man, and hoped that he got away in time.

Such treatment, less violent but still unfair by our standards, was not limited to Chinese. As time passed, cracks began to appear in the promise about protecting the lives and property of foreigners, as well. In factories and offices alike, the roles of managers and workers were being reversed. Claims for large amounts of money, rejected under the law years earlier, were resurfacing. What were effectively kangaroo courts found for the Chinese employees in nearly all claims against the big, rich foreign company. This was reinforced by a related labor law that prohibited businesses from dismissing employees, no matter how serious the damage they caused.

When full payment could not be made for lack of funds, or because the overseas head office refused to be blackmailed any more, the unionized staff held the foreign manager hostage. One senior manager for the big Caltex oil company told us how this worked. With no warning, he was imprisoned in his office with all communication cut off and no food or water available. He had been locked up there for two days and nights before he escaped. When he joined our dice game a few days later, he told us how he survived.

"I spotted an assistant in a mob under my window and dropped her a cord with a message attached. This asked her to tie on a package of water, food and pills I have to take. She brought this, and I pulled it up. I was lucky to see her there–and that my office was on a low floor!"

We gave him sympathy when he lost the round, but still made him pay for the drinks.

Breakout of *H.M.S. Amethyst*

At the end of July two events happened. One brought bad news and the other good news.

The bad news was the visit of typhoon *Gloria,* whose eye, packing 110 mile-an-hour winds, passed directly over Hungjao. The strongest storm in recent history, it caused the Yangtze to flood into the city until the main roads were submerged under three or more feet of water. Dad and I and the tenants in his building were marooned for a full day, until driver Wong turned up in a pedicab. People in most of the other big buildings and hotels were also marooned, and the electricity, telephone and water were cut off even longer. The poor homeless Chinese refugees suffered the most, and we saw many dead bodies floating away.

The good news could have literally been a heaven-sent blessing. *Gloria* kept on depositing water, as it whirled westward up the Yangtze River, adding several feet to the depth over sand bars and shallows normally impassable to ships. This fact did not escape John Kerans, Captain of the *H.M.S. Amethyst* a hundred or so miles up the Yangtze.

For weeks he had been waiting for a chance to break out. His crew had cut down and lightened the ship's superstructure to reduce the draft and the risk of being spotted in the dark. Now, with several feet of draft added by the storm, he challenged the Communist warning that his damaged frigate would be sunk if he tried to escape. As soon as it became dark his ship slipped her greased cable and tore down river at maximum speed. She had several near misses, survived fire from shore batteries, broke through a boom and had to sink a junk, but made it to open sea.

The escape of the *Amethyst* on August 1 should have been impossible: the stuff that legends and movies are made off. Again and again Kerans took chances worthy of Captain Hornblower's most outrageous stunts. Except that for this British Lt. Commander, this achievement really happened.

Dad and I heard the account of the thrilling breakout on BBC on our secret radio at home, including the Captain's famous, and characteristically terse, report to his commander-in-chief: "Have rejoined the fleet."

The commendation from the British Consul-General Urquhart, heard at a party, was just as succinct: "The laddies did a fine job!"

I drink at the Longest Bar in the World

This was the first really encouraging news that Shanghai's foreign community had received for months, and all of us–and especially the British–rejoiced. The next day Dad asked me whether I would like to join the festivities inside the Shanghai Club. "Some of the members are having a drink to celebrate the escape of their ship," He said. "Not many Americans are members, and I'd like you to meet some of the club officers."

That noon he led me through the columns and heavy doors of Shanghai's most prestigious building, Number One The Bund, into a solid mass of laughing, joking, and loudly talking people. Most were smoking pipes or cigars and every one of them was a white man. Noticing my puzzled expression, Dad explained, "No women or non-whites are allowed in here. That has been the rule since the club was founded in 1911 as a British gentlemen's club."

He indicated a dark brown wooden bar on the left, jammed with several layers of men pressing against it. "That is the Long Bar, about 110 feet. It is famous as the longest bar in the world." Then Dad pointed toward the window facing The Bund. "Notice there is no crowd at that end. Those few men you see there are the River Pilots. We depend on them to navigate every ship that comes in from the ocean. Ever since the club was built they have occupied the seats of honor by the front window. Probably one of those pilots there brought your ship up the river.

"You will recognize some of the men next in line. They are the Tai-pans of Jardines, of Swire, Mac and Mac, The Bank, and so on. Most of them are Scottish and the others English. Next to them are lesser managers, and so on down the line to the far end, where the newest members are placed. None of them would try to sit at a seat higher than his pecking order."

We returned to the top of the bar where Dad introduced me to John Keswick, the Chairman of Asia's leading company. Jardine Matheson. When James Clavell's novel *Noble House* came out a few years later, he was rumored to be the model for Ian Dunross. They talked and laughed like the friends they were. We continued down the line where I met several others whose pictures were often in the news. Dad ordered us drinks, which we sipped as we walked and talked. At the end we came to the billiards room. Looking at the tables, I noticed that they all had short legs and were mounted on wood stands. Puzzled, I asked Dad why.

"Good question, son. Could only have happened here. During the war the Japs used this club and pretty well wrecked it. They were too short to reach over the top to play billiards, so they cut off the bottom half of the legs to lower them. We had to mount the tables on those little platforms to bring them up to normal height. One reason why some people refer to them as little dwarfs."

The Screw Turns Tighter

The burst of pride injected into our world by Captain Kerans and his crew quickly passed. Only days after the turnover came a mass of new bureaucratic organizations, each issuing its own confusing regulations that could impact our lives. These sprang from the office of General Chen Yi, who was now appointed Shanghai's mayor, Chairman of the Shanghai Military Control Committee and two other powerful committees. The mayor then established a Political Department and the Foreign Affairs Bureau, which directly affected us.

Bureaucratic offices sprang up in different parts of the city, often requiring hours of travel to get from one official's desk to another for multiple signatures on any form. In time, this function became more onerous as we were required to go personally for repeated interviews and to submit many documents, including contracts and leases. All were required to be written in Chinese. The sudden changing of street names from English lettering to Chinese characters didn't help, either.

Yet within this web of bureaucratic controls, foreigners were treated formally and correctly. The lowest office clerk was afforded the same attention as a managing director. There was one significant development: the authorities announced that diplomatic privilege did not exist. Nor did diplomats. Letters addressed to titles like "Ambassador" were routinely returned or simply vanished. This did not affect John Cabot, however, who had already destroyed our consulate's confidential files and left the country.

We continued to enjoy personal safety, as promised. But this required careful obedience to the law. Anyone not carrying a new I.D. card was arrested and questioned in the former Broadway Mansion, now called the interrogation center. The Shanghai Chinese tended to wear drab colored clothes to avoid attracting the attention of zealous police who might bring them in for interrogation. Mah jong and similar home games were banned, and subject to discovery by police who would burst into homes, offices and even the sacrosanct Shanghai Club to check identifications and search for illegal radios. Dad and I had our Halliburton well hidden.

Our round table lunches at the American Club continued, but more and more the conversation focused on this bureaucratic nightmare. "And only a few weeks ago we were bitching about the crazy regulations of the last crowd!" exclaimed a senior bank manager.

"Their regulations are smothering business," added another player. "Especially the confusion the petty officials create poking around in the office, bothering our staff with questions."

"No one can even play bridge any more."

"At least they haven't stopped liar's dice."

"Don't be so hopeful. When they learn what the game is, they probably will."

I shared their frustration. With shipping halted, my marine insurance business, which had been a profitable sideline, dried up. As if the new bureaucratic regulations weren't bad enough, our problems were now compounded by actions of our own former allies!

From their base in Taiwan, the KMP announced a blockade of Shanghai. This would be enforced by warships stationed off the mouth of the Yangtze River with orders to capture or sink all traffic attempting to enter the delta. The shipping community quickly learned that this was no bluff. Three small freighters made runs at Shanghai. The first, a foreign flag, was captured by a Nationalist frigate, taken to a Nationalist-owned island, and released weeks later after her cargo had been removed. The second made the round trip and escaped intact, but only after intervention by the British frigate *Cossack*. The third was captured and confiscated with all her cargo.

Our Blockade Runners

When I came in that morning Pat was standing in front of the big wall map, studying the locations of his Isbrandtsen ships. It was October 15, and all the model ships were in place, about two weeks apart on their round-the-world pattern. The *Flying Trader* was at the mouth of the Yangtze with her bow pointing up river. Still looking at the chart, Pat said, "The *Trader* was fired on coming into the Yangtze delta last night. The captain thinks it was a 20 mm gun on a single patrol boat. No hits." He looked at me expectantly.

"If that's all they use, there shouldn't be any trouble coming in. Or leaving later."

"That's what I recommended to her captain. She will be in this afternoon with a full cargo, including several thousand tons they lifted in Hong Kong from ships whose owners refused to run the blockade."

"I hope we're getting a good freight for it."

Pat studied me for a moment. "If the conference rate is, say, ten, what would you charge?"

I kicked myself. I should have known he would do this. Cautiously I tried, "More than the regular Hong Kong/Shanghai rate. I would shoot for double, that's twenty."

"You lose," Pat said. "I asked for 24, and they paid. There is no competition and opportunities like this don't come often. The way to success is to extract the maximum when they do pass by, as one does with a winning poker hand." He peered at me with a trace of a smile. "*Carpe diem*."

There was no ship until a month later, when the *Flying Cloud* brought in a full cargo. The delay was due to a problem in Hong Kong when some of the crew refused to run the blockade. The owner of the company, Hans Isbrandtsen, displayed his tough character from New York, and the mutineers backed down.

Hans had less success in his frequent and impassioned attempts–including large ads in the newspapers–to persuade the state department and our Navy to intercede. No meaningful action emerged from Washington to protect American ships.

Bombs Ahoy!

Pat and I had a memorable experience on November 28 aboard the next ship, the *Sir John Franklin,* which had anchored in the Yangtze just off the mouth of the Whangpoo River. The Nationalists had apparently singled her out and she was hit several times on her way in. Pat decided to go on board and took me on a fast launch with several of his shipping staff and an English marine surveyor to check the damage.

An hour later we passed out of the Whampoo into the broad Yangtze. The *Sir John Franklin* appeared just ahead, surrounded by empty barges and lighters crowded against her black sides in the classic "hen and chicks" formation. Winches on the ship's fore and aft decks were lowering cargo nets crammed with crates and barrels into their holds. As each barge was loaded it was moved away and another took its place. Our pilot navigated carefully through the pack to a Jacob's ladder suspended over the ship's side.

We climbed aboard into a world which I never tired of relishing: sights of rotating winches gushing steam, scents of strong creosote and other ship smells, ear-splitting shrieks from winches, shouts in English from the ship's officers and curses in Shanghai dialect from laborers sweating far down in the dusty holds and unpacking cargo nets on the barges.

I sat in the officer's mess with Pat and his shipping people and the ship's officers while they discussed the loading of outbound cargo from Shanghai. Then we joined the English surveyor who was directing simple repairs to the exterior. "Nothing serious," was his first report. "From the shell fragments and the size of the holes in the sides, it is very likely that 20 mm guns did the shooting. The sand bags you have placed around the bridge will continue to provide adequate protection, unless larger guns are used."

After a light lunch, we were talking shop when a crew member called in, "Captain! A big plane–looks like a bomber–is circling overhead. You better come see." Others of the crew had stopped working and were standing in groups watching the plane.

We hurried out to an open deck. The caller was right. I recognized the silhouette of a B-24. It was no more than half a mile high and making runs over our ship. I was waiting for word from Pat or the captain when I heard, "Look!"

There, under the bomber, two small objects were tumbling down toward us. I knew they were bombs. Instinctively I wanted to rush down to the engine room to gain the protection of three decks overhead. But Pat was there and I had to control myself. I looked at him for guidance. He and the captain were calmly watching the falling missiles, exchanging a few words.

Apparently noticing that I showed nervousness, Pat smiled, "The captain tells me they will miss by several hundred yards. He was often bombed during the war, and should know."

He was right. They hit the water several hundred yards off the stern. The only disturbances I noticed were some muffled booms and frothing water. Everyone waited for more bombing runs, but instead the plane headed south, probably toward Taiwan.

Back in his office Pat returned to the subject of the failed bombing attempt. "The bombardier on that plane could have easily hit us. The responsible officers in Taiwan must know that we appreciate this. That being the case, their purpose in sending the bomber was a warning: 'Stop trying to run our blockade or we'll hurt you next time." I will prepare a report for Hans which I'll want you to read."

PART TWO

Tsingtao – The Dangerous Journey

The *Flying Arrow* Sends an SOS

A headline in the January 9, 1950 *New York Times* read:

FLYING ARROW HIT 12 TIMES BY
NATIONALIST WARSHIP SHELLS

The account that followed was illustrated by a map of the China Sea off Shanghai and a photo of the ship's captain, David Jones, who looked glum and angry.

In the meantime the newspapers in Shanghai and Hong Kong fielded sensational headlines and stories about the attack on our ship. There were the usual exaggerations, but Pat, waiting for me when I arrived, had already pieced together a factual summary for us to discuss.

First, the ship had been damaged, but was in no danger of sinking and the fifteen passengers, including seven women, were safe. Next, Hans Isbrandtsen had just ordered Captain Jones to take his ship on to Tsingtao for shelter from the January storms while repairs were made. The *Arrow* should arrive at this former German colony the next day.

"Finally," Pat said, "We have no one there to handle her and as far as I can ascertain there is no shipping office left there that I could appoint sub-agent. Our marines seem to have taken with them everyone with shipping experience when they withdrew."

"I guess you'll have to send someone from your shipping department here."

"Not possible. They speak only Shanghai dialect and I am told the people in charge there are all eighth route army soldiers from North China who speak only Mandarin. Also, the new Shanghai authorities refuse to issue travel permits to locals."

A pause followed. What the hell would Pat do? I wondered.

I found out fast enough. "I've decided to send you. You will have a full power of attorney to establish our temporary office in Tsingtao and handle the ship. There is no consular presence or any other American still there who could be useful, no telephone or wire communication, and God knows if mail will get through. So you will be isolated, on your own. You speak their Mandarin dialect language and should be able to handle the job." He looked at me questioningly, "How soon can you leave?"

I couldn't believe it. Pat must be playing his whimsical games again. He knew that I had no more experience handling ships than his office telephone boy. But realization that he meant this sank in fast. Pat was clearly desperate. I couldn't let him down by failing to at least try.

"I'll need training before going. At least a week..."

"We don't have that luxury, John. I will assign my best man to work with you here until we can obtain your travel permit. We will prepare a folder of back up information specific to C-2 class ships like the *Arrow* for you to study on the train there, and a travel guide showing hotels and so on. You can ask the ship's officers for guidance.

"You will need access to money–probably a lot. It is not possible for us to remit this to Tsingtao, so you will have to carry it with you. This had been made feasible by the new currency. We will arrange for you to take several hundred large denomination bills, most in a money belt and the rest in a duffel bag for you to carry."

After a moment he added, "Let me know if you think of anything else."

I did. "If I have to stay there for more than a couple of weeks, I would like to have someone there with me. My friend Louie has had no job since Tim O'Sullivan left. You could hire him on a temporary basis for this trip." Pat listened, but said nothing. I saw Big Louie the next day and suggested that he make an appointment with my boss.

Our Marines in Tsingtao

Dad's first advice was about my health. "Take plenty of warm clothes and a heavy hat and coat. It will be bitter cold. There's always an icy wind from Manchuria."

He was obviously concerned. I had never undertaken any project so difficult–and, I realized–so inherently dangerous. I was going alone into hostile territory where Americans were said to be hated, and with no support available if I needed help.

Dad continued, "I wish I could provide you with contacts there, son, but our friends in the marines who came here from Tsingtao, have obviously left. I strongly suggest, though, that if you are questioned about American marines by Tsingtao officials, or by anyone else, you deny any knowledge of them."

In fact, I *did* know nothing about our marines in China, except those that were my parents' friends and what I had heard from visiting correspondents at lunches. There had been some up north and, of course, in Shanghai. Thinking it over, I wondered why any marines had been in China at all, when their war was in the Pacific. I would find out.

I was amazed at what I learned.

In 1945, right after the war ended, 25,000 marines came ashore at

Tsingtao en route to cities all over north China to receive the surrender of several hundred thousand Japanese soldiers, and oversee their repatriation to Japan. The last 10,000 of these Japanese, from Shantung Province, were embarked from Tsingtao. This accomplished, the marine force was rapidly drawn down and by 1947 Tsingtao, garrisoned by the 2nd battalion of the 4th marines, was the only base left. The port was also the shore base for our seventh fleet, whose many ships' crews on shore leave had made it a prosperous city. Playing on the port's name, meaning "green island," Tsingtao was sometimes called "a thriving green island in a red sea."

After winning a series of battles with the Nationalists, the Communist eighth route army controlled the rest of Shanting Province. Only the foothold around Tsingtao, the prize jewel, was denied to them by the muscle provided by our marines, and became a sharp thorn in the sides of the Communist leaders. Day after day, the marines' presence in China interfered with their plans. Units of Communist soldiers ranging from dozens to hundreds of well armed troops continuously attacked much smaller marine forces wherever they might be vulnerable, even those riding guard on freight trains. They closed around Tsingtao, but did not take the port.

Finally, in 1947, the last garrison force in China was sent from Tsingtao to Shanghai, then back home. This left only one company aboard the *U.S.S. Chilton,* anchored off Shanghai with Admiral Badger's ship, *U.S.S. El Dorado.* With their departure in 1949, the last American marine had left China. But American marines were not forgotten by the Communist military, whose plans they had stymied for so long. I would soon find this out.

"Your Boat Stays There Until It Rots and Sinks!"

Dad's warning may have saved me from a serious problem. I had no sooner stepped down from the railroad car onto the frozen platform that several soldiers, wrapped in heavy fur jackets, came up to me. They took me into a room where one said in Mandarin: "Papers."

I extracted my American passport and several large documents in Chinese covered with stamps and chops which Pat had managed to have approved at various bureaus in Shanghai. They took these with a letter from the Shanghai Foreign Trade Bureau confirming my employment and that I was involved in imports for China's industry. The letter was shoved back at me and the documents taken away. The apparent leader said harshly, "You are *mei kuo shui chun!*"

This meant American marine, and I recalled Dad's admonition. Other soldiers milled around and I heard them muttering "*shui ping*" and "*shui chun.*" meaning "sea soldier."

"*Bu shih*!" I exclaimed.

They were not convinced, and passed my documents around, examining them again.

I had planned a tactic, which turned out to be critical, for just this situation. "How can I be a marine?" I demanded. "Look at me! Marines are all very big men and I am a very little man."

This seemed to register. When I saw them vacillating, I spoke again. "I work for the company that owns the black ship that was shot up by our enemies, the KMT. I must visit the commander of this port to discuss ways that I can help unload the valuable cargo that the factories in your country are waiting for. I am very tired after my long train ride and must rest before meeting him. Can someone please help me go to the guest house that was the former home of a German official?"

I had looked this up and it seemed the best place to try.

My "big marine, little man" tactic worked! After some grumbling and insults, I was put into a taxi and delivered to an old but comfortable 30-room inn. There was no way to check my duffel bag, so I held it while devouring an excellent Chinese dinner. Then, after my nineteen–hour train ride, I slept solidly all night. My money belt stayed on and I held the duffel bag with me.

The next morning, January 15, I called on Military Control Director Wong. The senior port official was a tall northerner, totally bald, and wearing glasses on his long, thin face. He was meticulously dressed in uniform–and he was also spitting mad.

When I introduced myself his first words, shouted at me in Mandarin, were: "Your boat stays there outside the harbor. Not one person will go on it or go off it until it rots and sinks!"

Naturally, I thought I had mistaken his Chinese words. "Excuse me, Mr. Director. I don't think I understood what you said."

"Get out! Go back. Tell your manager that we Chinese are not used to that captain's foul language!"

I had no idea what he meant, but had to separate myself from the captain fast and took a chance that I hoped would work. "Perhaps, honorable director, you will give me an opportunity to prove to you that my family and I are different from ordinary rough sailors who use foul language. We in my company are gentlemen. We have lived among Chinese in Shanghai as close friends all our lives.

"If you will do me the honor to tell me what the rude captain of this boat did to bring shame to me and my associates, I will do everything I can to apologize to you on behalf of my company. I have not met this shameful person before, but understand that he is only a sailor, and not educated in the ways of gentlemen." I held my breath, praying that I had not overdone this.

By some miracle I seemed to have struck the right note. The director gradually changed his tone, but after two days of meetings with him and other officials I still had not received the go ahead to even visit the ship. The *Flying Arrow* was still there, anchored far off the harbor mouth, cut off from all communication, now and then visible behind sheets of spray, pitching and rolling.

My break came when a new player entered our discussions. He had some government position in industry and started asking me questions. For the first time I was able to extract from my bag the ship's cargo manifest that Pat had prepared for me in Shanghai. His voice became excited as he translated into Chinese: "Bales of cotton, caustic soda, oil in drums, many more industrial chemicals. Value American dollars six million!"

Turning to the others, he said excitedly, "Our factories are closing for the shortage of these! We must get these goods landed and delivered."

That was the breakthrough. From then on things slid into place. The next morning I went out into a sleet storm aboard a small tender. We pulled up to the ship's leeward side behind the dubious shelter of the hull, which was rising and falling with each passing wave. It was too rough to hang out a Jacob's ladder, so I had to go up a rope ladder, which swung in and out from the side. I waited until it was out over the tender's deck, grabbed the frozen ropes and held on for a wild ride–flying out over the foaming ocean one moment then crashing in against the iron hull, over and over. Fortunately, I was not burdened by the duffle bag, which the hotel had safely locked away.

I finally crawled up the ladder to the deck rail to be helped aboard by the crew wearing wet yellow slickers. Into a scene from a horror film. Although wet and bruised, I was appalled, besieged by panicking passengers screaming to be let off. I struggled loose, pushed my way into the saloon and met the ship's captain, "Davy" Jones.

Pat's briefing in Shanghai had given me some background on this notorious sea captain, but scarcely prepared me for what I encountered.

"Those filthy yellow bastards tried to wreck my ship!" he shouted. I almost laughed at the similarity to Director Wong's greeting. No wonder they couldn't get along! "I was boarded by some Commie general with a group of dirty soldiers waving around submachine guns who tramped into my saloon and made a frigging mess of it.

"I kicked them off and sent them packing in a lifeboat. We hadn't even finished cleaning up their mess when they came back–with twice as many dirty soldiers, and started busting up everything! My crew and I threw them off again, and the next day they sent a message that my ship was quarantined. Permanently."

There was no question that this was the genuine Captain Davy Jones. Stout and pugnacious, he conformed with everything people had told me to expect. He was a mix of the vulgar roughneck of his reputation and–I would soon learn–a cultured gentleman. By nineteen, David Jones had already become a King's Point Marine Captain and a reserve commander. In the WWII merchant marine, he survived four ships sinking under him. Before he left Tsingtao, he had helped negotiate the Communists' return of 12 U. S. Navy pilots. He was also a hard disciplinarian: he ruled his crews with a firm hand and, in fact, had once shot and killed a seaman for good cause.

Calming down now that he had a sympathetic audience, the captain gave me a summary of his experience.

"We were in international waters, nineteen miles off China, when two Nationalist frigates started shooting. One followed for half a day pumping shells at us. Someone counted thirty-eight hits, and we know that seventeen were forty mm shells. Some of the holes were two feet in diameter, one only four inches above the water line. I had the mid ships housing protected by those 250 bales of cotton," he indicated some of them piled on the deck. "So no one was injured.

"They kept on shooting until the sloop *Black Swan* interceded. The Brits sent over some of their crew and used their hoses to help put out the fires, mostly in holds number four and five. Then finally our DDs, the *Stickwell* and *Bausell*, sent over some salvage equipment–welding equipment and wood plugs. By the time we got here the fires were pretty extinguished, but two holds were flooded with seawater from the pumping.

"We could have handled that ourselves if the caustic soda barrels hadn't been ruptured. Now all that water swishing around down below in holds four and five is a deadly caustic soup. No one can work there without wearing strong diving equipment.

Looking at me almost pleadingly, he said, "But first, you must give me your help. Get those crazy insane passengers off my ship! Their welfare is my responsibility and they are driving me crazy with their bitching and demands! Other things can wait, but never the passengers. I think you know one of them–Richardson."

I had met Wayne Richardson, the jovial, stout, grey-haired A.P. Bureau chief, only a few times, but was pleased to have the chance to answer some of his questions for his report to the *New York Times*. I had a few minutes to reassure the passengers that their ordeal was no fault of my company, and would soon be over. Nearly half, including Richardson, planned to continue their voyage on the ship. I took the names of those destined for Shanghai to make their train reservations when they disembarked. A week later they had arrived there.

Soon after I met Davy Jones, the first employee of Pattison's Tsingtao office joined me. His name was Ching and he had been a senior shipping manager. Serendipitously, he also turned out to be a nephew of Director Wong, which may have had something to do with the fact that Ching was waiting for me in my hotel after work. Also, that on the next day, January 18, I received permission for the *Arrow* to come in and dock.

The whole character of my work changed. Up to then most of my efforts were directed toward getting information and problem solving. Now Ching, who I had titled Pattison Office Manager, and several assistants he hired, handled this work efficiently. As soon as the *Arrow* pulled up to the dock, a ship repair crew arrived, followed by two divers with full gear that looked suspiciously like former U.S. Navy property.

Trucks pulled up to take on cargo as it was unloaded from the ship. A hundred other tasks essential to ship handling were performed. Finally, after only a few days had passed, we had a small office. Although no telephone or telex service was available, we did have a bold, hand made Pattison logo right over the entrance.

Visit to the *Brooklyn Heights*

The next vessel in the chain of Isbrandtsen round-the-world freighters, the *Brooklyn Heights,* was diverted from Shanghai to Tsingtao after the attack on the *Arrow*. She anchored off the harbor near where the *Arrow* had been and I received permission to visit her to deliver ship documents. First, there was the matter of communicating. The *Arrow* was prohibited from using her radio, so the only method we could try was Morse code messages sent with a signal lantern mounted on the bridge.

I had seen these while in the Navy. They projected a strong focused beam that could be turned on and off by moving a handle on the side. The idea was to use this to flash dots and dashes. I had never used a signal light, but remembered most of the Morse code and aimed ours in the approximate direction of our sister ship. During each break in the rain and sleet storm, when the vessel came in view for a few minutes, I started pushing the handle back and forth.

After several sessions blinking "Can you see this?" no response had come. My eyes were swollen nearly shut and my hands–even with thick gloves–were frozen to the handle. I went back to the saloon and was busy de-icing when one of the ship's officers came over. "Never used a signal light, eh?" he said.

After a short exchange of words, the older man accompanied me up into the storm and flipped a switch underneath the device. Bright light shined through cracks in the top. I realized that I had never turned it on!

My new friend aimed it and blinked a few dots and dashes, explaining, "That's the standard recognition phrase." He repeated this several times, then, like a miracle, a light flashed back from beyond the waves!"

"OK. What's your message?"

"We are forbidden to use the radio. If you come in you will also be shut down." After a few minutes an acknowledgement came back. My friend asked, "Anything more to send?"

"Yes. The company agent will try to bring documents and messages to you and bring back anything you have destined for forwarding to Shanghai."

Before the ship was lost in the sleet we had signaled that I would go out with the mailbag when the storm abated enough for me to reach the ship. They would keep a watch out for my boat.

I thanked my friend, and later explained to Davy Jones what we had done. In view of my earlier experience, I decided to travel light. No senior port officer was interested in accompanying me, so I took along Office Manager Ching and two junior port officers, probably bullied into going.

The trip was, if anything, more terrifying than my earlier excursion to the *Arrow*. This time I had another big duffle bag full of documents to shepherd–and to manhandle onto the freighter. Again the pilot held the tender near the lee side of *Brooklyn Heights,* which rose and dropped sharply with the rocking of the ship. It would be impossible to leap onto the gyrating rope ladder carrying the heavy bag, so we tied on a cord. When I jumped I would hold the other end, and, when secure on the ladder, would haul it up.

At least that's what we planned. But it didn't work. Before I could grab the ladder, I slipped and fell on the ice sheet formed by spray on the deck–and nearly slid off into the sea. We covered this with wood boards from below and I could just stay afoot in the wild motion of the bouncing launch. Barely able to stand, I again leapt for the rope, but dropped my end of the cord before I caught it. Again and again I tried, each time dropping the cord in terror. The thought of sinking into that frigid water–to be immediately frozen or crushed between ship and tender–was so terrifying that I shivered just thinking about it.

It was Ching who saved me. In his passable English, he suggested, "You go catch ladder first, climb up so you legs not in water. When you get up top I throw this end cord, you catch." He had lengthened the cord and tied on an iron bolt, which surely would be easier to grab than a piece of string. Freed from the cord and with my *Arrow* experience, I was able to grasp the swinging ladder on my first try. A few minutes later, on the ship's deck, I had plenty of help catching the bolt and pulling the bag up. Ching climbed on board and the two port officers followed. We received a warm welcome, followed by a delicious American meal with the ship's captain.

Mail to and from the ship and Isbrandtsen was exchanged. Since the *Brooklyn Heights* had booked neither cargo nor passengers for Shanghai, she set off to do her China business at Taku Bar, off Tientsin in the north. Before she sailed, though, I seized this opportunity to communicate with Pat and bring him up to date. Pat had just informed me that Big Louie was on his way here when I was sharply interrupted by Director Wong's junior officers. "Stop this communication to Shanghai or we will shut you down!" Before the ship sailed I had a final meeting with the captain, and was able to place in his hands an envelope from Ching for delivery to New York.

This experience opened the way for us to invite Director Wong aboard the *Arrow*, where he was treated like an old friend and thanked effusively for the hospitality of the port.

On January 26 the *Flying Arrow* departed for Japan, where freedom of the press permitted Bureau Chief Richardson to finally send full, uncensored dispatches covering the attack on the *Flying Arrow*. Big Louie arrived, bringing a belt full of cash, a stack of shipping documents, a load of happy enthusiasm and Pat's congratulations. I had been in that freezing outpost for nearly a month, and left immediately for home.

PART THREE

The Train (Conclusion)

Exhausted, I slumped into a deep, peaceful rest right after the train left Tsingtao's southern station. Not even a dream disturbed my sleep. Then, suddenly, the screeching of emergency brakes and the jolting of the carriage shocked me awake. Before I could realize what was happening, soldiers were dragging me away.

Details of the relentless 15-hour interrogation that followed were described in the "Prologue: The Train" at start of this book. It would be months after my release, until I was well away from China, before I could shake loose the grip of worry that soldiers were closing in to throw me into solitary.

PART FOUR

The Aftermath

Dad

No one met me at the station in Shanghai since there had been no way to communicate that I was returning. In any case, it was curfew time. My travel documents, which had been returned, gave me safe conduct so I took a curfew-licensed pedicab straight home. Number one boy seemed to go into shock when he opened the door and saw me. "Master, Master!" he called. "Young master come back!"

I had never seen my frail Dad so emotional. I could feel him trembling while we held each other. We had grown very close since Mother sailed to America and I knew he had been worried for my safety. Remembering his words before I left, I said brightly, "You saved me, Dad, with your advice. They asked me about marines, and I answered just the way you told me to–that I knew nothing. Thanks. I might have been thrown into jail if you hadn't warned me."

Dad nodded in satisfaction. It was close to midnight and we were both tired, so I gave him only a quick run down on my trip, passing lightly over my arrest and interrogation.

Then, after a short roughhouse with my hysterically happy Cindy, I went to a deep, dreamless sleep. I had the feeling that Dad slept well that night, too.

We continued our talk at breakfast before leaving for our offices. I sensed that Dad was nervous. Finally, after beating around the bush, he said, "I have wanted to tell you something, but didn't want to make you worry. Now, after your Tsingtao trip, I know that you can handle this.

"Some time ago a good Chinese banking friend warned me that my relationship with some of the Nationalist leaders who have fled was being investigated. Depending on who is doing this, I might end up facing trumped up charges of espionage against the state. If convicted, the sentence could be severe. As you know, my salary from the bank stopped when it was taken over by the new government. Now my other incomes are drying up as Shanghai's businesses die off. So, by remaining here I have little to gain but possibly a great deal to lose.

"I have decided therefore to try to leave China as soon as I can. This would best be started through the standard process of applying for an exit visa. The authorities are not issuing many, and if I am refused, I may ask your manager to take me out on one of your ships when they begin coming here again. There are unofficial ways I could slip aboard under another name." Dad gave me a sad smile. "After all these years, to end up like this."

"Of course, Dad. I'll talk with Pat when the time comes–if the blockade ends."

As we were walking to the car Dad stopped and impulsively grabbed my arm. "It is *you* who I worry about, son. I have lived my life. You still have yours ahead." He lowered his voice and said urgently, "Get out, John. This is not our world any more. Get out. If Pat won't send you, apply yourself for an exit visa. I'll guide you through the process and your whole family will help. But don't wait."

I didn't know what to say. All of my interests were here–friends, business, Cindy. And now Olga, who had become very close. Finally I said, "I'll talk to Pat as soon as we have a chance. Also about you."

Pattison the Sleuth

Pat and his senior staff were assembled in the boardroom when I arrived. For the next several hours I gave them a day-by-day report of our shipping activities in Tsingtao, describing the benefits of my hiring Ching as office manager and confirming Big Louie's arrival. Asked about complaints of Davy Jones' behavior from several returning *Arrow* passengers, I gave the captain high marks for managing a very difficult situation, emphasizing his concern for the safety of his passengers. Decisions for future actions were made and recorded by Pat's executive assistant, Margaret.

Pat asked me to join him for a hot lunch in his office. As soon as we were alone, I said, "There is something important I have to tell you," and started talking.

My boss listened carefully as I spoke about my arrest and interrogation. He stopped eating and lowered his huge chin into his concentrating position. He said not a word until I had described my return to the train. He asked a few questions for clarification, then brought his head up, peered at me and asked, "What aspect of this is the most urgent to explore?"

I had obviously thought about this. "Why they pulled this off in the boondocks, far away from any city."

"Have you found any answer to that?"

"Only that whoever organized this might have wanted it kept secret."

"From whom?"

I shook my head. "No idea."

Again, Pat lowered his chin and went back to ruminating. Then he looked at me and announced, "We shall see. Some other questions come to mind.

"Why did the culprits believe that you are sufficiently important to immobilize that first class train, and passengers, for all those hours? Who are those culprits? Was your arrest caused by something personal or paternal, or because of your association with my organization? Or for some other reason?

"And most important," he concluded, " What is the degree of your personal peril now, and would you be allowed to leave on short notice?"

"Leave what, Pat?" I asked nervously.

"Communist-controlled China, of course. Whoever engineered this probably has the clout to lock you up. Yet they choose to let you go–for the time, at least. Could it be because of that crafty tale you told them about preparing to dance arm-in-arm with their soldiers, that would have done justice to Baron Munchausen?" Pat shook his head, smiling. "Good try, but unlikely.

"No, the reason for your arrest probably still lurks. You have follow-up work to do from your trip. Do not discuss this experience with any-one. And I will make a few calls…"

"Meanwhile, I suggest that you think about steps you would take if you were planning to leave. Nothing firm–just loose ends you would tie up, such as what you would do with your dog, your insurance business.

"You might also brush up on your French. There is a possibility that we may establish a loose business relationship with Emperor Bao Dai's court in Vietnam. I knew him slightly in France and he has asked me to send a representative. Interesting, but only if business prospects war-rant your visit and Bao Dai is able to inject sufficient gravitas into his playboy image to gain support from France. Meanwhile, assuming that our blockade continues, I have concluded that China commerce previously anchored at Shanghai will be rerouted to Taku Bar, the seaport of Tientsin.

"We are the only major shipping company with no office there yet and–considering the way you handled the difficult Tsingtao assignment–I would like you to set one up. Your first task will be to meet and evaluate a former German shipping manager seeking employment."

My Tientsin Adventure

The train ride was even longer than the one to Tsingtao, and the wood seats just as hard. There was still no effective banking relationship with Shanghai, so I strapped on my trusty money belt, well concealed under layers of warm clothes. Tientsin, just south of Mongolia, was even colder than Tsingtao.

The candidate, Herr Oberstrasse, had previously represented the Nord Deutsche Lloyd, owners of the *Mosel* on which we had sailed as children. Absolutely business minded, he addressed me only as Herr Potter and I would have never dared to call him Hans, or such. We spent the next week organizing Pattison Tientsin–basically a branch office to service the Isbrandtsen ships, which–like the *Brooklyn Heights*–would moor at Taku Bar until Shanghai opened up.

Things went so well under his competent handling that I was free to socialize. One of the first Americans I met was Bob McCann, a big man nearly six and a half feet tall, who owned a major automobile distributorship. We were comparing the takeover of Tientsin with that of Shanghai, when I remarked on the politeness of the Communist soldiers that I first encountered.

"I have a slightly different recollection," he chuckled. "I was on the front steps of my office building with a friend who happened to be about my height, when a troop of them marched into the square in front. They were little fellows, probably fresh from the countryside, who had obviously never been in a city. Their eyes were popping out at everything they saw.

"Some of them noticed us standing there. They just stared, shaking their heads. Finally one asked the others, 'What are they?' Well, I like to be helpful, so I answered in their language, 'We're Americans. But we're only *little* Americans.'" Bob roared with laughter. "They took off like a flock of geese!"

"That's the best I've heard." I said. "I suppose you've heard about the toilet?"

"Where they poured their food rations into the toilet, thinking it was a cooking stove?"

"And flushed it down, then thought the machine was stealing their lunch and smashed the toilet bowl to get their rice back!"

Our good laugh was one of the last I had with Bob. Only a few months after I left Tientsin, he disappeared. Later it became known that he had been arrested for espionage. From then on there were rumors that he was being held incommunicado somewhere in China, in solitary confinement. But I knew nothing certain until 1961, when Bob McCann was finally carried out of China on a stretcher, dying from lung cancer. I reacted in deep sorrow–but also couldn't help wondering whether his captors could be the same ones who had picked me off the train.

Compared with Bob I got off scot-free–in this case, for breaking one or more of the new laws. My crime took place in my hotel bath tub, where, after a great meal and several drinks, an attractive American woman named Helen, whom I had met through new German friends, and I were busy splashing each other with warm water.

There was a heavy banging on the door. It burst open and some green-clad gendarmes rushed in.

"What the hell!" I exclaimed.

For a moment all was still. Then Helen was standing in the tub, stark naked, brazenly shaking her fist and screaming curses at them, the gendarmes were cowering in embarrassment and I was scrunched as far down under the water as I could get and wishing the tub was deeper. What should have concluded with Helen and me in jail and my assignment aborted, ended with the police apologizing to Helen and backing out practically kissing the floor. As if nothing had happened, Helen, laughing in amusement, pulled me to bed. Not a word would she say to address my raging curiosity as to what type of *mojo* she employed to pull *that* one off.

In less than a week my Tientsin assignment was completed, entirely through the efforts of Herr Oberstrasse. Pattison Tientsin was up and running before the next Isbrandtsen vessel pulled into Taku Bar, and was fully functional with manager and staff a month later when our *Empire Glencoe* and subsequent vessels passed through.

Dad Escapes Arrest

Dad was certainly far-sighted in applying for his exit permit when he did. At the time he made his move, Shanghai's new military government was still getting organized and he was able to clear all the hurdles before its various bureaus were functioning together efficiently. He made arrangements for me to continue living in his apartment, to provide for his various company employees and household staff to live comfortably, and to settle countless other matters I was not aware of. He would not attend any farewell parties to avoid attracting attention.

Meanwhile Herr Oberstrasse arranged for Dad's accommodation in Tientsin and booked his passage on our *Empire Glencoe* leaving April 24 to New York. I smiled, thinking of the conversations in German that he and Dad would enjoy.

Dad had only been away two weeks, but was safely at sea, when an event occurred that caused me both amusement and concern. A troop of soldiers, led by an officer of some sort, barged in. The officer demanded to know whether I was Potter John.

"Yes. I am Potter John," I replied.

"You must come with us for interrogation," he announced, waving what appeared to be a warrant of some kind.

"Why?"

"You are China bank manager. We have questions for you."

Nearly falling over with relief, I said, "I am not banker. I work with American shipping company. The banker is my father."

"Where is he?"With a stroke of genius, I feigned outrage. "How do I know? You took him away. You tell me what you did with him!"

Ignoring my outburst, he announced," We look," and they all trooped through the apartment. Finally, convinced that Dad was not hiding there, they demanded again, "Where is Potter John the banker?"

"You should know. Your police took him away! You tell me where he is!" The troop milled around, discussing the new situation, then left. To my relief they didn't return. Dad's prescient move in applying for exit when he did spared him from interrogation and possible imprisonment.

An Unexpected Offer

Pat's investigations were as thorough as possible under conditions where he had to assume that his every move was being monitored by paranoid authorities. As relevant information emerged he kept me informed. "So far, nothing has surfaced that points a finger at possible culprits, let along identifies them. Furthermore, we have been unable to identify any other occurrence similar to yours that might suggest a pattern. Confusion with your father was considered, but discarded when he was cleared for his visa. We may never learn who were involved, and why. Or what might still lurk ahead for you."

It was not long afterward, during a private lunch in his office, that Pat mentioned casually, "My Hong Kong office performance has been bothering me. The manager, van Beveren, seems quite content to rely on commissions from imported cargo, which as you know is only 2 ½ percent. The freight manager is only rarely able to book 5 percent export cargo. And in a port city where business depends heavily on trading business, ours never got started.

"I need a dynamo there to build up export bookings and import-export business–effectively starting from scratch." Looking at me sharply, Pat said, "You have been tested, and have proven yourself. For this reason, and your personal safety, I have decided to offer you a position there."

I was not completely surprised, and he continued, "Shanghai is dying, John. Certainly from the blockade, but also from the controls being imposed by the new authority. Hong Kong, on the other hand, is booming and my office there needs your energy. I would move there myself if I could obtain a visa. But I cannot. I am solely responsible for my employees' welfare. Moreover, no visa would be approved for Mae and our child, for whom you are the godfather."

I fully shared Pat's pessimism. Nearly everyone who could get an exit visa was bailing out. Senior managers were not so lucky. They had to run a gauntlet that was a nightmare. Most who controlled their company's money were flatly refused. Others were being abused and intimidated by their employees and their unions, and had to spend days at a time at "people's courts" being judged by former clerks who casually awarded extortionate payments for drummed-up crimes like cheating on taxes, with no evidence.

These payments, plus salaries for employees who had no work but could no longer be dismissed, were exhausting cash reserves in Shanghai and causing more and more calls to overseas headquarters for funds. Even a short delay in responding usually resulted in the manager being squeezed–often locked in his office for days without food, drinks, electricity, heat or communications–until even the most outrageous demands were met. The Caltex manager I had met earlier at the American Club was only one of the first of many suffering this abuse.

My visa application was less complicated that Dad's because of my junior position in the company, but months would pass until it was approved, if ever. This gave me many precious days and nights with the girl I had come to love.

Olga

The dam holding back my emotions broke the evening when she told me, tearfully, that her American husband Brooks had stopped communicating with her. His final message was from some discharge point on the West Coast, promising to return to get her. He sent her no money, and her efforts to locate him disclosed that his insurance policy, originally in her favor, had been cancelled.

The upshot was that with the twin barriers of her marriage and Dad's resistance gone, she moved in with me. Even Cindy, ferociously jealous of women in my life, played happily with her. As a wife, she was more than perfect, forever producing extras to please me.

I soon changed my habits from spending my three-hour lunch at the American Club to having Wong drive me home, where Olga had prepared my favorite treat. This was a thick sandwich full of caviar–the red pearls, which she had discovered were my favorite–with eggs, onion and all the other fixings.

Handing me a plate full as she helped me to undress behind my closed bedroom door, she would smile seductively, "Eat plenty, *Pop-chick,* and hurry up. You will need it all to satisfy me! Someone else is hungry, too!"

She had cried out this nickname for me the first time we made love, and used it frequently. When I asked her what it meant, she giggled like a naughty girl, "It means your backside, but no one uses it but me–and only for you."

Oddly, when I would return to the office three hours later, I felt stronger than when I had left. That caviar! I thought, laughing to myself. Pat, of course, knew of my relationship and liked Olga–provided that she did not interfere with his plans for me.

We fell deeply in love during the several months we had together. Despite the threat I might be facing, and Pat's opening in Hong Kong, when my exit permit was finally issued, I was reluctant to leave because of her. She would not receive any travel document for at least two years and there was nothing I could do to speed this up because she was legally married to another. Although she would probably have to return to her UN compound, Pat assured me he would pay her enough of my salary each month to live comfortably.

On our last morning, after a long night of love making, she cried bitterly, "I'm afraid, Popchick. I'm afraid I will lose you!"

My reply was heartfelt. "I don't care how long it takes, darling. As soon as you can travel, I'll meet you and we can be together again!"

It took a little over three years for her to receive papers to leave Shanghai. Within days from her departure, we found each other again at the Excelsior Hotel in Rome.

Bye, Bye, Shanghai

Before boarding the train again for Tientsin, I arranged for my insurance accounts to be handled by Winston. Other matters, such as the car and our servants, had all been taken care of by Dad.

This left me with the most important, Cindy. She would go with me on the train, stuck in a large dog house, except during stops when I was able to take her out for brief walks. Herr Oberstrasse used his influence to arrange for us to share a single room at my hotel in Tientsin, and again when booking Cindy's kennel aboard the Butterfield & Swire coastal ship *Cheefoo.*

Cindy was given a free run of the ship's fantail for several hours every afternoon, where I kept her in check with an extra strong harness and tether. Again and again she lunged at the sea gulls that dive-bombed us. One swung low across the deck and flew off one side, closely pursued by Cindy–so close that she sailed high over the edge still snapping at her prey.

Cindy was hanging far below, a few yards above the ship's boiling prop wake, when I managed to bring her fall to a halt. Heart pounding with relief that the harness had held, I pulled her up to the deck.

Here, utterly nonplussed at her adventure, Cindy started jumping at the passing gulls again. My Guardian Angel must have adopted her, too. I lost her to the Hong Kong quarantine for six months, but visited her in the government kennels frequently until she was released.

Life Six: Hong Kong 1950-1951

PART ONE

The Hong Kong Business World

Re-entry into Civilization

After a refreshing night's sleep I joined Wimpy and his wife, Winnie for a full breakfast. This was served by Ah Kwok, their cheerful cook-boy, wearing the standard black trousers with white top and flashing a gold tooth. After preliminaries, Wimpy invited me to stay with them until I found permanent quarters. My only cost would be a share of the household expenses. I accepted their generous offer immediately.

Wimpy lent me his Austin and the driver, who took me to the government quarantine facility. I found that Cindy was being well treated and spent a half hour exercising her. She would be held there for six months like all domestic pets entering the Colony. I disliked this, but had to admire the wisdom of this British regulation, which had just about eliminated rabies in England and their territories.

Then we picked up Wimpy, crossed the harbor on the Star Ferry to the Hong Kong side, and finally parked in front of an office building. As with all such colonial architecture, the ground floor façade in front of us was set back some fifteen feet from the side of the building. The overhang sheltered the sidewalk underneath from both monsoon rains and tropical sun.

A boisterous mass of people filled the walkway–vendors hawking cigarettes, counterfeit watches and Chinese newspapers, peddlers offering bowls of steaming noodles from mobile stoves, beggars, ragged coolies struggling under heavy loads. All seemed to be pushing and jostling and shouting angrily. We elbowed our way forward, assisted by the tall Sikh guard wearing a red turban.

Wimpy led me up the front steps, through a narrow lobby crowded with businessmen and messengers and into an ancient grid cage. The uniformed operator slammed shut the door. We jolted and began a slow trip upward, creaked past three open landings and finally jerked to a stop. The door opened and I followed Wimpy into A.P. Pattison & Co. (Hong Kong), Ltd.

The Pattison Office

My workplace was on the third floor of the American International Underwriters building in the heart of Hong Kong's commercial district. The office had four rooms bordering an open area where some twenty male clerks sat at small desks clicking away at abacuses and scribbling in ink, pausing now and then to exchange words in Cantonese. Most wore western clothes with ties but no jackets. Three older men had on traditional Chinese robes. Revolving ceiling fans sent down tepid air in a losing battle against the sweltering heat, just as bad here as in Shanghai.

Wimpy showed me the side rooms. One contained shelves with office supplies and scattered consumer product samples, and a table holding a clattering telex machine and telephone. The next room housed three Chinese secretaries wearing neat skirts and blouses. On their desks sat Remington typewriters with extra wide carriages to accommodate shipping manifests. The girls stood up, smiling, as Wimpy made introductions. He singled one out. "This is Pamela. She will help you."

The third room was occupied by his two "foreign" managers who were working at crowded desks. Wimpy commented as we walked past, "I give them time to finish business. You will have a table there."

Then we entered the master office at the end. Here Wimpy presided from a heavy teak-wood desk carved with Indonesian designs. Behind him, three large windows framed by colorful batik curtains overlooked the harbor. All about us the walls were decorated with antiques. Seeing me admire a carving, he explained, "Winnie finds these in Hong Kong. She likes such things." He shook his head sadly, "We had so many beautiful pieces in Java. All lost. The *verdomde* Japanese soldiers…"

Wimpy sat me down on a sofa and summoned his managers. The senior was "Mac" MacCorkindale, the short, rugged Shipping Manager responsible for the smooth operation of the Hong Kong agency. Looking me over appraisingly, he announced in a strong Scottish accent, "So you're the laddie who handled the *Flying Arrow* in Tsingtao. We'll find plenty for you to do here."

The other manager, Johnny Meade, would indoctrinate me into the freight business. He was English, about fifty, medium height and glowingly bald. Both managers welcomed me politely, yet I could not help sensing a reserve about "the guy that Pat sent from Shanghai" intruding into their cozy world and giving them more work training me. Also there was little extra spare floor space in their office.

Wimpy then walked me through the main room and introduced me to three older men in Chinese robes, the section heads. Each described in halting but passable English his department's responsibilities and presented me to his clerks. It was clear that Pattison's main business in Hong Kong was handling the Isbrandtsen Line vessels, which came through every two weeks. I could see no evidence of the trading activities that Pat had wanted me to invigorate.

I spent the next hour with my new secretary. To my surprise, she welcomed the prospect of adding me to her other "bosses." Pamela was just over five feet tall, slender, in her low twenties and very bright. She took short hand and transcribed accurately. Apart from Cantonese, she spoke both Mandarin and Shanghai dialects.

Until two years earlier she had attended a convent school near their home in north China. Then her father was publicly executed for the crime of being a landlord. She and her mother, destitute, had escaped and crossed illegally into Hong Kong.

Pamela handed me a manila folder with correspondence. I was happily surprised to find a letter from Pat reiterating his interest in developing import-export business in Hong Kong. Knowing that it would be delayed en route by the censors, he had sent it from Shanghai weeks before I left so that it would be here when I arrived. Pat had hand written a footnote: 'I am counting on you and have plans for you'.

Wimpy took me to lunch at the Parisian Grill, acclaimed as Hong Kong's–and possibly Asia's–finest restaurant. After savoring the *crepes suzette* which topped off a delicious chateaubriand with béarnaise, I excused myself and wandered around the city to get a feel for my new world.

The store windows captivated me. I stared into bright, colorful displays, marveling at the abundance of consumer goods in this free market society. During my confinement in Shanghai, I had become inured to a colorless, drab environment devoid of luxuries, with nothing in the shops but ceramic pots, kerosene lamps, basic blue clothes, medicinal herbs and occasionally a foreign magazine which had escaped confiscation. The few films permitted were black-and-white propaganda efforts showing Communist Chinese heroes vanquishing foreign imperialists.

Now, like Pizarro overlooking his hoard of golden Inca treasure, I stared at the overwhelming variety and quality of the merchandise on display–stylish clothing, shiny new utilities, cameras, golf clubs, Johnny Walker whisky, English magazines with up-to-date news of the world. And movie theaters showing real American films! I didn't recognize the titles, but still remembered the stars like Bogart.

That night I had difficulty getting to sleep. My head was a kaleidoscope of brightly colored clothing, cameras, golf clubs, watches, and so many other suddenly-available items that welcomed me into this exciting new world.

PART TWO

Lessons Not Taught at Business School

The Calcutta Crook

Pat had good reason to focus me on import-export. In a city practically living on trade, this office had no trading department nor anyone interested in starting one. When I asked Wimpy for guidance he suggested that I begin by reviewing correspondence. Pamela produced files of letters and telexes from importers and exporters all over the world. Few had been acknowledged. I remembered Pat's admonition: "A telex deserves a telex reply the same day; a letter within a week."

I then turned to the *Commodity Review*, a weekly trade publication listing hundreds of offers and requests for everything from cotton clothing to watch bracelets. From this I zeroed in on products most in demand. One was Hong Kong-manufactured sewing needles. Pamela and I made a list of the most interesting requests for offers.

I also made the rounds of needle manufacturers, visiting their warehouses and factories on back alleys in Kowloon. Many were businessmen from Shanghai. They invariably showed interest when I threw a few words in their dialect at them. One elderly patriarch had known my father. He took me under his wing and introduced me to the needle business. Our bank gave Mr. Chang a clean bill of health, and he became my designated supplier. Now I needed customers.

One Calcutta importer who had written to us looked particularly inviting. I answered his most recent letter and four days later received a telexed request to quote for a big order. Excited, I took it to Wimpy. His reaction was puzzling. "Be careful," he cautioned. "See me before you make any commitment."

Mr. Chang confirmed that he could supply the whole request ex stock. "You still young man," he said with a warm smile. "I know you Daddy and I help you." He gave me a competitive price, to which Wimpy included a huge 15% profit. Thursday afternoon I telexed our offer giving our account at the Hong Kong & Shanghai Bank as recipient of payment. Wimpy insisted this be by banker's confirmed irrevocable letter of credit. Early the next morning our telex chattered:

> ACCEPT OFFER STOP HAVE ARRANGED CALCUTTA BRANCH YOUR BANK OPEN IRREVOCABLE L/C NUMBER (SHOWN) FOR AMERICAN DOLLARS 29,800 TELEXED YOUR ACCOUNT HONGKONG REQUIRE SHIPMENT PER S.S. NAGASAKI MARU VOYAGE 16 DIRECT HONGKONG CALCUTTA STOP TELEX CONFIRMATION CARGO LOADED.

I should have heard warning bells and seen red flags at such a facile acceptance, but was too excited. The ship was already in Hong Kong and scheduled to depart in two days. Mr. Chang had just enough time to make the delivery dock side and complete export formalities if we signed the purchase order by 6:00 p.m.

But first, I went to the bank. The L/C had not yet arrived so I asked for a credit report we had requested on the buyer. This was also not yet available. With neither L/C nor credit report, I decided to postpone shipment until they came in. I telexed Calcutta that their L/C had not arrived and asked for a later sailing date. Their reply was prompt, reiterating that their L/C had been opened and stating that their customer refused to accept any changes.

Remembering Wimpy's instruction to see him before making any commitment, I went to his office. The room was empty–he had left on the ferry to Macao. Now, what the hell to do? It was decision time, and I had to make it.

I reasoned that even if the ship sailed with our cargo before the L/C arrived, we would have the security of owning it until paid. Then there was that hefty 15% margin. Confident that Wimpy would have given me authority to commit, I went for it and signed the purchase agreement.

We worked Saturday mornings and just before noon Wimpy unexpectedly walked in. I filled him in and explained my reasons for going ahead on my own. His reaction stunned me. His face darkened and he demanded:

"Where those needles? Are they loaded?"

"I don't know," I stammered.

"Why you don't know? You bought them!"

"I signed, but we haven't paid. We have credit until the L/C comes."

"L/C?" he exploded. "What L/C?" Wimpy gave me a withering look. "Where is this L/C of yours? You think those Calcutta crooks open your L/C?" Scornfully, he continued, "There is no L/C. They trick you to put your *verdomde* needles on a boat–to Calcutta! Why? They steal them!"

"But they can't, without documents –"

"Documents–bah." He shook his head in exasperation. "When you learn?" After a moment he calmed down and grabbed his phone. "I try to stop this."

A few calls later Wimpy turned to me, suddenly relaxed and genial. "It is done. Those crates are still on the dock. They go back to the godown." Offhandedly he added, "Now you can decide what you do with your needles," and walked away looking positively cheerful.

It dawned on me that Wimpy meant what he said–Mr. Chang's purchase order had my signature. With a shock I realized that now I was the owner of hundreds of thousands of sewing needles! Where do I find the money to pay? What do I do with them? My best hope was for Mr. Chang to take them back.

To my surprise–and huge relief–Mr. Chang seemed not in the least perturbed when I told him my news. In fact, his chubby face actually broke into a grin.

"Young Mr. Potter," he chuckled. "You have good luck today. You don lost money." A sudden shortage of needles had developed in the Hong Kong market and the price was rising. He could sell at a good profit. I immediately agreed to cancel our order.

He then asked how I wanted my commission paid. Cash would be best, he said. Being still naïve in these things, I thought it dishonest to accept any part of his profit and politely said so. He laughed merrily, "So honest, just like you Daddy!"

I told Wimpy my good news. When I added that I had refused a commission he turned on me with an incredulous expression.

"You do what?" he demanded. "*Godverdomme*, that is my company profit!" Then, realizing he had relinquished any claim to the cargo he subsided, shaking his head in disgust. "You lucky," he muttered. A moment later I thought I saw him actually masking a smile.

A few days later a heavy box was delivered to my office. Mac and I opened it, and stared in awe at a full case of very expensive Johnny Walker Black. I offered six bottles to Wimpy, who did not show the slightest hesitation in accepting.

This experience taught me what a key role luck can play in business. What would have happened, I wondered, if Wimpy had not returned in time to stop the loading? Or if Mr. Chang would not bail me out?

A few days later Wimpy called me to his office for a review. The L/C had not arrived, but I still couldn't understand why he had reacted so violently. We would still own the cargo. It would be safe until we could find a buyer. I told him so.

"Yes, safe on board," he agreed with a smile. "The vessel is now in Calcutta, discharging. But no L/C has come. We say you loaded your needles and your Calcutta crooks cannot take delivery without documents. So you don't worry." He leaned forward and looked sharply at me." Now, what happens to them?"

As I started to answer he interrupted, "They will go on a nice, slow voyage. They will sail to Bombay, Suez, America, Panama, Japan... maybe back to Hog Hong." He stopped, watching me closely from under his heavy white eyebrows. "Unless the shipping company off loads them. Maybe in Djibouti or Karachi? You know the port conditions there? But you are lucky–they don't. So what do you do?"

I was thinking when he continued sharply, "I tell you what you do. You work like hell to find someone to take your cargo. You will send twenty, thirty telexes every day to importers at every port on the ship's route to find someone who will pay.

"And all this time will your supplier wait, maybe for months? Or will he sue you? Do you think about freight? You must pay the steamship company. Every new port the freight goes up and you must pay more. And insurance? Who will give you insurance, with no consignee and no destination? And after the ship has left port?"

Without waiting, Wimpy came to the point. "Your Calcutta friend tricks you because you are not experienced." He paused, "Of course your needles are safe. Mr. Calcutta knows he cannot steal them. But he also knows he can give you big headaches and make you lose money. So? He blackmails you!

"As soon as your needles leave Hong Kong you will get a telex. He will say, 'Your price too high stop buyer will open L/C...' and offer you half price. You know his game, but what can you do? You counter-offer fast because soon your ship leaves Calcutta and your chance is gone. Your crook knows this and waits while you try to bargain. On the last day when he has your lowest price–*then* he opens his L/C."

Wimpy saw my humiliated expression and finished softly, "This happens to me once, John. I was young like you. My cargo was Indonesian spices. But I was not lucky–nobody stopped me."

The Opium Pipe

The commission that Isbrandtsen paid Pattison was 5% on outgoing freight which we booked, but only 2½% on incoming freight. Most of our bookings were incoming, and the 2½% barely covered our expenses–probably the reason that Wimpy assigned me to assist Johnny Meade.

Johnny worked hard, but ran into resistance everywhere. He explained that most exporters refused to use our ships because Isbrandtsen was a "non-Conference" line. As was the case in Shanghai, all the other big shipping companies were banded together into a cartel–called "The Conference"–that controlled most of Hong Kong's exports. To be able to ship on any of their vessels, exporters had to agree not to ship with us. If caught doing this, they were punished.

To break the Conference stranglehold, we would need to offer exporters timely service to ports all over the world. This was impossible–our round-the-world sailings came by only twice a month and omitted too many important destinations. Our only real chance to succeed would be with exporters whose major customers were located in ports which we regularly serviced. Johnny and I set about looking for them.

One by one we called on shippers that Johnny felt offered the best chance. Most visits ended abruptly when the exporter heard "Isbrandtsen." After two weeks we had lined up only a few small prospects.

Until one day, when we found a Chinese exporter who might be interested. Access to his office was gained through a curtain at the rear of a tiny noodle shop. Inside was a flight of darkened narrow wooden steps. We climbed two flights and walked into an empty room. Johnny called in Cantonese and received a mumbled reply to wait. Ten minutes later, a man shuffled in through a door at the rear.

I was startled to see the reincarnation of the Chinese Mandarins who once had bought opium from clipper ship traders in Canton. But this one was frightening–very tall, thin, his face a mask of yellowed skin stretched across a bony skull. He wore a shiny dark blue silk Chinese robe and a round cap with a button at the top.

On his feet were dark blue silk slippers. His arms were crossed in front, folded into the robe's loose sleeves. There was no expression on his face as he nodded us to round stools facing a wooden table and sat on the other side, arms still folded into his sleeves. No servant offered us tea. No calling cards were exchanged.

Finally, through stained yellow teeth, he demanded, "Why you come?"

Johnny noted the poor command of English. He responded in Cantonese and was sharply cut off. Then the host turned to me. "What you do my house?"

I explained in pidgin English. Our host listened without interrupting and I realized we had a common *lingua franca*. Johnny also switched to pidgin English. We learned that his name was Mok. After we had introduced ourselves, and our purpose for coming, he explained that he was an exporter of Asian produce to customers in North Africa. His main business, he added, was shipping Chinese green tea to Casablanca. "You savee?" he prompted. "Gleen tea?"

This seemed too good to be true. We did indeed savvy and in fact our ships had carried large quantities of green tea from Shanghai to North Africa. I replied, "Likee gunpowder, chun mee?"

At this he started, clearly surprised. When Johnny offered sailings to Casablanca. Mok asked us about sailing dates, frequency, freight rates, and so on. Johnny answered in general terms since we were unprepared for this. Finally Mok said that he shipped thousands of cases of green tea every year. If satisfied with our freight rate and service he would consider placing some on our ships.

He would start with a trial shipment. This would be made through another exporter who had already broken with the Conference. We would have to convince him that we could handle his exports with no problems. Scarcely able to believe our luck, we left with an agreement to return in two days with our firm offer.

On the street, Johnny and I patted each other on the back. This could be a million dollar business. And, apart from the revenue, we would have succeeded in prying loose the first important shipper from the Conference. Telexes went off to Pattison in Shanghai and Isbrandtsen in New York. Replies confirmed there would be cargo space aboard our next sailing, the *Flying Cloud*, scheduled to arrive here in six days. Isbrandtsen's telex quoted an unusually competitive rate including the cost of diverting the carrier to Casablanca. Clearly they also appreciated the significance of getting this business.

The next morning I was fully prepared, waiting for Johnny, when his wife phoned that he was sick with a high fever. Wimpy agreed that I should go alone–we did not want to risk antagonizing Mr. Mok by breaking our first appointment. This time my reception was quite different. Mr. Mok stood up from his stool and, withdrawing an arm from its sleeve, waved me to a seat. A small boy brought us cups of steaming tea. I waited politely until Mr. Mok raised his cup, then joined him. Mr. Mok suddenly asked, "What this tea?"

I swished it around the little cup and sniffed. The aroma was familiar but I couldn't quite place it. Then, reaching back to a tasting session when Pattison took me to a tea factory near Shanghai, I took a chance: "I think this chun mee tea."

His thin lips spread into a form of grimace which I took to be a smile. It made his face more frightening than ever, but clearly conveyed satisfaction. This led into business. As each point was covered Mr. Mok nodded. Twice he referred to our willingness to make direct shipments to Casablanca, which most competitors would not offer. Our discussion continued easily until he asked, "How muchee?"

I named our rate per measurement ton with a three percent buffer built in for negotiation. Predictably, this was too high. We continued and bit by bit I dropped our price until I reached my limit. He still shook his head. Knowing how keenly the Chinese enjoy negotiating, I had not been concerned until then. But he was clearly serious and I had given away all my bargaining chips. It dawned on me that we could be headed for stalemate. I was considering how we could persuade Isbrandtsen to lower the rate when he stood up and turned away.

"You come," he said, leading me to the room's back door. When he opened it I was shocked to find myself looking into an opium den. A real live den with sofas, cushions and all the trimmings! My nose confirmed this–the room was redolent with its heavy sweetish odor and I began to feel queasy. I started backing away when Mr. Mok pointed to a dark stained sofa and pressed me to sit. I hesitated, but the chance for a last shot at his business overcame my revulsion.

He went to a wall cabinet and pulled out a long black opium pipe. He pressed a dab of brownish stuff into the small brass cup at one end and lit it. Then he sat down across from me, puffing silently. For many minutes no words were exchanged. I could see his body gradually settling back as the opium's effect took hold. I began feeling light headed and nauseated. The drug's fumes were also getting to me.

His next move took me completely by surprise.

He leaned forward suddenly, his gaunt face relaxing into an odd smile, and handed me his pipe. Every instinct in my body rebelled. But the urge to succeed–perhaps nudged by the opium fumes–was too strong. As Mr. Mok watched intently, I took the pipe and gingerly touched my lips to the mouthpiece. I did not inhale deeply, but gave an imitation that apparently pleased him. Presently he retrieved his pipe and continued to puff. Then he announced quietly, "You last plice can do. You come tomollow bling paper." Our meeting had ended.

Wildly excited, but nearly overcome with nausea, I backed out as quickly as I could and rushed down the stairs. I had barely reached the sidewalk when it came. Doubled over at the curb, I vomited my guts out. Opium clearly did not agree with me. After that, my nausea returned whenever I smelled its aroma–or even marijuana. Years later, at a party in Madrid, it nearly cost me a legendary night with an English secretary. We had scarcely begun preliminaries when I was jarred by the taste of pot on her lips. I felt nauseated, but spurred by the inducements that lay ahead, managed to soldier through.

Johnny and Mac both agreed that my willingness to "share the pipe" had sealed Mok's decision. It resulted in the most profitable contract Pattison had ever booked here.

PART THREE

Fun and Games in Hong Kong

The Clubs

The American Club

For the first months my boarding arrangement with Wimpy and Winny, which implied "civilized" hours acceptable to an older couple, went well. Then I joined the American Club and adopted the habit of drifting to its Men's Bar after work. Here I met a number of single men about my age. Bit by bit I settled in with them at the big table. We played liar's dice while discussing such important matters as which horse would win the feature race Saturday at Happy Valley or whether a new nurse at the British Military Hospital put out.

The leader of the group was much loved Uncle Ted, about forty, a portly, easy going joker who despite his title of regional director for an insurance company acted no older than the rest of us in our late twenties. Among the Americans were two bankers–Frugal MacDougal and Lee–with Chase and City respectively. Shipping was represented by Mickey O, with an American shipping line; Charlie was PanAm's marketing manager, and Eddie managed a trading company.

Swiss were represented by Hans and Ziggy, with the big Swiss trading companies Emile Ott. Our Canadian explorer, Dave, traveled for the mining group Ventures, Ltd. English members were Superintendent of Police Johnny, who cheerfully quashed our traffic tickets and arranged complementary "special" massages, and Lieutenant Patrick, *aide de camp* to the head of the RAF here, who offered me an unauthorized ride in a new Meteor jet which was passing through. As with the American Club in Shanghai, most payments for drinks were determined by liar's dice, and each of us had his own inscribed leather dice box.

Now and then our dice sessions led into other activities with the result that I returned late for Winny's family dinner. She tolerated this silently for about three months. Then, clearly annoyed, she said, "John, the cook is not happy that he must make another dinner for you. Also you left the door open last night. This is dangerous."

Wimpy, on the way to the office, followed up with, "You are young and I understand. I think you would be happier if you stay at another place." By good fortune, a place was ready for me.

The Foreign Correspondents' Club

This was the Foreign Correspondents' Club, universally known as the FCC and featured in the movie *Love is a Many-Splendored Thing*. My membership in the Shanghai FCC automatically qualified me for membership in the Hong Kong Club, where one of the eight guest rooms upstairs had just become available. I grabbed it and moved in with a legendary assemblage of characters from all over the world.

The manager, Peppi Pauzen, was universally beloved and often presided on Friday nights at the dining room piano with guest musicians for sing-a-longs. Behind the long bar, welcoming everyone, was Liao. His association went back to Chung King in 1943 where he had made drinks for the Flying Tiger pilots, including some now with Air America who visited him here. Liao had worked at the Shanghai FCC, and when the Communists threatened he carried that club's records to Hong Kong.

When I arrived he sent my bag up with an assistant and fixed my scotch while I went to the long bar. The first person I met was Walt. I had not seen him since Shanghai and greeted him with the standard opening, "Your smell's gone."

He made his standard response, laughing, "It'll catch up soon."

I could never forget his account of the incident. He was a junior with the National City Bank in Shanghai when WWII started and the Japanese took the city. They imprisoned my Dad and the other Americans. But not Walt.

"When I heard the damned Japs were actually rounding up American businessmen," he told us. "I decided to escape. Of course there wasn't any normal transportation, but I got a lead to the guerrillas and they hid me.

"Then Japs started snooping around and the guerillas told me I had to be moved. They couldn't hide me in a cart because the soldiers bayoneted all the loads they carried. So they sneaked me onto a big sampan in the river. They knew I spoke Chinese and one of them laughed and told me, 'They won't look for you here.'

"Damn tootin' they wouldn't look!" He exclaimed. "That sampan was a frigging honey barge! The whole thing was a big tub of crap–thousands of gallons of fresh steaming human crap! They lit a lantern and showed me a space about six inches high under the wood bottom of the tub. *And* told me to crawl in!" As we doubled over laughing, Walt challenged, "Have you ever been squeezed under a load of crap? With the damn stuff dripping all over you through cracks in the bottom? It stank so much I was actually crying! Just trying to breathe I was choking.

"Well, after the boatmen sculled us a few miles up the Yangtze they finally told me I could come out. Then–just as I was starting to breathe again–they shoved me back in! A Jap patrol boat was coming. I heard jabbering and shouting, then the Japs bugged off at top speed. You got to hand it to those guys. They were really smart–no way would those Japs come aboard to search *this* boat!

"I was stuck there for days, and had to go back in my hole every time a Jap patrol boat came by. Finally we got up the river past the Jap lines and I could go ashore. My God, the air smelled good! I took a big breath–and then suddenly that stink came and choked me again. The only way I could escape was to run like hell, then take a breath before it caught up to me. Not just a short run–it had to be at least ten steps for one fresh breath. With fifteen steps, I could usually get two breaths.

"Well, when I got to our guys we tried everything to clean off the smell: industrial soap, kerosene, you name it. Showers–one after the other. And of course new clothes. Finally, after a few days, we got rid of it. But I still dream about it."

I had heard Walt's story before but let him tell it again and pay for my drink. Then I settled in my room upstairs. That evening, after a good meal in the dining room, I met the first of many correspondents I would come to know. The dean of the press corps was Australian Dick Hughes, nicknamed "Old Craw" for being the model for John le Carre's character in *The Honorable Schoolboy*.

Years later, Dick would give his book *Hong Kong: Borrowed Place, Borrowed Time* to my pregnant wife, amusingly inscribed: "To two and a half Potters." In the bar here, on my birthday September 1, I would also receive the inaugural edition of *The Asian Wall Street Journal* published that same day. Its editor, Peter Kaan had inscribed the newspaper's covering page: "To John. On our joint birthday."

The bureau chiefs of all the major publications such as *Time, Newsweek* and *The Economist* came here along with droves of diplomats and military officers from several nations, and even people who were–rightly or wrongly–called spooks. One day I was pleasantly surprised to meet a CAT pilot widely known as Earthquake McGoon because of his heavy, dark appearance. In fact he was a soft spoken gentleman named James McGovern, greatly missed after being shot down later while flying supplies to the French Foreign Legionnaires in Dien Bien Phu.

The bar at the FCC, apart from being the most boisterous in town, served drinks to accommodate all tastes. One was particularly popular here with groups of liar's dice players bent on suicide. It was played in three rounds: the loser of the first round named a drink, the loser of the second paid for it, and the loser of the third drank it. Since the person who named the drink was exempted from drinking it, he usually ordered the one guaranteed to inflict the most damage: the *pousse café.*

Served in a tall, slender glass, the contents were a series of six or eight different liquors, each brightly colored red, blue, green, or what have you, sitting in half inch layers on top of each other from the bottom of the glass to the top. The position of each layer depended on its specific gravity: the heaviest liquor on the bottom, and so on up. It looked like a beautiful coral snake–and was just as lethal.

This drink contributed to a fatality while I stayed there. The victim was Jock, a popular US Navy chief who joined us one Saturday after dinner. That afternoon he had been at the Royal Hong Kong Jockey Club race meet when a jockey friend gave him a sure thing after swearing him to secrecy. The horse, called *Straight Arrow* and running at impossibly long odds, was to be shooed in to provide a financial cushion for the widow of another jockey recently killed at the track.

Jock was, as usual, skeptical but he liked the story. He bet a week's pay on win and watched his horse stagger in first. The judges allowed the result to stand although there was a near riot from losing betters who had watched the favored horses being held back so hard they nearly strangled. His wallet bulging with large denomination bills, Jock drove his Jeep to the FCC and proceeded to buy drinks for the house. By midnight, these included *pousse-cafes*. When Jock finally left for home he was intercepted by Liao, who offered him a room and begged him to stay. Jock refused, and stomped out to his Jeep, roaring with laughter.

He never returned. The next morning his body was found beneath his overturned Jeep on a ledge below a bend in the Peak road. A bittersweet comment made the rounds: "At least he died happy."

Soon after the Korean War started the British aircraft carrier *HMS Arc Royal* put into port after a tour off Korea. My RAF friend Patrick asked me to go aboard with him. "You will have a chance to see British naval tradition in action," he said.

After arriving on the barge, we joined a group of senior British naval officers for a drink in the boardroom, then moved to the flight deck. It had been cleared. The lights went off and in the dark Patrick whispered, "Some of their pilots were shot down over Korea while bombing and strafing the Commies. This is to remember them."

At that, two spotlights came on, aimed at the ends of the long deck. Each illuminated a single Scot piper dressed in full military regalia. As I watched, spellbound, their pipes skirled with the sound of *Amazing Grace* played as I had never heard it–as a proud lament.

The pipers advanced in slow step until they met in front of us. Then they circled, with dignity, and marched back–still in slow step– to where they had appeared. The spotlights went out and they disappeared into the darkness as the last notes of their haunting dirge faded away. We stood in respectful silence, deeply moved.

Finally the main lights came on and we walked silently back to the boardroom. Every one of us had wet eyes, and wasn't the least ashamed of it.

Other Adventures – Mickey's Revenge

One evening after work our group was sitting around a table at the American Club bar playing the usual liar's dice for drinks. Frugal MacDougal had the center stage, protesting unconvincingly to Eddie that he really had a full house under his dice cup; Eddie, nodding skeptically, waited happily to pounce on it; Lee, Charlie, Uncle Ted and I watched with amusement. Our Swiss friends, Hans and Ziggy, were commenting softly in a combination of French and English.

Another regular, Mickey O, walked over from the long bar, drink in hand. About twenty-five, medium build with jet-black hair over a handsome Greek face, he was fair–and quite willing–game for foreign and Chinese women alike. Mickey's outgoing, cheerful manner blended with superb sales skills to make him an ideal marketing manager for his big shipping line. But today Mickey was not cheerful. He glared sourly out the window at the company's majestic flagship berthed at the Kowloon Dock across the harbor. Then he snapped, "The bitch is on that ship."

"What do you mean, Mick?"

"That damned bitch. Some VIP's daughter. Traveling alone. We got a telex from head office to take good care of her, show her around, all that shit. I got stuck."

Heads nodded in sympathy. We were all familiar with these requests to entertain visiting VIPs–a job nobody wanted. It was usually passed down to the lowest bachelor on the office totem pole who met minimum standards of appearance and manners. Mickey shook his head, "I have to feed her tonight. And you know, that stuck-up bitch wouldn't even talk to me this afternoon? Probably expected the country manager to kiss her ass and take her out." Mickey took a large swig from his scotch and soda and repeated, "That is one snooty, spoiled little bitch."

Mickey left, we shrugged exchanging sympathetic comments, and the game continued. It turned out that Frugal MacDougal really did have his full house and Eddie howled in mock agony at being suckered into calling him.

The following evening we were back at the same table when Mickey arrived.

There was no resemblance to the miserable person who had stomped out the day before. The man who strode into the bar was grinning happily, puffed up with excitement. He plunked himself down, shouted for a double scotch and soda and beamed at us, waiting. I bit first, "OK, what happened?"

Frugal asked hopefully, "Did you get laid?"

"Better," Mickey exclaimed. "Remember I said she was a snooty bitch? Well, she just got worse. First I took her to the Gloucester Lounge for a drink. Now how could anyone not like that? But not her–it was too noisy. Then I took her to Jimmy's for Russian borsch and beef stroganoff. Chang saw us coming and sent his special high proof vodka. We must have had a half a dozen drinks when we left. I figured the booze would soften her up if anything could. But no, she just got drunk and nastier.

"Then she wanted to see the local atmosphere! Well, I thought what the hell? She wants to see local atmosphere? I'll show her local atmosphere. So I took her to Wanchai."

We hooted with appreciation, picturing Mickey and the spoiled brat elbowing their way through hundreds of drunken sailors, whores, tourists, and pimps in that warren of bars, massage parlors, tattoo shops and God knows what other types of distinctly non-Junior League places.

Mickey's scotch arrived and he downed the glass. Then he grinned smugly and waited until someone finally demanded, "So what happened?"

"What happened? Well, let's just say little Miss Snooty isn't so snooty anymore. She must have had an awfully sore ass since she sobered up this morning." He convulsed with laughter. "Hah! The job is beautiful. The tattoo guy spent at least two hours on it after she passed out. Right across her back, just over her ass, he stenciled the small boat warning 'TWIN SCREWS - KEEP CLEAR.' And right underneath, on each pretty white cheek, he tattooed a beautiful bronze propeller–just like on her Daddy's big ships." Mickey lay back choking and weeping with laughter.

We were stunned. Finally Uncle Ted murmured, "Jesus."

"It's been fun knowing you," Charlie said.

When Mickey got control of himself he gasped, "Nothing will happen. If that girl was you, would you run and show your big shot Daddy a couple of bronze propellers tattooed on your ass? No way. She's going to keep her precious little tush hidden top secret until she can find someone to clean it up." Mickey paused, then added thoughtfully, "That would be too bad, because those propellers were really beautiful."

He was right. He kept his job and was even promoted not long afterward.

Other Adventures – Uncle Ted's Birthday Gift

Mickey never stopped amazing us with wildly unpredictable stunts. One evening after dinner about ten of us dropped in at the Paramount Ballroom. This was a large, noisy dance hall with a live band where high-class whores could be bought out for a fee–but from that point on, you bargained with the girl, who might or might not. Or might agree, accept the money, and disappear. Or might even agree and keep her word. Most were peasant family refugees from villages around Hong Kong, in their twenties, reasonably attractive and clean.

That particular night there were no big ships with sailors in port and business seemed slow. We were on the point of drifting out when Mickey stopped us, "Wait, I got an idea!" We listened over the din of the band as he continued, "It's Uncle Ted's birthday today. He wouldn't tell anybody, but I learned this from his secretary."

"It's too late to get him a present now." Rumor was that Mickey was screwing Ted's Eurasian secretary, but he denied this.

"Besides he's probably in bed, sleeping."

"So maybe he is. That makes it all the better." Mickey pointed at the clusters of taxi dancers talking in small groups along the walls. "Look at those poor girls standing there without any customers. Breaks my heart. Why don't we give Ted a package of them for a birthday present?"

The idea was fatally appealing. In just minutes we had rounded up nearly a dozen with the promise, "Only talkee, talkee. No fukkie, fukkie." Over the months we had built up a certain credibility there and since business was lousy and we appeared to be sober, this assurance was accepted. Hans, the shrewd businessman, negotiated the group buy-out fee and individual payments to each. Within half an hour we had herded our covey into taxis and were winding up the Peak Road to Uncle Ted's flat.

Two of us stood at the door of his twelfth floor apartment when his sleepy amah responded. We greeted her by name and she let us in after a yawning protest that master he go sleepee. Then she disappeared into her servant's quarters at the back. We motioned the others in from the fire escape landing where they had been waiting, and slipped silently into the living room. Mickey, who visited frequently, brought out a fifth of Ted's expensive Black Label and pressed full glasses on our visitors with soothing assurances, "Good for you...."

Being somewhat nervous, the girls tossed them down. Another round seemed to make them more comfortable. Then just before opening Ted's bedroom door, Mickey told them to strip naked.

It was touch and go there for a while. Had there been transport back into town the girls would have no doubt fled. Finally, with classic Chinese finesse–and after a second bottle of Scotch–a compromise was reached. Some would strip naked for an additional "special service" payment. The others would go along, but insisted on keeping on their panties. For our part, we reiterated assurances that this was all a velly funny birthday plesent and no one would be molested–let alone raped. Ted's bedroom door was gently opened and naked girls, now giggling with excitement, crept in. We flicked on the light.

What followed was more than we could ever have imagined. As we watched from inside the door this mini hoard of harpies, apparently overcome by a mass hysteria, swooped down screaming onto Uncle Ted. Before he realized what was happening they had swarmed into his double bed alongside of him, on top of him, and probably even under him. He let out the loudest roar of terror I have ever heard. Then he struggled to throw the girls off, or at least escape.

But his six-foot frame had acquired too much fat and soon lay helpless as they stripped off his pajamas in a feeding frenzy, shouting gleefully in their local dialects. Ted was soon submerged under an undulating tangle of naked thighs, breasts, buttocks, and other body parts. Their enthusiasm grew as they became carried away with this novel game. The more daring were soon exploring Ted's body as he doubled up trying to escape grasping hands.

It was soon apparent that some of the girls had themselves become worked up. They jumped off the bed and ran over to us. I was amazed how stimulating naked young bodies wriggling against a suit can be. One girl apparently knew Hans and they slipped out into another bedroom. Before long others had paired up and disappeared.

There were birthday presents aplenty that night for nearly everyone except the intended recipient. Uncle Ted regretfully did not share in the evening's happy finale and it took weeks for our warm camaraderie to return.

Nina and I are Attacked on Repulse Bay

Mickey often led us into games at our weekend parties. The participants ebbed and flowed around our hard core of liar's dice players and our dates, and each evening's activities depended, naturally, on how long we had been drinking and the enthusiasm of our partners. These were usually American, English and Eurasian employees of our companies, consulates and hospitals. Some were married couples. Others, married women with husbands out of town. Some of the single ladies were looking for a husband. All wanted a good time.

One Saturday night after the usual drinks at the American Club we assembled at Lee's apartment overlooking Repulse Bay. His amah had prepared a table load of trays loaded with "small chow" snacks on which twenty or so of us were gorging between drinks.

At that time I was dating a Dutch woman named Nina, who was as usual surrounded by eager men. She was slightly younger than I, blond and blue-eyed with a strong resemblance to Marilyn Monroe. I had met Nina some weeks earlier when Winny, my boss' wife, had brought us together at a Dutch gathering. My initial impression of sweet innocence on her lovely face was shattered by a knowing, seductive smile and a soft, "Allo, John." This woman simply radiated sex.

From her appearance it did not seem possible that just a few years earlier Nina was suffering the worst kind of hell in a Japanese concentration camp in Java. For month after month the teen age girl had been ravaged and bullied by a hoard of brutish Japanese army captors. Her striking beauty and youth had made her the target of every sadistic act that her cruel captors could inflict on her. She had lost everything a woman could lose–except her determination to survive. While her fellow internees were being starved and beaten to death, she was able to scrounge enough food to stay alive.

But tonight it seemed that Nina had forgotten those horrors. She joined in enthusiastically as Lee's party continued until late. It was well after midnight when we noisily tromped out.

Nina and I headed for my car. Then, as we passed the darkened, deserted beach, she announced, "I want to swim." It seemed like the right thing to do, so we stripped in the dim moonlight and leapt, shouting and laughing, into the warm water of Repulse Bay. Of course things didn't stop there and soon we were sprawled on the wet sand, feet splashing in the wavelets.

All went well and after a while we broke for a rest. Then, as we were about to have an encore, I became conscious of sharp bites along my flanks and thighs. Nina's angry Dutch exclamations indicated that she was under attack as well. We decided to get the hell out of there. It took several minutes to find our sandy clothes, which stuck to our wet bodies as we struggled to pull them on. We were scratching furiously by the time we returned to the car.

In her hotel room we discovered that our legs were covered with angry red welts. Fortunately these had subsided a bit by morning. We never did learn what had bitten us, but we did find that a bed made a far better playground than a wet beach.

The Guys and Dolls Mint Julep Gala

Mickey will always be remembered for his inspirational gift of enriching our evenings with brilliant sporting ideas. But not all happy events were spawned by him, and probably the most memorable of all was held right at my house.

I had recently moved from the Foreign Correspondent' Club into a 14-room mansion on the Peak that Pat arranged for me to occupy until he received his exit visa from Shanghai. This was one of Hong Kong's great show places, with white marble floors and circular staircases, elaborate reception rooms, and a long verandah fronted by tall white columns over a sweeping lawn. In many ways it resembled Tara in the movie "Gone with the Wind."

One early summer Sunday, after I had settled in and learned the names of the five domestics on the house staff, I had a visit from an old

Shanghai friend. This was Ace Smith, proprietor of a liquor and club supplies business with offices in Hong Kong and Okinawa.

Ace was some fifteen years my senior and was well connected with business and diplomatic leaders. He was a prominent member of the exclusive racing set and owned several horses. Once, in Shanghai, Big Louie had told me that he was a senior CIA officer. When I asked, he merely laughed, "Johnny, every American here is rumored to be a spook–half of your friends think you are right now."

Ace–unchanged from Shanghai–stood well over six feet of solid athletic build. His weathered face was crowned by a full head of sandy hair which tended to be unruly. He spoke in a lazy relaxed manner with a trace of Dixie coming through now and then.

We toured the interior rooms, then walked across the lawn commenting on the spectacular view of the harbor far below. Ace turned toward the house and gazed up at the tall white columns. After a few moments he mused, "My old mammy would have really loved this...so much like home in Virginia." His mother was said to have been a congresswoman from the South. Ace inhaled deeply and smiled, "I can smell the magnolia blossoms...yes, and mint juleps–tall frosted glasses garnished with sprigs of fresh mint...crisply uniformed attendants passing silver trays among our fashionable guests right here in the garden...soft music..."

"You sound like you've already had some of those juleps."

The dreamy look disappeared. Suddenly he was all business. He swung around to me and said, "Johnny, it was meant to be–mint juleps on this lawn. And it just happens that last week I was able to pick up a consignment of the perfect bourbon from a distress sale in Okinawa. Twelve-year-old Maker's Mark, which the good Lord created just for mint juleps." He beamed, hair waving in the breeze. "There's plenty of mint. And Loopy Wong–that old bartender at the club–makes a flawless julep. I know," he chuckled. "I taught him."

"I'm sure Pat wouldn't mind our using this place," I offered, intrigued. "At least if Wimpy comes."

Ace laughed, "Free drinks? Of course he will."

Preparations were easily managed, with logistics delegated largely to clerks at Ace's organization. Loopy Wang would bring some American Club bartenders to help him prepare hundreds of juleps, and the experienced house staff would serve.

Now we needed a theme to set our party off from the countless others given every month. The answer came out of America. Suddenly Hong Kong's foreign community was swept by hit tunes from the Broadway production of *Guys and Dolls*. Here was the peg to hang our party on. The next day Ace produced one of very few long playing records available. "A Pan Am stew brought it over for me," he said. Soon we were humming, "I've got the horse right here"–and the Guys and Dolls Mint Julep Gala was born.

Nearly a hundred Americans, Europeans, and wealthy Chinese accepted. By late afternoon of the Gala, the Peak roads around the house were clogged with everything from chauffer-driven Rolls Royces to little Mini Minors. My list produced a mostly younger group from the American Club, journalists at the Correspondents' Club, and business associates I had come to know in the multinational trading and shipping companies. Most of the men were single party animals who brought attractive dates. From my company came the MacCorkindales, Johnny Mears - and of course, Wimpy and Winnie.

The guests invited by Ace tended to be more senior, some with titles like "sir" and "the honorable." These included officers from our Consulate General, diplomats of other countries, Hong Kong government officials, Chinese tycoons, company directors, stewards of the Royal Hong Kong Jockey Club, and other members of the elite who ran the colony.

As they came in, the guests were pleasantly surprised. At the door, welcoming them to the music of Guys and Dolls thundering from speakers throughout the house and garden, was Hong Kong's champion Australian jockey Billy Marshall, crop in hand, dressed in his famous orange and green racing colors. He greeted several by name. His winning betting tips were parceled out to only a favored few. Rumor was that he always received full value of one kind or another from the recipients, who ranged from Hong Kong billionaires and international gamblers to beautiful actresses.

Each guest was immediately handed an icy frosted julep containing two full ounces of Kentucky's finest. Not being accustomed to this delicious, but sneaky, Southern drink, many were soon sipping their second tall glass. The effect was spectacular.

The first indications that this would not be your typical run-of-the-mill garden party came just before sunset when a prominent French couple, formally dressed in dinner jacket and gown for a late-evening ball, toppled screaming over the low garden wall into a vegetable bed below. Fortunately they landed in soft mud and strong hands hauled them back up. The rescuers recoiled as the soggy brown-stained lady tried to embrace them.

Then a distinguished English judge, known for sleeping at his bench after a lunch of red wine, lurched into a designer-clothed Chinese lady and unloaded his icy julep down her neck. Her frightened shriek attracted her shipping tycoon husband who rushed up and angrily smacked His Worship in the face.

The festivity progressed into a noisy bacchanal. Everyone seemed to be shouting at once. Some danced on the lawn to the music. Others stood embracing or collapsed in each other's arms. Those with empty glasses wandered after waiters who carried trays of frosted juleps. Here and there arguments broke out. A group of young sports shouting "Nathan, Nathan Detroit" pranced across the lawn banging into everyone. They collided with a pair of US Marine guards, made the mistake of telling them to get stuffed, and were soon rolling on the grass.

Darkness settled in and the party raged on with no indication that the guests would leave by the accepted departure time of nine. In a usually respectable garden party setting, some very improper behavior was going on. Wives slipped away into shadowy corners to embrace other husbands–or younger men like Mickey. Husbands found plenty to occupy them among single girls looking for excitement, and perhaps more. Around me more and more of the guests wore disheveled clothes and smudged lipstick.

Two girls walked by, giggling, and I caught the words "... he was super–and I don't even know who he was..."

Ace and I cut off the drinks before our bacchanal degenerated into a full-blown orgy. By then most of the diplomats and businessmen had walked, or been helped, to waiting limousines, leaving us with a younger hard core. Some of these lay crumpled peacefully on the grass–suits hanging loose and colorful party dresses bunched to the hips. Others, in various stages of drunkenness, stalked around the garden in groups looking for drinks.

The staff and I were challenged by couples trying to slip upstairs to bedrooms. I had just enough sense left not to permit this in Pat's house.

And all the while our record played, and off-tune voices continued to bellow out "I've got the horse..."

By midnight we had finally eased out the last of the live partygoers, calling taxis to send them home. The not-so-live guests lay where they had settled on the grass. They rested peacefully thorough the night and probably had the mildest hangovers of all. Many were still asleep the next morning when the staff collected articles of clothing strewn about the garden.

The Guys and Dolls Mint Julep Gala would be talked about for weeks and even acquired a certain degree of prominence–or perhaps notoriety–in the annals of Hong Kong party giving.

The definitive comment was uttered by Ace when he stopped by to collect his few remaining bottles of bourbon. Leaning back in a reclining chair with a frosted julep in hand and a seraphic grin on his face, he announced, "That, Johnny, was one hell of a party!

Life Seven: Voyage to the South Seas 1951

The *Laurie Pattison:* Ship and Crew

She was an ordinary little tramp steamer, built in 1902 at Connells Shipyard on the Clyde in Glasgow. For nearly fifty years she had been moving cargoes of every kind between ports all over the world. When Pat entered negotiations with her owner, the rusty old lady was nearing the end of a long career, lying at anchor off Bristol waiting for a buyer–or the scrap yard.

Pat, unable to leave Shanghai, bought her sight unseen and named her *Laurie Pattison* after his mother. Then, with his uncanny business acumen, he recovered the entire purchase cost on just her first voyage.

At that time, when I was still in Shanghai, no ship owners would consider running freight to Shanghai through the dangerous blockade by KMT Nationalist Chinese warships cruising off the Yangtze River. The closest port of discharge they offered was Hong Kong. Yet in face of this, Pat instructed his British agents to issue through bills of lading for a sailing direct to Shanghai.

Shippers in England fought for space, and the *Laurie* was fully laden with eleven hundred tons of cargo, booked at exorbitant freight rates, when she left Liverpool for the Far East. Freshly painted on her funnel was the flag of the Pattison Lines: a bold red "P" on a white background bordered on each side by a Navy blue stripe with two white stars.

This voyage was the first stage of an enterprise which Pat had been planning for years–to organize a fleet of coastal vessels that would run between Pattison branches in China, Hong Kong, Korea, Japan and Taiwan. Their shipping staffs were already handling the round-the-world Isbrandtsen vessels that passed through every fortnight. They were capable of taking on other ships as well. In time, Pat hoped to see

Pattison-flagged vessels crisscrossing the Far East carrying his cargoes to ports ranging from Inchon to Balikpapan.

Soon after she sailed it became apparent that the *Laurie* was not built for speed. Racing at her maximum six knots, she might have kept pace with Columbus' *Santa Maria* if things had gone well. But they didn't. Her engine failed just after she entered the Mediterranean, costing several days for repairs in Gibraltar.

She broke down again in the Suez Canal, nearly blocking the busy passage. This idled the ship for two weeks in Port Sudan where her iron hull roasted in that equatorial hell. The entire ship's complement moved up on deck. The engineers making repairs could remain below for only minutes at a time, since the blowers were not working and even the jerry-built canvas wind scoops could only send puffs of more hot air down the ventilator shafts.

The worst problems laid her up for a full a month in Singapore. Critical engine parts could not be patched and needed replacing. Some had not been manufactured for years and had to be reconstructed in a Singapore foundry. By the time the *Laurie* was ready to leave, news had arrived of the attack on the *Flying Arrow*.

The crew rebelled and refused to sail to Shanghai despite the best effort of their Captain Ian MacGregor. But Pat, in character, had protected his company against such a development. The bills of lading contained a clause permitting discharge at the nearest free port at the discretion of the captain. The *Laurie* dropped off her cargo at the Kowloon Docks in Hong Kong, fulfilling the contracts with the shippers.

Here, under the close supervision of shipping veterans MacCorkindale and Captain MacGregor, the ship was thoroughly surveyed, repaired, refitted and made ready for sea. John Means booked several hundred tons of cargo and she left for Kobe.

An Unexpected Assignment

I became acquainted with the *Laurie* several months after arriving in Hong Kong. By then the old lady had been in the Far East for several months, barely covering operating costs by shuttling low-value cargoes around the China Sea. She was lying at anchor in port one day waiting for a cargo when Wimpy called me in. He was shaking his head, feigning puzzlement. "Why? Why he gives this to you?"

Then he sighed, "Pat says you must have a holiday. A nice ocean voyage."

Through an old connection in Malaya, Pat had booked nearly a full cargo of RSS-3 rubber from Singapore to Hong Kong at a good freight rate. He was sending the *Laurie* to bring it back and had instructed Wimpy to arrange for me to go as "Owner's Representative."

Owner's representative? I didn't even know what an owner's representative was. But not for a moment did I question Pat's wisdom in picking me over others with more experience. Quickly I tied up pending office work and prepared for the trip – buying summer clothes and, among other things, a copy of Hughes' *Handbook of Admiralty Law*. Back in Shanghai Pat had suggested that I become familiar with its contents. The voyage ahead should give me time to go through its 531 pages.

Outward Passage

When I climbed the *Laurie's* gangway I left Hong Kong–and entered a new world full of surprises.

The transition was easy thanks to the warm welcome aboard by Ian MacGregor. The captain was truly unforgettable–short, with a craggy face, full head of unkempt brown hair that belied his age, and a brusque, authoritative manner. His forceful personality distracted attention from a wooden leg showing below his khaki shorts. Despite this handicap, when he led me to my cabin he stepped easily over the foot-high bulkheads protecting the midships section from seawater that could surge across the main deck. I put my suitcase on the bunk and followed Ian to meet the other officers.

There were two. The Chief Engineer was an Englishman named Bobby Jones. He was tall, balding, cadaverously thin and the most harried looking man I had ever met. All the way over from Liverpool, Bobby had shouldered the responsibility of keeping the ship running–often making repairs in turbulent seas while the tossing ship banged him up against a hundred sharp metal objects in the engine room.

He still had the scars. He would glance toward the engine room and growl, "If I knew what a bloody disaster was down there I'd a stayed home drawin' me pension." The fact that Bobby had been able to keep the old ship running was, as Captain Ian would say, "A fawkin' miracle."

The other officer, Joe Strong, was an Anglo-Indian Eurasian. He was the only officer carried over from past service. Short and chubby, always relaxed and cheerful, the middle-aged First Mate was a storehouse of information. I would often listen to him while he recited stories from the ship's past when she was registered as *Maya Christina*. One afternoon he told a bloodcurdling tale of fighting off Indonesian pirates who boarded her in the Straits of Malacca, which I believed until I knew him better.

One story I did believe was how the captain lost his leg. I dropped careful hints to Ian but he refused to open up. Joe Strong was glad to. "He'll never show you his medals," Joe said. "But he has plenty of 'em."

Ian MacGregor had joined the British merchant marine at the start of WWII and spent the next four years aboard freighters. He survived seven North Atlantic crossings on the Murmansk run despite having two ships torpedoed and sunk from under him. He had been promoted to captain when he made his last voyage.

His convoy had fought past several U-boat wolf packs and was off Norway nearing the end of the run, when a squadron of low-flying Nazi Heinkles attacked and killed the front deck gun crew with machine gun fire. Reacting with fury, Captain MacGregor rushed down from his bridge, manned the idle brace of Bofors 20mm guns and fired at the next approaching plane. By a near miracle he connected. But he didn't see the bomber splash. Before it hit the sea, bullets from another plane had riddled his body and he had lost consciousness.

Later, at his trial for deserting his post on the bridge, he was exonerated. But one mangled leg could not be salvaged.

These three, the captain and his two officers, were the only Europeans. The rest of the crew was a medley of Chinese, Malays and a few Lascar stokers in the black gang who shoveled coal into the steam boiler down below.

They did their job well. By evening Hong Kong's Lyemun Pass had dropped from sight and we were crossing the Pearl River estuary, off Macau, headed into the South China Sea. I had grown used to the lulling throb of the engine, and the gentle pitching of the vessel brought back happy memories of other voyages. I leaned over the iron rail watching the muddy spume drift past. The water seemed close enough to scoop up, although I knew that our freeboard was a full four feet.

Earlier, before we weighed anchor, Joe Strong had walked me around the ship. I noted that her brightly painted colors reflected those of Pat's flag: white over the entire three island superstructure, Navy blue covering the hull and funnel, and Chinese red for the bold word PATTISON displayed in yard high letters across each side.

The main housing amidships rose two levels above the deck to the navigation bridge at the top. There was a long cargo hold forward and another aft, secured with hatches. Alongside each stood a mast and boom from which cables reached down to a steam-powered winch.

Aware of the engine's questionable performance record, I made a point of locating the lifeboats. I could find only one hanging from davits at the stern. When I asked Joe Strong where the others were, he shrugged, "Never needed another. Just use this one to get about in the harbor."

I found Captain MacGregor at his usual station on the bridge. He was sitting at the chart table giving directions to a young Chinese helmsmen standing at the wheel. He noticed me, nodded, and said, "I'm breaking him in. Signed him on in Hong Kong. He's good but needs seasoning.

"Come over here. I'll show you where you're going." He tapped a line on the hydrographic chart spread out before him. "This is our course. Southerly until we round French Indochina then down the coast of Malaya, past Singapore island. Then northward through the Straits of Malacca to Penang. We'll discharge our cargo there." I nodded. I had helped book that six hundred tons.

"How long do you think the trip will take?" I asked.

"Depends. Depends on the cargo handling. Don't expect any trouble with the engine so it shouldn't be much over four weeks."

After a few more instructions to the helmsman he showed me around the bridge. It reminded me of a maritime museum. The navigation instruments were obviously old. It seemed like they had been here since the ship was launched–and some might well have been.

I was drawn to the binnacle mounted just forward of the wheel. The compass rose in its center was decorated with designs of mermaids and whales often seen on old charts. This must be a collector's item. A Seth Thomas chronometer and matching barometer also looked like antiques. Everything was carefully maintained and the brass was polished to a mirror finish on these, the engine room telegraph and speaking tube, and all the other instruments. The only modern instruments I could see here were the radio and radar.

The Old Three Banger

A few days after sailing, near the coast off Malaya, my first excitement occurred. Earlier that morning Joe Strong and I had been amusing ourselves watching sharks attack chunks of jettisoned refuse a few yards off the rail. Now I was back in my chair trying to focus on Hughes' *Provisions as to Risks and Perils*. It was hard to concentrate, sitting there in the shade with the warm sea breeze in my face.

My reading was interrupted by an unusual sound from down below–a muffled boom followed by a loud shrieking hiss. Then, terrifyingly, gushers of steam poured out of the engine room ventilators around me. Survival instinct took over and I dashed toward the stern determined not to be crowded out of that lifeboat with all those sharks around.

I passed some crew members squatting on the deck working on something or another. Seeing me rush by, they looked at each other, laughing. What the hell was wrong with them? I thought. The boiler must have exploded and the hold is probably half flooded already.

Still, I hesitated. No one else had appeared. Either they were all deaf and blind or this explosion wasn't any big deal.

Captain MacGegor, obviously amused, set me straight. The boiler was perfectly fine. It had not exploded; it was just the condenser blowing again, releasing high-pressure steam. Of course this looked bad and made a noise, but it was not serious.

Later Bobby Jones showed me what had happened. I followed him down two tiers of iron ladders into the sweltering heat of the engine room. Two stokers, soot-blackened and stripped to their shorts, were shoveling coal from a bunker into the furnace fire doors. Their sweating bodies glowed red in the hot light that shined out from the incandescent beds of coal. They seemed to be automatons, working in a trance, and did not notice us.

Bobby led me to the ship's power plant–a massive iron monster that towered over me. Three huge cylinders ran along the twelve-foot side, their pistons swooshing rapidly up and down in three–foot strokes as they turned the heavy crankshaft underneath. Bobby snorted, "This is the bugger that made all the trouble comin' out. Won't play games any more–we fixed her good in Hong Kong."

An expression resembling fondness crossed his face. "Johnny, you're lookin' at a grand old relic from the last century, built in the '90s. Not many of these three bangers still runnin' today. Scottish, of course, built by Lamont."

With my senses under assault from the engine room noises, heat and smells, I strained to understand as Bobby lapsed into marine engineer's lingo. This power plant, he explained, was technically known as a triple expansion reciprocating steam engine.

And over there, Bobby pointed, was where my "boiler explosion" that had sent me scurrying for the lifeboat took place. It was no more than the rupturing of an expansion joint at a condenser. "They blow quite often," Bobby said casually. "We fix them in half an hour."

Shipboard Amenities

During the next days, as we crawled down the Malayan coast, I learned about shipboard living *Laurie* style. We had none of the amenities of passenger liners–not even a simple movie projector–so eating was the main diversion. Meals were prepared by a Hong Kong cook who did a fine job with the available resources.

When we left port everything perishable was stowed in a large wooden icebox. The ice was in large blocks and kept the food fresh until we entered the tropics and temperature climbed into the 90's. At that point it melted quickly and our menus changed.

Fresh vegetables and fruits gave way to mulligatawny soup, heavily spiced with curry powder. Curry powder was also used on eggs–possibly giving birth to our deviled eggs *hors d'oeuvre*. Meats like beef and lamb spoiled quickly but we continued eating steaks and chops by covering them with that essential shipboard staple, A-1 Sauce, to disguise the smell.

Now and then our diet was varied with fresh flying fish that took to the air to escape larger predators. The unlucky ones landed on the deck, and were delicious.

Despite long hours of boredom, little hard liquor was served at sea. We did, however, drink the finest European beers, taken on board duty-free as ships' stores. My companions, being good Brits, savored it warm; I tried to cool mine by dragging the bottles on strings over the side, but lost most of them. The sea was too warm to do much cooling, anyway, so I finally gave up and drank mine warm like a good Brit, too.

The three officers and I usually ate together at a table in the "officers' mess." This was a cramped cabin with a simple wood table and chairs. Dinner was one occasion when Captain MacGregor exerted his authority: no matter how much we were sweating, he insisted that we wear a shirt. Joe Strong led the conversation, usually basic shipboard chatter and comments about the news. This came from the BBC, which was the only station we could always receive on the scratchy radio in the mess.

Our listening highlight was a wildly successful English program, "*Much-Binding-in-the-Marsh.*" I first heard this at dinner the first night out. It sounded like a bunch of crazy drunks screaming and cackling in English accents that I couldn't understand.

When I asked what the hell was going on, Joe exclaimed: "You mean you don't know *Much-Bindin*? Good God, lad, where were you brought up? This is what holds the empire together!" Joe went on to describe the program as an irreverent spoof on a bunch of WWII RAF types. Most people loved it; the rest wanted it banned. Before long, when I could understand what its characters were saying, I became just as addicted as the others. Years later I learned that this and *The Goon Show* launched the school of alternative British humor featuring Peter Sellers, Spike Mulligan, John Cleese and the Monty Python gang.

I Become a Shellback

On the ninth day out we passed several islands to the starboard. They were inviting, with lush green vegetation piled up above shining white sand and coral beaches. The next morning we rounded the flat shoreline of Singapore island, only fifty miles north of the equator. Just before noon one of the crew gave me the message that the captain wanted to see me on the forward deck. When I arrived I found all three officers lined up waiting for me. They wore strange paper hats, the Captain's resembling a crown. On the deck before them was a large water barrel.

The Captain greeted me solemnly. "Pollywog Potter," he intoned. "You and all other Pollywogs are poor creatures who have never crossed the equator. Pollywogs are soft and weak. On the other hand, sailors who have crossed the equator and received the ceremony become Shellbacks. Shellbacks are strong and bold. We shall not cross the equator on this voyage and you should remain a Pollywog. However, King Neptune has taken pity on you and has given me special dispensation to initiate you into the order of the Shellback."

He nodded to Joe Strong, who dipped a bucket into the barrel. Wide grins broke out as Joe dumped gallons of seawater over my head. "Welcome aboard, Shellback Potter!" they laughed.

At this, the captain unrolled a wide scroll and read its message:

> K*now all ye by these presents that I, Neptunus Rex, Imperius Ultimus over All the Seas, doth hereby decree that Shellback Potter, in compliance with ye olde Traditions, hath been ceremoniously inspected and initiated aboard ye grande shippe* Laurie Pattison, *and so possesses my blessing and protection to travel freely the seas and to pass unaccosted the Equator.*
>
> *By order of his humble servant,*
> *Ian MacGregor, Captain*

I treasured this hand-scribbled certificate.

For the next two days we crawled northward through the Straits of Malacca, the busy shipping lane that separates Sumatra from Malaysia. We were usually in sight of land, flat and low on the horizon. Sometimes we passed close enough to recognize stands of coconut palms and rubber trees. The sea was smooth, shimmering under the equatorial sun. There was no breeze.

Our only relief from the daytime stifling heat came in the afternoon, when for a few blissful minutes a deluge of tropical rain hammered down on us. The downpour was so heavy that from the bridge we could no longer see the ship's bow. Then the sun came out and sweltering heat enveloped us again.

It did cool a little at night and we would stand on the stern gazing at the green-blue trail in our wake. In these tropical waters the phosphorescence seemed bright enough to read by. On all sides small explosions of color marked the splashing of fish. Our world out there was peaceful and silent, barely disturbed by the gentle prop wash and the muffled engine.

Penang Island

Two weeks after leaving Hong Kong we anchored in the Penang roads, the three-mile-wide strait separating Penang island from Malaya. Within minutes bum boats appeared with fresh papayas, mangoes, pineapples, bananas and other tropical fruits and vegetables. Joe had his moment of glory battling the vendors. "Thievin' barstads," he would shout at them as he drove down prices with tactics learned in long experience.

A few hours later lighters came alongside to offload our Hong Kong cargo. To the rumble and shrieking of the steam winches, and shouts from the laborers on deck and down below, rope slings containing cases and bales were hoisted out of the holds, swung over the sides and set down into the lighters. As they filled up, tugs pulled them away and brought up empty barges. Joe supervised the operation to insure an accurate accounting.

With the cargo discharge in experienced hands, Captain MacGregor suggested that we go ashore. "The agent couldn't come aboard because he was out of town," he said. "We'll meet him in his office later this afternoon. Except for this, there is really very little to do here, but you might find the snake temple and crocodile farm interesting. And of course we'll have a drink at the E&O."

This was the first (and I hoped the only) time that I used the lifeboat. Ten minutes later we stepped ashore on a jetty so old that the cobblestones were worn smooth. The captain hailed a pre-war taxi. "You go snake temple," he instructed. "You understand? Snake temple." The old Chinese driver nodded and we set off.

Honking furiously, he maneuvered through a tangle of narrow lanes, dodging bicycles, carts, rickshaws, scampering naked children, animals and even other cars now and then. On both sides a wall of ancient whitewashed storefronts, grey with time, pressed in. None were higher than three stories, and all very old. Penang had been fast asleep for years–and still had not awakened into the modern world.

After more traffic dodging we reached our destination. This turned out to be a typical Chinese Buddhist structure with red roof tiles and walls and a few saffron-clad monks sitting in front. At the doorway I was struck by the pungent smell of incense, which intensified inside. It was dark, the only light coming from candles. After a moment I could make out some dim figures which appeared to be statues of Buddhist deities. Then I saw the source of the suffocating aroma-row after row of incense sticks planted around an altar. Some were three feet long and they were all belching out clouds of cloying smoke into the confined space. But where, I wondered, where were the famous snakes?

As my eyes adjusted to the gloom, they began to appear. We had been told to expect cobras and pit vipers, but I couldn't make out any details. They were all around us, curled up on altars and draped over statues. Not one of them moved. They all seemed to be in a stupor. I wondered why. Then I realized that if I had to spend my life breathing that damned incense, I'd probably be in a stupor, too.

After this less than memorable event we skipped the crocodile farm and went straight to the E&O. Now here was something worth visiting. The European & Oriental Hotel had opened in 1885 and was soon famous as one of the great hotels of the British Empire. Over the years its guest list became a who's who of the world's celebrities: Noel Coward, Rudyard Kipling, Somerset Maugham, Douglas Fairbanks and most of the rich and famous that visited this part of Asia. Seeing these big names, I remarked to Mac, "Don't you think we belong here, too?"

"Of course," he chuckled, so we added our names to the register.

We enjoyed a whisky soda and a smoke. Then Mac glanced at his watch and stood up. "The agent should be in now. Are you ready to go?"

His name was Kwok and his office a typical Chinese *hong* opening onto a crowded street in Penang's business district. As soon as we entered he excitedly asked the captain if our ship had space for some Hong Kong cargo.

I watched Mac, curious how he would respond. Instead he turned to me. "You're the owner's representative. This is your pidgin."

With a shock I realized he was right. Mr. Kwok spoke fair English and described the cargo as fifteen hundred bales of firewood. The shipper urgently needed an on–board bill of lading to meet terms of a letter of credit. Knowing that we had a full cargo waiting in Singapore, I asked if shipment as deck cargo would be acceptable. It was, and Mac confirmed that this deck cargo would not interfere with the loading of rubber later.

At this, Mr. Kwok sent a messenger who returned a few minutes later with the shipper, a Mr. Cheung. Negotiating a good freight was easy since he was under time pressure and we seemed to be the only vessel offering prompt sailing to Hong Kong. I demanded the full conference rate, no discounts. After the expected haggling, I shaved it slightly to give him face.

Mr. Cheung's company maintained an account with the Hong Kong & Shanghai Bank's Penang branch, which was nearby. It took only a few minutes for their manager to transfer the freight payment, in Malayan *ringgits*, from Mr. Cheung's account to one that Pattison had opened here. Then, using my power of attorney from Pat, I transferred 5% of this payment to Mr. Kwok for his booking commission. He had already received another 2½% inward freight commission for handling our cargo from Hong Kong, and was understandably quite pleased.

At Mac's request Mr. Kwok telexed the Singapore agent that our ETA would be delayed one day, and arranged for the firewood loading to start the next morning. Then we telexed the news to Wimpy, who would copy it to Shanghai for Pat, and returned to the ship.

Later that afternoon Joe Strong, his duties for the day completed, asked me to have dinner with him ashore. I accepted and he took me to a Malay restaurant where I encountered an amazing assortment of dishes I had never heard of. The only word I recognized was "*satay.*"

There were bowls of rice, beef, mutton, fish, shellfish, chicken, and all sorts of vegetables (but never pork, Joe said, which was considered unclean in this Muslim nation). Everything was highly spiced with curry and chilies except for a sweet tapioca dessert in coconut milk called "*gula Malacca.*" Its delicious flavor more than compensated for the raging fire in my gullet from all those curries, chilies and other spices. A few bottles of Anchor beer helped, too.

The winches were again screeching at 6:00 the next morning, and by noon large areas of the fore and aft decks–but not the hatches–were buried under stacks of firewood. Each pile was covered with a strong cargo net anchored to deck cleats. For additional security heavy cables, also secured to cleats, were laid crisscrossing the cargo nets.

Joe carefully surveyed the work. "That'll hold," he announced confidently. "Not even water across the deck will loosen that lot. The empty lighters were towed away. We hoisted anchor, sounded one long "I am going forward" blast on the horn, and began to move, leaving behind a cloud of black smoke hanging in the air. Not much later the pilot climbed down onto his boat, and we were off to Singapore.

Singapore Island

Three days later the *Laurie* sailed past Palan Bukum island and hooked up to a buoy in the mooring zone near Sentosa. Our cargo for Hong Kong was already stacked in lighters awaiting our arrival. After the usual formalities with our agent and the authorities, our hatch covers came off and the winches began their work.

The cargo turned out to be bales of rubber strips shipped over from Malaya, partly processed after tapping from the tree by beating the sap into long sheets and smoking them. The designation RSS-3, I learned, meant ribbed smoked sheets grade three, the standard quality.

We were surprised again when our Singapore agent asked the captain if we could take some last minute cargo here. This time it was described as a small parcel of tropical fruit. Again Mac passed the buck to me, but he clearly was not enthusiastic. There was little space available, and only on deck. However, this parcel measured only a few tons, so I asked, "What kind of fruit?"

"Durian."

Mac snorted, "I knew it. No wonder no one will take it."

The agent persisted, "Shipper say he pay plenty. Two times conference freight."

"He damn well should. Durian!"

And so it went. Finally, Mac–obviously reluctant–asked Joe Strong, "Think you can make some space on the fantail? Up against the aft railing?"

The First Mate could. They both looked at me expectantly. That extra freight income determined my decision. "OK," I said. "If they'll pay that much."

During the next two days as the rubber was coming aboard I learned why Mac was adamant that stowage should be at the very back end of the ship. I also learned why durians have a singular place in Malayan life and folklore, where they are known by many as "The king of fruits." In appearance they resemble coconuts covered with long sharp spikes.

What gives durians their prominence is the unique qualities of their meat. This has an overpowering, nauseating smell that has been described as "a cross between stinking feet and human excrement." I soon confirmed this personally. Yet millions of people in Southeast Asia are addicted to durians and will pay handsomely to eat its fruit. To them, durians are aphrodisiacs and "a taste of its flesh sends them into ecstasies."

Humans are not the only addicts. A popular name for durians is "Tiger fruit," because tigers cannot resist them and cut their mouths on the spikes trying to crack the shell with their jaws. I was told of instances where tigers died from infected mouths as a result.

The cargo loading was Joe Strong's responsibility and he remained aboard while I went ashore with Mac and Bobby. This was my first trip to an island where, in a later life, I would live for many years with my full family. But on this trip we were visiting a newly established country which had only recently been an important hub in the British Empire.

Our first stop was a courtesy call for Bobby. A year earlier he had spent days at a marine foundry supervising the construction of replacement parts for the engine. Bobby took the time to thank those who had helped him.

Then we found our home ashore at the Raffles Hotel. This, like the E&O, was steeped in history. The Singapore Sling had been born here, and its long bar was also famous for its gimlets (with Rose's lime juice, of course) and pink gins (with Angostura bitters). Sitting there, we listened to accounts about life here in British colonial times and during the brutal Japanese occupation.

My favorite tale was how Somerset Maugham, sitting right where we were, was nearly beaten to death by an enraged English planter from Malaya. Maugham would pick up material for his stories at this bar by listening to conversations taking place around him. He overheard this planter tell a friend about an affair he was having with a Malayan woman. Then, in one of his stories, Maugham described the whole episode in accurate detail. The story was read by the planter's wife, who recognized her husband, and there went the marriage.

Defeated by Tiger Fruit

After three days the *Laurie* moved out on the return leg to Hong Kong. She was fully provisioned with fresh tropical foods, and her hold and decks were crammed with rubber, firewood and even a small pile of durians at the stern. No question about this being a profitable voyage.

For the first few days, as we steamed northeast up the Malay coast, the heat was moderated by a northerly breeze which strengthened that from the ship's motion. Then the wind shifted to a following breeze strong enough to carry forward across our deck. It did not take long for us to be aware of this. Up to then any odor from the durians had been blown back away from ship. This, of course, was the reason for stowing them at the extreme rear. Meanwhile, directly exposed to the tropic sun, the fruits had been ripening to the point where they emitted the full-bodied aroma for which they are famous. Now with the breeze flowing forward, the stench swept up across the decks, permeated the cabins to the last nook and even seeped down into the boiler room where the stokers toiled.

Feeling close to nausea, I discovered that the human body is simply not capable of co-existing with that durian miasma. Bobby Jones spoke for us all when he demanded, "When is this bloody wind going to turn around so we can get rid of that fookin' smell?"

But it didn't turn around. Finally, responding to unanimous demand, the captain swung the ship back into the wind to give us an hour of respite. We were just beginning to breathe normally when we returned to our course and our suffering resumed.

This unbearable stench continued for another day and was clearly affecting the efficiency of everyone aboard. The crew seemed on the point of mutiny when Mac called his officers and me to the bridge. "We all know that this ship's complement has gone through a bad two days," he said. "I have tolerated this hoping for a shift in the wind direction. However, as of thirty minutes ago the marine radio weather report indicated no change.

"Therefore," he continued bluntly. "By my authority as master of this vessel I am ordering the durian cargo to be jettisoned. Immediately. You are my witnesses."

The word was passed and in minutes the crew, jabbering in excitement, gathered at the stern. They lifted the durians carefully to avoid the spikes and, shouting with glee, flung every one of them overboard. I looked back and smiled with relief as I watched those stinking little green balls bouncing around in the wake all the way back to the horizon. The thought struck me: tigers try to eat them. Maybe our tiger sharks will, too.

There was no shortage of lively conversation at dinner that night. At the end Mac asked, "John, how're you coming with that admiralty book?"

"About half way through. It's heavy going."

"Do something for me, will you? See what you can find about penalties for ships' captains who jettison durians." We all roared with laughter.

Later, for the hell of it, I looked up the section on jettison in Hughes. After wading through a preamble in Latin I came to: "If, in a storm, a ship must be lightened in order to save...and part of the cargo is thrown overboard..." But at this point it became totally confusing. Besides, there was no storm.

I mentioned this to Mac the next morning. Looking at me with obvious approval, he said, "Ye'll do well, lad–just tried the wrong place. Now keep this to yourself, will ye? I would have dumped those damned fruits much earlier but first wanted a reading on our liability. So I radioed Wimpy to check with our underwriters. As soon as the reply came back I ordered the jettisoning."

"So we're covered."

"Not necessarily. But wouldn't you agree that the crew's welfare and morale is more important than the value of that smelly cargo?" No wonder he was so respected, I thought.

The Run Home

The final days of the trip went by quickly and soon we were passing the rocky islets marking the approach to Hong Kong. At my favorite spot on the bow I reviewed the events of the past weeks. How fortunate I was to have been given this opportunity by Pat. It seemed like every day brought new experiences and opportunities to learn, and I hoped that before long I would be able to use these for the benefit of my old friend confined in Shanghai.

I realized that I had established real bonds with my shipmates Mac, Joe and Bobby. If offered another chance to travel with them I would jump at it.

It was hard to accept the reality that tomorrow I would leave our heady shipboard environment and return to the plebian life of the Pollywogs. I smiled, anticipating the kind of remarks Wimpy was sure to make. But for all his boasting at the Parisian Grill about receiving full value, he would never understand how much my own life had been enriched by this unforgettable voyage.

Life Eight: Pattison South Korea 1951-1952

Goodbye, Hong Kong

Pattison's loyalty to his friends extended to Henry, a former star foreign correspondent. Like Pat, Henry enjoyed roaming Shanghai's rowdier watering holes. Their drinking bouts in bars along Shanghai's Blood Alley were legendary. Pat could handle huge quantities of alcohol without even a hangover. But Henry–like so many veteran journalists–deteriorated from the effect of so much alcohol. By the time of the Pearl Harbor attack he had become a pathetic parody of the brilliant correspondent he had been.

The war saved Henry from being fired. Like most Americans in Shanghai, including my father, he was interned in the *Pu Tung* prison camp where his physical condition worsened. After the Japanese surrender he was lucky, with Pat's help, to be employed by an American weekly. Their friendship continued in the booming post–war Shanghai, as did their visits to Blood Alley. During this time Pat added to his growing enterprises the Far East general agency for the Isbrandtsen Steamship Lines. This expansion led him to open new offices in Hong Kong, Korea and Japan. At each he recruited a staff of competent local nationals, headed by an experienced American or European. Except in Korea. Experience had taught him that it was particularly important to find a country manager there whom he could trust, but in that chaotic post-war environment none could be found. He would have to bring one in from outside.

At about this time Henry was fired by his newspaper and again turned to his old pal for a job. Pat had reservations, but because of the urgency, decided to take a chance. He felt that Henry could handle the job if he stayed sober. Henry agreed to stop drinking and joined Pat's experienced shipping managers for on-the-job training. He managed to stay sober throughout the two–month training session and took a ship to Pusan.

Despite this promising start, after two years in Korea's deadly environment Henry had become a drunken derelict. The staff did their jobs well, but without a competent leader things went wrong. Finally, after a blast from Isbrandtsen Pat knew he had to replace Henry, and remembering my handling of the Tsingtao crisis, picked me.

About that time I had just returned from my "pleasure cruise" on the *Laurie* and was looking forward to a normal life in Hong Kong. The last thing I expected–nor wanted–was another surprise assignment when Wimpy called me in and handed me a letter. I read, under the blue seal and letterhead of the Foreign Service of the United States and signed at our Consulate General in Hong Kong:

> TO WHOM IT MAY CONCERN:
> This is to certify that, in accordance with telegram No. ZX-35967 dated September 8, 1951, from the Supreme Commander for the Allied Powers, Tokyo, Japan, to this Consulate General, Mr. John Stauffer POTTER, Jr., bearer of valid American Passport No. 129547 issued at Washington, D.C. on November 18, 1947, has been granted clearance to enter Korea for an indefinite period.

Stunned, I looked at Wimpy. He was shaking his head slowly. "John," he said slowly. "I did not do this. I am not happy."

The most difficult part of leaving Hong Kong was to part from Cindy. I thought about leaving her at Pat's premises, where she would be pampered until I came back. But there were too many uncertainties. So I arranged for our next round-the-world freighter to carry Cindy to New York. Dad would take her to Pao Hai, their beautiful estate in Southampton. A few months later I learned that Cindy had endeared herself to my parents and was happily chasing clusters of birds around their acres of grassy lawn.

I Learn the Situation in South Korea

I knew nothing about Korea and before going there I wanted to find out what I would be getting into. So I crammed. After several days of reading and questioning a confusing, brutal picture developed. It had started with the Japanese surrender after WW II when the Soviets tried to take over the country. America stopped them at the 38th parallel, splitting the country roughly in two: the northern half a dictatorship under Russian puppet Kim Il-sung, and the southern half a democracy headed by President Syngman Rhee, supported by the UN.

This was the status quo until June 25, 1950. Then, without warning, eight seasoned divisions and an armored brigade of the North Korean army, spearheaded by tanks, smashed across the 38th parallel demarcation line and overwhelmed an unprepared South Korean defense and 500 supporting American advisors. In two months they powered their way 230 miles down the peninsula, conquering all of South Korea except a 50 by 100 mile enclave at the southeast tip. Here, along the "Pusan Perimeter", the defenders made a critical stand. Pusan was the only port where reinforcements could be landed in a race to build up defenses before superior forces drove them back in another Dunkirk. The first American reinforcements to arrive were units of the 24th and 25th infantry and 1st cavalry divisions from Japan, followed by combat teams from Okinawa and Hawaii and finally units of the powerful First Marines.

Despite many desperate battles the perimeter held until mid-September when MacArthur's bold Inchon landing behind the Communist line forced back the Pusan attackers. The marines retook the capital, Seoul, in ferocious fighting. Then, with the arrival of the 2nd and 3rd infantry divisions and other United Nations forces, the combined Inchon and Pusan forces drove a disintegrating North Korean army all the way to the Chinese border.

Warnings that the Chinese would come in were not taken seriously by MacArthur's HQ group in Tokyo. Then, in November over 300,000 troops of the regular Chinese army attacked. The brilliant fighting withdrawal from the Chosen Reservoir by the marines, and the 2nd division's heroic defense of Chipyong-ni, were just two of many actions that followed. Driven back across the 38th parallel, the UN forces were able to hold a line south of Seoul.

By March sufficient reinforcements had arrived for forces under the new UN commander, General Ridgeway, to recapture Seoul and most of the "Iron Triangle" battlefields to which American troops assigned such names as the Punchbowl, Bloody Ridge and Heartbreak Ridge. Here things stabilized for several weeks as General Ridgeway replaced MacArthur in Tokyo as overall commander and General Van Fleet took his place as UN commander.

In a final major attack, elements of twenty-one Chinese and nine North Korean divisions crossed the front. Through a series of short withdrawals to prepared positions General Ridgeway gained his objective of weakening the enemy's ability to fight by exploiting his most powerful weapons: massed barrages by artillery pre-positioned for "time-on-target" shelling and non-stop air strikes. Again and again Chinese "human wave" assaults were shredded by concentrated shelling and napalm bombing. Ridgeway's strategy of exchanging a few miles for many enemy lives worked.

In June, 1951 a cease-fire was proposed by the Soviets and truce talks began. No further full-front attacks took place and the fighting diminished to skirmishes and artillery duels. In a single year of fighting the North Koreans and Chinese had lost one and a half million soldiers–and gained nothing. It was not until July 23, 1953–long after I arrived–that the armistice was signed.

Good Morning, Korea

Carrying one suitcase, my passport with U.S. entry authorization, a power of attorney from Pattison and a book of travelers' checks, I descended from the Northwest Airlines flight into Pusan's mud and filth. It took me a good hour to elbow my way through the pushing, shouting mob, wearing a mix of American and Korean clothes and uniforms, that jammed the customs area. I was forcibly introduced to the pungent smell of *kimshi* -- old fermented cabbage with a powerful aroma. This seemed to be on everyone's breath.

I finally broke clear and was met by a delegation of three young Korean men neatly dressed in dark suits. They politely led me through a cold November drizzle to a pre-war Ford with driver. We squeezed in and set off down a crowded road, the driver playing chicken with a hodgepodge of military and civilian vehicles–all honking angrily–as he splashed across the sunken tracks. I held onto the jolting back seat and wondered what the hell am I doing here. Presently one of my escorts, apparently their spokesman, said, "Mr. Potter, we are happy you have come. We have been waiting for you. My name is Kim." He smiled, "You can call me 'Small Kim'. We have three Kims in our office. I am the shortest. Kim Number Two is the driver and you will meet 'Big Kim' in the office." Small Kim had the appearance of a teenager and spoke softly. Yet he conveyed an inner confidence that gave me reassurance that he could be depended on.

For the next half hour I was briefed–first cautiously, then eagerly–about the situation. I had known that things were not going well, but could not have imagined the state of chaos there. As details emerged, I felt like the new captain of a rudderless ship being swept against a reef.

We ran the gauntlet of Pusan traffic and out onto a long pier into the harbor designated Pier Two. Our trip ended alongside a small wooden building surrounded by trucks, cranes and all sorts of machinery run by gangs of Korean stevedores noisily unloading supplies from lighters alongside. U.S. military personnel moved about directing the flow of traffic. Although the fighting war was ostensibly halted by a cease-fire, "negotiations" continued and skirmishes broke out frequently.

Pattison's office consisted of two crowded rooms and a bathroom. There were two telephones: one was on the local system and worked part of the time; the second had been arranged by the American Military Sea Transportation Service (MSTS) for communications regarding the unloading of military cargo from the Isbrandtsen ships. This one worked all the time.

Pattison's staff of seven were all men, most in their twenties and well enough connected to avoid military service. They spoke and wrote English fairly well. Small Kim was their *de facto* leader, although no one had ever been delegated any authority. He introduced me to Big Kim (the third Kim), and to the other four: Cheung, Ho, Lee, and Yong. He then explained, smiling, "We have nearly all the Korean family names here. My name, Kim, is the most popular. It was originally Chinese and means gold."

My Heartbreaking Assignment

My first task–the most distasteful I ever experienced--was to fire Henry and get him out of the company house. The office and old company car were no problem, since Henry never left home. But the house was another matter. Although old and badly maintained, it was one of very few Western style structures here. The driver dropped me off and I was led upstairs by an old crone to a bedroom. Here I met Henry.

The elderly man with thinning white hair was sprawled on a bed, wrapped in a Korean gown. He peered at me, frowning, them mumbled, "Who are you? What are you doing here?"

The many instructions from Pattison had made no impression on his alcohol-soaked mind. This gentle old man had lost contact with reality. For hours I tried to explain my reason for coming. Usually he could not talk coherently. At other times, slurring his words, he would insist that Pat had never sacked him, there was a mistake. Again and again he would plead with tears running down his drawn face for "the milk of human kindness." I tried to reason with the pitiful fellow, my heart rebelling against this task. But he would not leave.

Unable to move into the company house as I had hoped, I returned to the office. Small Kim had anticipated the outcome of my visit and arranged a temporary place for me in the cleanest available hotel. There was no legal system in place for eviction during those chaotic times, and in any case neither Pat nor I would have considered force. So I rented three rooms in a wooden firetrap near our office and moved in with my suitcase.

Small Kim arranged a kerosene heater and an illegal phone connection. Then he miraculously produced a housemaid who had worked for an American family before the war and remembered a few words of English. Her previous employers had trained her well, and she set about industriously cleaning my apartment. The first meal at my Korean home consisted of the several tins of food that I had brought from Hong Kong and eggs boiled in their shells. There was little else available locally, she explained, since most of the food at the stalls along the alleys was unsafe for foreigners.

Happily our *Flying Enterprise* put into port and for several days I feasted on American food with Kurt Carlson and other friends among the ship's officers. When I went ashore they loaded me up with enough meat, vegetables and fruits to last until our next vessel came in. This arrangement provided my meals until I arranged access to military commissary facilities.

The company car and driver gave me transportation when I needed it. This was infrequently, since I worked 12 to 14 hours per day whittling at a huge backlog of unfinished business and getting the office organized. I was greatly helped by a bilingual former accountant who could take dictation–possibly the only such person available in Pusan. He was an emaciated old man named Park who Small Kim found and brought in after a heroic search.

Unfortunately Park was racked with TB and would not be able to live much longer unless he received treatment with the miracle drug PAS. To be effective large doses had to be taken every day, but there was not one pill available in all of Korea. I contacted Wimpy and soon our Hong Kong office had located a supplier. From then on several cases of pills were sent on our ships every month, saving Park's life and gaining a valuable and loyal asset.

Organizing Assets for Growth

Pattison's office work was routine, consisting of discharging MSTS cargo from two Isbrandtsen vessels which called each month. The commissions from these shipments covered expenses and small remittances to Hong Kong, but that was all. Unless I could find ways to earn more revenue, my Pusan posting would never grow unto the successful business that I wanted for Pat.

So I looked for growth opportunities. It was easy to see that we had one big asset: our people were all intelligent, experienced and motivated by the Korean work ethic. Yet ironically, they were idled for days at a time with little to do between ship visits. They were clearly frustrated and I was determined to get them occupied productively.

My training with Pat and Wimpy had prepared me for just this situation. Two areas of opportunity appeared: expanding our shipping and developing import-export business. From a survey of the staff's capabilities I learned that nearly all of them had worked earlier with Korean companies. Big Kim and Ho had managed an export business in Seoul. All the others except the driver and Small Kim had been in shipping.

Small Kim turned out to be an enigma. His documents showed no previous employment or education history and my questions were neatly dodged. Yet he was familiar with Pattison's business and clearly commanded everyone's respect. Over the following months I benefited again and again from his exercise of invisible authority–sometimes bordering on ruthlessness–in dealing with government and civilian groups alike.

With the skills of our personnel identified, I could organize. Our priority was to regain the confidence of Isbrandtsen and the local MSTS officers. I assigned this critical task to Cheung, who communicated best in English. At the same time he and the other experienced shipping men would look into possible future shipping opportunities for Pattison. Big Kim would head the new trading department, with Ho as his assistant. They were to explore import and export opportunities.

Small Kim seemed pleased to have his position formalized with the title of Executive Manager. He would continue to keep things running smoothly, but would also search for business opportunities and provide political contacts. The company driver was designated his assistant.

My secretary Park had not lost any of his accounting skills and eagerly accepted the responsibility of managing our finances. He would produce monthly profit and loss statements, follow up on overdue bills and oversee our two bank accounts. I gave him co-signing privileges with me on our Korean won account in Pusan. The other was in US dollars at the branch of an American bank in Hong Kong, where Wimpy and I were the only signatories.

By the time our new organization was in place, the Siberian winter of 1951 had swept down on us in earnest and the weather was miserable. I realized that Christmas had arrived and decided to send belated news of our progress to Pat as a late present.

But this was not to be. No phone, telex or mail service existed between Pusan and Shanghai. Even a message to Pat via Wimpy was stopped. When pressed for an explanation, Wimpy warned that censorship was stricter than ever. Any message from me would be intercepted and could endanger Pat.

I thought gratefully of Pat's tremendous efforts after my arrest to make possible my own safe exit from China.

Pusan's Foreign Business Community

Bit by bit I entered into Pusan's little community of American and European civilians. Nearly all held special permits like mine and had been authorized entry to Korea on a need basis to keep the stream of military and related supplies pouring into port on MSTS ships. They managed Pusan offices for major shipping companies like Isbrandtsen, American President and American Export Lines as well as a mixed bag of European companies. All were single, since families had no place in this dirty and dangerous enclave.

There were also others outside the shipping world: Jimmy, a tall, sandy-haired Californian, ran an American trading company. He spoke Korean fluently and relished *kimshi.* Another was Tom, a white haired sweetheart who represented Northwest Airlines. Now and then Gene, a former Flying Tiger and now chief pilot of the Korean National Airline, turned up with his co-pilot Slim. A senior U.N. officer, Obie Mueting, was our United Nations contact.

This group remained unchanged until a year or so into my stay. Then, suddenly, Big Louie stormed in to manage a Philippine shipping agency. After several near-fatal confrontations in China, he had the good fortune to have gotten himself arrested, then booted out of the country as an "undesirable element." Louie brought bitter news from Shanghai that Pattison, prohibited from leaving, was drinking heavily, and another American had disappeared.

We Enter the Trading Business Arena

Our first trading effort was an offer of Korea's biggest exports, dried cuttlefish and graphite ore, which I sent to Wimpy with high hopes. His discouraging reply was that Hong Kong was saturated with such offers. We would have to slash our prices to succeed. Experience had taught me that Wimpy might be up to his old tricks trying to squeeze us to increase his own profit, so we cross checked. Our prices were competitive, indeed.

I decided not to spar with him, and contacted Pattison's Japan office. Their active trading department was run by a German named Otto. I had met him earlier in Shanghai, where Pat stole him from an American multinational. Since then we had built up a good working relationship.

Otto's import manager, a Japanese-American named Nishi, interested a customer in taking the whole lot if we could slightly reduce the price. Otto and I shaved our margins and the business was confirmed. Our Tokyo office arranged for the buyer's letter of credit and insurance. We provided certificates of quality and made the shipment on a Japanese coastal freighter.

I gave our team a Korean dinner to celebrate our first business success. The staff was overwhelmed by this unprecedented gesture of appreciation, which gave great face to Big Kim and Ho and even greater incentive to the others.

Otto

Our Japan trading manager, Otto, would have made the perfect recruiting poster for Hitler's master race. He stood nearly six feet tall and sported a full head of bright blond hair over a clean-cut, handsome face. But Aryan or not, there was nothing Nazi about Otto. As soon as Hitler came to power, he and his family had left Germany. They traveled the world for several years, ending in Shanghai. Along the way Otto had received an American education and now acted like just any other American 30-year-old. Soon after we met I recognized that Otto became bored with routine work and looked for challenges, as I did. This entrepreneurial bent had brought our first venture to fruition. We could not have known it then, but it would soon lead to business successes beyond our wildest dreams.

Our fish and ore shipment had opened the door into the Japanese market. Our traders, Big Kim and Ho, obtained more offers from the most reliable exporters while Nishie contacted Japanese importers of Korean produce. Soon we had enough tonnage to fill a small coastal freighter. The *Laurie* was not available so our Shipping Manager, Cheung, chartered a small Korean vessel. The shipment went well and our offices shared a tidy profit.

Learning the "Rules" of the Game

While we were focused on exports, Small Kim had been meeting friends in the government ministry that arranged tenders for bulk commercial imports. Returning from a visit, he said, "John, I have information. It is not yet announced, but next week there will be a notice for a cigarette paper tender from Hong Kong. It is a big amount so all the importers will be making offers."

We decided to bid. I let Wimpy know that we had no chance with his inflated mark-up and asked for his understanding if we bought direct from another supplier. His reply was immediate and indignant. We went back and forth and finally I obtained his promise to quote us an honest net price, with the understanding that we would evenly split any profit.

Sure enough, two days later Wimpy telexed a truly competitive offer. Big Kim submitted our sealed bid and was sitting among the other bidders when the envelopes were opened. We came in second, with the winner exactly one per cent lower than we were. Small Kim investigated and–to no one's surprise–reported that the tenders had been opened and resealed just before the deadline. We agreed that we would have to play by new rules.

Some months later another cigarette paper tender was announced. All the bids were again submitted–except for one from the previous winner, which was conspicuously missing. The deadline approached with much excited speculation about the missing bid. Then the envelopes were opened. Our bid, shaved to the bedrock, won.

A few minutes later a frantic messenger from the absent bidder rushed into the hall, waving the missing envelope and screaming that he had been held prisoner in the elevator. But it was too late. I asked Small Kim for his take on this. He shrugged sympathetically and gave me a half smile.

This introductory experience prepared us on how to compete when attractive tenders were offered. I was happy to learn that the bidding process was usually conducted honestly. Our traders, now strongly supported by Pattison's Hong Kong and Japan offices, were able to win enough tenders to make this business attractive without resorting again to dirty tricks.

A few weeks later our earnings increased substantially when the *Laurie* was approved for direct Hong Kong/Pusan sailings. This gave us a real competitive advantage by controlling the freight rates and schedules. Exporters who previously had to transship their cargoes at Kobe were happy to pay a higher freight, and kept our ship loaded to the Plimsoll line.

We Add General Insurance

Through an acquaintance in the shipping business I met a Korean-American with the improbable name of Charlie Chan. But this Charlie did not resemble the then-popular movie detective of that name. Instead he was short, round and prematurely bald. But always jolly. People loved to be around him.

Charlie had picked up Culbertson and a bit of Goren at college in

California and brought me into the local bridge group. After returning from America he had joined a Korean insurance company in Seoul. His skill and popularity soon earned him promotion to sales manager. Then the Communist attack wiped out his company and clients. He escaped and was anxious to get back into insurance, but could find no opening here.

This was interesting. I had recently been approached by a major British insurance company with which I had worked in Shanghai, and sounded out Charlie. He was immediately interested, and I put him on our payroll as insurance manager. It didn't bother him that his desk was a small end table crammed into a corner. He was busy making the rounds of potential clients.

I visited the British insurance company's Tokyo office with my power of attorney and arranged for us to be their Korea agent. Then I flew back to Pusan with a briefcase full of insurance forms and promotional material and Charlie and I developed a marketing plan. His canvassing soon paid off. Local traders liked the availability of insurance in American dollars from a reputable British company, and our insurance business got off to a good start.

Colonel Dow: Provost Marshall of South Korea

My first impression when I met Dow was his size: a huge, powerful body and giant head crowned by wavy dark black hair. I could have been looking at a Big Ten fullback. He projected power–an appropriate quality for the man who controlled most of the military police in the country.

I had called on the colonel to obtain some permit or another, expecting to be passed on to one of his junior officers. Instead, our meeting took place in his Provost Marshall's office overlooking Pusan Harbor. Dow sat me down on a sofa and joined me. He asked me a few superficial questions about my activities. Then he said, "That ship of yours, the *Laurie*. I had the crew checked before I OK'd it for entry here. I'd like to meet that captain, the Scot who lost a leg in the war. Think you could arrange it?"

Surprised at the scope of his knowledge, I replied, "I'd be glad to. She's due here in a couple of days. I could bring Ian–Captain MacGregor–over to meet you."

"I'd like that." He walked to a cabinet, returning with two glasses and a bottle of an off-brand Scotch and poured us each a straight drink. After we sipped our drinks he shook his head with disgust. "This damn piss we have to drink. It's all we can get here."

"How's that?"

"It's the distribution system. Class Six items are sent over from Japan. They're distributed down the line. By the time we get our deliveries, this..." he gestured at the bottle, "is what's left."

"That sounds rough. What's Class Six?"

"That's the term used to describe liquor, beer and some other items which don't have military priority."

I had a thought. "Our captain carries a few cases of Scotch on board. Usually his personal stock, Johnny Walker. Most of it is under seal in port, of course. But I know he has a few bottles available and would like to have a drink with you if you would visit the ship."

Soon after the *Laurie* moored in Pusan harbor Dow came aboard with me for an "inspection trip" followed by a simple lunch. When Ian poured the Black Label, Dow grinned, "Now that's what I call whisky." He and the veteran captain hit it off immediately. When the colonel left, Ian refused to take more than a thank you for the package that Dow took ashore.

The next day I received a message to stop by the Provost Marshall's office. Without wasting any time on preliminaries Dow asked whether I had a source of good Scotch that could be imported on our ship.

I thought of Ace and his liquor business in Hong Kong. "Yes. I think I can."

"Good. I'd like you to run up to the EUSAK headquarters in Taegu and talk with a friend of mine, a major in Special Services."

I had no idea what he was getting at. "Excuse me. What's EUSAK?"

"It's an acronym for Eighth U.S. Army in Korea. EUSAK headquarters is in Taegu, about eighty miles north of here. It was moved there when the war started and will stay there until it gets reestablished in Seoul." We agreed that I would go the next day.

I Visit EUSAK HQ

Our old car could not survive the bad road to Taegu, so Dow lent me a military police jeep with driver. After some three hours we pulled into a building fronted with the sign EUSAK HQ. An MP guard directed us to the Special Services offices nearby. There I met Major Bill, who controlled the army's distribution of Class Six materials throughout Korea.

The informally dressed officer rose from a littered desk and shook my hand. "Dow warned me to expect a visit from another of you liquor-peddling carpet baggers." Then, seeing my alarm, his chubby face broke into a warm smile. "Welcome to Taegu, John. Sit down and tell me why the colonel decided to send you here."

"Thank you for seeing me, major."

He laughed, "Call me Bill. We don't put much stock in formality here. Dow asked me to take good care of you and I'll see what I can do."

I was introduced to his staff and their system of importing and distributing Class Six consignments to military units around Korea. Again and again I heard the word "pilferage" and realized that this must be a big problem. I was also briefed on the tricky topic of money. Our forces were paid in military payment certificates, called MPCs, instead of US dollars. Usually these bills were valid currency only at military establishments. Personnel wishing to exchange MPCs into real dollars were required to use authorized banks, and to justify any amounts considered excessive.

"But why couldn't everyone just be paid in regular dollars?" I asked.

"Doesn't work. We tried it in Europe." MPCs had been introduced in Korea to discourage black market activities, and I was alerted to report any offers of bribes for the use of our money transfer facilities.

Before leaving I had a final meeting with Bill. We reviewed my visit, then he spoke seriously, "O.K., Mr. Potter. I've given you our blessing to sell Class Six in areas under our jurisdiction. You are the first civilian to be approved for this and we will advise the Korean authorities accordingly. I've put this in writing for you to use if necessary." He handed me an official looking envelope, adding, "This will establish your *bona fides* when you visit our military units and may come in useful if there is any problem.

"But I must caution you that your actions will be monitored. One infraction and your permit to work in Korea will be immediately withdrawn. I want to make sure you understand that."

"Yes, I understand."

"Your hardest task will be to control pilferage. I will accept the theft of a few bottles now and then. God knows we have thefts every day. But anything that resembles selling into the black market will not be tolerated."

Then, suddenly, he reverted to the warm, friendly person who had welcomed me. "Personally, John, I wish you success. Contact me if there is anything we can do. And if you hear anything I should know, be sure to let me know."

All the way back to Pusan my mind was racing with exciting plans.

Preparing for U.S. Military Business

Next morning I briefed my small staff on my meeting. Then I outlined plans to expand into the liquor business. When our team recovered from their surprise, I asked them to get to know the customs personnel whose support we might need. A budget would be available for meals and entertainment.

Privately I discussed with Small Kim the need to establish a control system. With a single bottle of VO selling for $80 on the black market, we would need tight control from discharge ex-ship to delivery receipt by the U.S. military consignees. Small Kim replied quietly, "I will make arrangements, John."

Dow was pleased when I thanked him for arranging my trip. He glanced over the letter which Bill had given me. "Good. Now come back tomorrow. I'll have something more for you."

The "something more" turned out to be Dow's strong endorsement on official stationery. It would certainly get attention. Also enclosed in the envelope was a signed requisition for fifteen cases of VO and one of Johnny Walker Black Label, with delivery instructions. This was followed the next day by a list of the military clubs for officers, NCOs and enlisted men in the Pusan area, with names of procurement personnel–often staff sergeants. Dow had scribbled on the envelope: "This should get you started."

I telexed Ace Smith to ship Dow's order on the *Laurie's* next sailing and to rush me quantities and prices of brands his company could send promptly. Ace telexed confirmation of Dow's order and airmailed an inventory of over 1,200 cases ranging from cheap gins to vintage *Dom Perignon*. Prices were surprisingly low, with popular brands like VO listed at under US$16 per case FOB Hong Kong. Park and I prepared our Korea price list, adding enough to cover shipping and insurance costs. And profit. I spent a long time considering this. With our near-monopoly I could easily tack on a huge margin. This would be expected of me by my Pattison associates. On the other hand, our customers were my own fellow Americans, many in real personal danger. In the end I settled on a price much lower than others would have set, while still giving us a generous margin. A collateral benefit of low prices was that this would make our business less attractive to others who might try to compete later.

I delegated to Park the task of producing our price list. As accountant, he transformed Ace's FOB prices in Hong Kong to our selling prices in Korea. Then as secretary, he found an acceptable printer and spent days producing a decent looking price list. Armed with copies, Small Kim and I were ready to set forth on an exciting new adventure.

Our First Military Sales

We reviewed Dow's information about regional clubs. Then, carrying our credentials and new price lists, we took the car to our first prospect. This was a large NCO club near the city. We saw a few disinterested sergeants loitering at the door having a smoke. Inside, the club was nearly empty. There were only a dozen or so men scattered around the tables; they eyed us with mild curiosity. I had trouble getting anyone's attention until I asked for the staff sergeant on Dow's list by name. Sergeant Booth was pointed out.

As soon as I showed him Dow's letter I had his undivided attention. He asked questions about us, then called to the others. "Hey, come over. There's a guy here says he can sell us decent whisky. He's been OK'd by the Provost Marshall." He passed Dow's letter around.

Soon we were surrounded by every man in the club. It was obvious that I was peddling a popular commodity. Booth took us into a small office and looked over our price list. Then he asked me, almost incredulously, "You mean your company can sell us these things at these prices?"

"Yep. That's why we're here."

"No shit?"

"Read that letter."

"You want to get paid in advance? If that's the case, forget it. We've been screwed before."

I explained that once we received the signed requisition we would import the order on our own ship. The customer would check it when he took delivery in Pusan and only then would he give us a dollar payment.

"OK… I want to check with the captain. If he OK's it we'll try you."

We left a copy of our list with Booth. After leaving, Small Kim said, with a rare smile, "He is suspicious. But he will make an order."

Early the next day Booth showed up at our office with his captain. He and I exchanged credentials. Our first club order, nearly all Canadian whisky, came to over $4,000. Two weeks later it arrived and was delivered. We received payment and airmailed the check to our US$ account in Hong Kong.

Small Kim and I continued canvassing the Pusan area, gathering orders at nearly every stop. After the first few shipments came in, word got around and buyers started visiting us. Things got badly crowded and I realized we needed a separate office for our Class Six and trading businesses.

By good fortune I ran into Tom from Northwest Airlines, whose office was on the second floor of one of the few decent buildings on the main street. He told me that the ground floor tenant was leaving and asked if I might be interested. I was. These premises would be able to comfortably house our trading and military sales departments, and also give Charlie Chan an insurance office. The shipping office would continue to operate on Pier Two.

I signed up the new premises and Small Kim again arranged telephone and telex facilities at the new site. We printed new Pattison stationery showing both locations. Everything seemed to be going great.

A Bombshell out of the Blue

The warning started with a message to telephone a former schoolmate on an urgent matter. We had been out of touch for years and I was surprised to learn that he was now in Korea, at our embassy.

I called on our military line. "Pete," I started. "What a pleasant surprise. What brings you to Korea?"

His response startled me. "John," he stated formally. "We knew each other at school, and because of this it was felt better that I contact you about your recent activities on behalf of Mr. Pattison."

"Pattison?" I exclaimed. "What activities?"

"Since you arrived here from Hong Kong, your behavior has been impeccable, conforming strictly with laws governing Americans here. But there is evidence that recently your company has committed infractions of American law. You may not be aware of this yourself," he continued. "For this reason it was felt best for me to communicate informally with you before any further action is taken."

"What the hell are you talking about, Pete?" I exclaimed.

"Money transfers." He paused, "Payments you have been remitting to your Hong Kong office which come from sales to American military personnel."

"That's perfectly legal." I had checked this carefully.

"Do you also know what your Hong Kong office does with that money?"

"Sure. Van Beverin, the manager, pays most of it to our liquor supplier and sends enough back here to cover our costs. The rest is held for Mr. Pattison personally to use when he finally gets out of China."

"Do you have proof of that?"

"Proof? I don't understand."

"Do you know how much is being held in Hong Kong for Mr. Pattison? Have you seen statements?"

I remained silent as the frightening realization loomed. I had not seen any statements. I had naïvely taken Wimpy's word that Pat's money was being held intact for him in his personal account. But what if Wimpy was sending the money we earned from American forces here to Pat in Shanghai? This money would go directly to the Communist Chinese, our enemies! And Wimpy might be perfectly capable of doing that.

At length I said, "Thank you, Pete. I'd never considered that possibility. I'll telex van Beveren to rush me an up-to-date statement confirming that all the deposits we made to Pat's personal account are still there. If any are missing, I'll stop sending money immediately."

"There's evidence that van Beveren has been relaying those transfers to Shanghai. But of course you should go ahead. See how he replies."

Wimpy's reply was a convoluted jumble of numbers–clearly an attempt to confuse. So I knew.

The more I thought about it the more furious I became. Before making a firm decision I asked Pete to check whether my permit to work in Korea would continue if I were not working with Pattison. He replied immediately, "Yes. Your clearance covers an indefinite period. You would be free to continue your military and other businesses here. And by the way, since our last conversation you have been cleared of any complicity in those money transfers."

I told Pete that this being the case, I would resign from Pattison.

But how to resign? There was still no way to communicate with Pat, and I did not want to inform Wimpy yet. So I postponed this action. I told my two key aides, Small Kim and Park, in confidence that I might continue with another business. When I explained the reason they insisted on coming with me. I knew the others would, too, but this posed a question of who stayed with Pattison to handle Isbrandtsen ships after I left.

I confirmed that the agreements I had signed for my apartment and the new office were in my own name. Then I cancelled Park's and my names as signatories on our Pattison accounts and opened a new joint account for us. Finally, I stopped accepting any new business until things got sorted out.

Carl & Shelly Mydans drive us past bombed ruins from Yokohama to Tokyo in 1947.

My Labrador puppy, Cindy. *With AFIA friends in Shanghai, Winston Chen presides.*

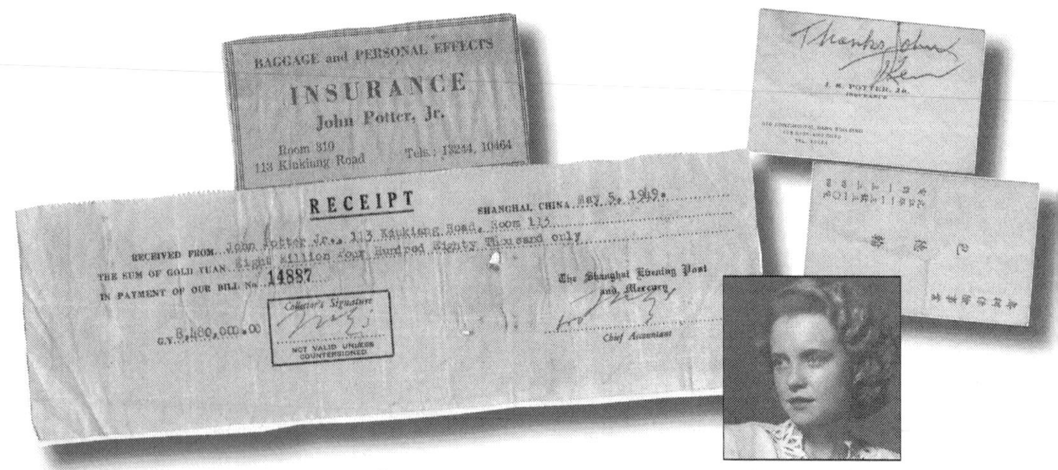

BAGGAGE and PERSONAL EFFECTS
INSURANCE
John Potter, Jr.
Room 310
113 Kiukiang Road
Tels.: 13244, 10464

RECEIPT
SHANGHAI, CHINA May 5, 1949.
RECEIVED FROM John Potter Jr., 113 Kiukiang Road, Room 115
THE SUM OF GOLD YUAN Eight Million Four Hundred Eighty Thousand only
IN PAYMENT OF OUR BILL No. 14887
G.Y. 8,480,000.00
Collector's Signature
NOT VALID UNLESS COUNTERSIGNED
The Shanghai Evening Post and Mercury
Chief Accountant

Shanghai insurance company with German assistant Josie; note receipt for 8,480,000 gold yuan.

Leigh Bishop

The sinking of the Flying Enterprise. *Capt. Carlson remains aboard until she slides under.*

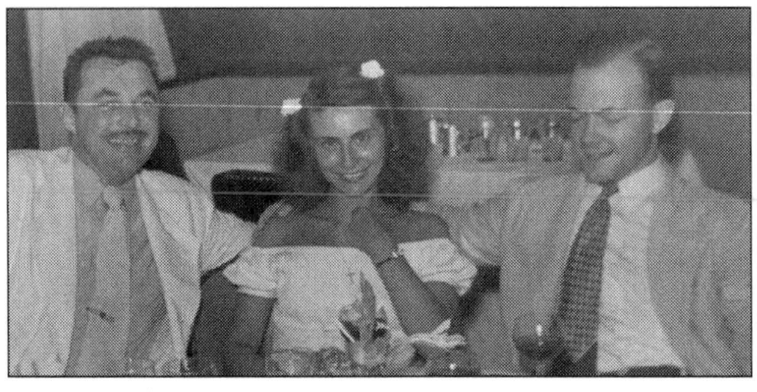

Big Louie & I enjoy the company of a sweetheart from Ralph's stable in Shanghai

Hasta manana, Louie!

Laurie Pattison *under steam.*

Out to dinner in Hong Kong.

Tientsin, China: a German acquaintance demonstrates the effect of his powerful Tientsin booze.

Flying to Pusan, Korea, on Korean National Airlines, with one suitcase and high hopes.

Tradeships' widely recognized pagoda.

"Executive suite" at Tradeship.

Tradeship's head office in Pusan and the view out onto Pusan's main street.

Dick Johnson on my right and Oley Olsson on my left.

Tradeship's first coastal freighter and our flag (the corner of the diamond logo is just visible on funnel).

I ride shotgun aboard a deuce-and-a-half carrying part of a 4000-case order of alcohol to the First Marine Division in Korea.

Life Nine: Tradeship South Korea 1952-1953

PART ONE

Putting Together the Organization

How Tradeship Got its Name

Otto had suggested earlier that we leave Pat to form our own company, but until now loyalty to my old friend had prevented me from considering such an idea. Now I had no choice. I flew to Tokyo where Otto met me at Haneda Airport and took me to my room at the Nikkatsu, a modern hotel with offices on the bottom floors. Without delay, we set about organizing.

Our prime business objective would be continuing to grow Class Six sales. So far we had scarcely nibbled at our huge potential market of military customers, who could easily take thousands of cases every month. Ace would keep on supplying us from Hong Kong. Later we might want to expand our sources, possibly buying from big liquor importers in Japan.

We would need bases in Korea and Japan. In Pusan, we would use my new office and continue unloading and delivery on the pier. Otto would rent a small office in Tokyo. Later, if we sourced there, he could rent storage space in a bonded warehouse. Wherever possible, we would use our own chartered ship to carry Class Six and any other cargo we could book. The Isbrandtsen agency for Korea could stay with Pattison, with shipping staff.

By the time we got around to selecting a company name, we had the benefit of quite a few rounds of the Class Six we would be handling. It was a tall pink potion which Otto ordered that inspired us to reach our goal. We had been tossing about words like "ocean" and "flying" and "sailing" when Otto burst forth: "Ship Trade! That's what we'll be doing: shipping and trading."

That seemed to be in the right church all right, but not quite in the right pew. Then, inspired, I sallied forth with the magic words "Tradeship!"

There was a moment of respectful silence. Then Otto and I, grinning happily, adjourned to the Queen Bee nightclub where a famous charmer named Dewy, in a bright pink gown, held court. Despite an exorbitant fee for her cocktails and titillating chatter we failed to book her out for the night–although not much later Indonesian President Suharto did and ended up marrying the girl.

It was only the next day that we fully realized the enormity of our undertaking. And money was right on top of our priorities. We each had several thousand dollars in cash and negotiable assets, but nowhere near enough to start an international business of the size we envisioned.

Now Otto made a major contribution: a working relationship with a Middle Eastern wheeler-dealer named Radakanaki. This financier offered to lend us seed money guaranteed solely by Otto's signature. His terms were 2% per month for a revolving credit of up to two million dollars. This was well above the going interest rate, but under the circumstances we grabbed it.

Other components of our new project quickly fell into place. Tradeship, Ltd. would be incorporated in Canada, far from possible confusion with Pattison. Otto would be president (I did not want any titles). We would open accounts for Tradeship, Ltd. with both of us as signatories at an American bank with branches in Hong Kong and Tokyo and a correspondent bank in Korea.

My Pusan staff would be active: Charlie Chan to take over all of Tradeship's insurance, and secretary Park, the accounts for both offices including salary payments to the staffs. We would deposit $200,000 from Radakanaki's credit line to Tradeship's Tokyo account to draw on at the start.

We spent a long and emotional time brainstorming the problem of trying to communicate with Pat, but the bamboo barrier stymied us. We knew his blackmailing captors would not let him out until convinced that they had drained him dry. If that day finally came, he would surely need money. So, with the hope that he would be finally released, we placed $100,000 in trust with a U.S. bank in Hong Kong for delivery to him when he arrived.

With the payment, I enclosed a heartfelt letter to my dear friend explaining the reason for my forced resignation and offering to do anything I could do to help him and his baby son, for whom I was godfather.

Years later I returned to Hong Kong and learned that Pat had died. He had passed through drinking heavily, and left for England still believing that I had stolen his Korea business. I was embittered to find no record of our bank deposit or my letter.

Assembling the Pieces

Back in Pusan I explained to the Pattison staff the reason for my leaving and my plans for Tradeship. I reassured them that the Pier 2 office, company car and driver, and company equipment would all remain with Pattison, along with the Isbrandtsen agency and enough of the shipping staff to handle Isbrandtsen's ships and the *Laurie.* Everyone would continue to be paid. I then asked if anyone wanted to join Tradeship.

They all did. I selected Small Kim and Park, the traders Big Kim and Ho, and two from the shipping group. To avoid disrupting Isbrandtsen's service, I reluctantly left our experienced shipping manager Cheung behind. He and the other shipping employees would manage until a new manager was installed. Then they could join me if they wished.

In my telexed advice to Wimpy I passed on only essential information, but made sure he knew that he was responsible. I also assured Isbrandtsen that the Pattison office would continue to handle their ships in Pusan.

I sent Ace all information necessary to continue our business and asked him to hold up any more orders pending new shipping arrangements. His latest consignment, valued at about $40,000 for seven customers, would arrive soon aboard the *Laurie.* I could not stop it, so Tradeship would receive the military payments and pay Ace direct. As a courtesy, I phoned Pete at our embassy to thank him and let him know our progress.

Dow already had the background but wanted full details of my plans. This done, he phoned Major Bill in Taegu. "Let him know everything," Dow told me, handing over the phone. "It is important for him to have the whole story direct from you now."

Everyone contributed to the organization of Tradeship's new "uptown" office after our new name was prominently mounted over the sidewalk. Charlie Chan plastered his insurance quarters with promotions and displays; Park had price lists printed with our new name; Small Kim arranged a fairly new Buick and driver. The car ran well, so we used it to visit and personally brief all our military customers in the area, leaving our new price lists.

By the middle of spring we had tied up most of the loose ends resulting from the change to Tradeship. Henry was recalled to be the nominal manager of the Pattison office, although the work of handling Isbrandtsen ships was managed by Cheung. We received threats and claims for money from Wimpy, but ignored them. The *Laurie* stopped visiting Pusan after discharging our last shipment of liquor. We were not yet ready to charter our own ship so Ace sent our orders on reliable ships, preferably American.

Small Kim Solves a Major Theft

Deliveries went smoothly. After checking their consignments, customers gave us checks made out to Tradeship, Ltd., signed receipts and customs forms, and loaded their cases on trucks–the ubiquitous 2½-ton "deuce and a half"–attached to their units.

Every now and then customers asked us to make deliveries with payment and receipts upon arrival. I wanted to accommodate them and checked with Major Bill. The Special Services chief replied, "We have no objection to your moving Class Six goods to military customers provided they are correctly documented. But I want to remind you of what I told you when you visited me. There will be risk, no matter how much security you arrange.

"Remember," he continued. "Until an authorized military buyer signs acknowledgement of receipt, any Class Six goods that you move away from customs control could be looked upon as illegally in Korea."

Keenly aware of Bill's admonitions, we used only Pusan's most reputable transport contractor, and only in exceptional cases. At my insistence they hired trusted guards to ride shotgun on our cargoes. All went well until a club manager phoned one afternoon asking when his order would arrive. I learned that it had left two hours earlier and alerted Small Kim. He agreed that there might be a problem and sped off in the car. I phoned the customer that there was a delay, sweating anxiously for news.

This came a few hours later when Small Kim returned. "John, it is settled," he said, exhausted but triumphant. "We have the truck and the whisky. One case broken but the bottles are there."

Unable to believe our good fortune, I asked for details.

He said carefully, "I did not think robbers did this. So we went to see the contractor's driver and also found the guard. We learned that the truck was in a garage near the guard's house," he continued. "Everything was still there. They did not have time to move the whisky after they took it."

"Good God! How did you know where to find it?"

"The driver told."

"But why? Why would he tell after he stole it?"

Small Kim paused and pursed his lips. "Electricity," he said calmly. "We did not have time to wait. They would have moved it."

The 110 volts current in Pusan was probably not enough to kill. But it would certainly persuade.

Early that evening the deuce-and-a-half, its whisky cargo still undisturbed, arrived at the customer's club. It was manned by a different driver and a different guard. Word quickly spread about the disappearance of the original driver and guard and what might have been their fate so I did not expect another such robbery attempt. But still, from then on we stopped such contracting and our buyers took delivery in their own vehicles.

Military Sales Take Off

Tradeship's sales increased exponentially as news spread about our service More and more military units became our customers. It was no longer just one truck at a time. Now there were mini caravans and even a 20-ton flatbed.

Despite Ace's efficient order processing, his operation could no longer cope with the astonishing growth in demand. Nor could any other Hong Kong supplier–there was simply not enough inventory of requested brands there.

Delays in deliveries also become a problem. With the growing volume of orders and the *Laurie* no longer available, we were dependent on a handful of small freighters with unpredictable schedules. This led to unreliable delivery dates. Consequently shipments to more than a dozen customers would sometimes be discharged onto the pier at one time.

As if this were not enough, despite immediate duty-free clearance facilities officially accorded to U.S. military, a suffocating barrier of delays was put up by underpaid customs functionaries. Customers from outside Pusan often had to wait overnight. Our protests were futile. Even though our customs brokers paid heavily in entertainment and gifts these delays continued.

I realized that we must change, and change fast. I had inherited an office staffed to service only two ships per month. Now I was building a dynamic, expanding organization capable of financing, importing, insuring, storing and delivering thousands of cases of valuable cargo to dozens of customers each month. Our sales had been growing largely because of word-of-mouth recommendations. But probably also, I realized, because we had no competition. Sooner or later others would come in and attack our monopoly.

I wanted to build the strongest barrier I could to fend off future competition. To achieve this we had to improve our business service by eliminating delivery delays. But this was not enough. When I thought of a sergeant curled up in his truck because he had no bed while he waited for delivery, I knew that we must also provide our customers with exceptional personal service: a warm welcome and comfortable place to stay overnight, good meals, drinks and entertainment. I summarized these thoughts into a proposal and mailed them to Otto, suggesting that he come over to discuss Tradeship's future with me.

Preparing for Growth

Otto arrived the day after a Japanese freighter discharged a typical large shipment for eleven customers. When I brought him to the office most of them were still milling around waiting for customs clearance.

Some were in a hurry but they all understood the reason for delay. The clearance documents finally arrived and we trooped down the dusty road to Pier 2. The whisky was being loaded onto trucks, about 125 cases per vehicle, as Small Kim gave orders to insure that each lot went into the right truck. His guards stood back, watching carefully. Despite the shouting and apparent confusion, everything went smoothly. Within two hours I had all the delivery orders and payments and the last truck had roared off.

At my apartment that evening Otto and I had a drink and a good dinner prepared by my amah. As we ate the salad, Otto looked up, surprised. "This tastes like fresh American lettuce. How did you get it?"

"Comes from a commissary in Pusan. They have plenty of good food and other things, too. One of my army friends got me a permit." I grinned, "Makes living here a hell of a lot easier."

We finished our coffee early and I began, "Well, you see how fast Tradeship is growing. And we're just getting started. I figure that in another few months, sales will be ten times more than we have now.

Otto's eyebrows shot up, so I pointed out that the army units we were supplying around Pusan represented only a tiny part of our market. We hadn't even approached a quarter million American troops deployed further north, plus personnel in many support units and the Air Force.

"It's hard for me to believe, Otto," I went on. "But just starting to reach this potential market means we'll be bringing in at least a thousand tons a month. And that's just liquor. When we add beer–which some of them want–we'll have one of the biggest liquor businesses in the world."

Otto nodded slowly. "Like you wrote in your letter. Go ahead."

"OK. You saw the way those guys were hanging around the office waiting for customs clearance. Sometimes they're here for days with no decent place to stay. We can't let that go on."

I then reiterated the steps that I had outlined in my letter, starting with a bonded warehouse. "Their shipments could then be cleared in advance giving them immediate delivery. Small Kim can arrange the guards. We could even hire customs officers to be there, if necessary.

"Then we're looking for a ship to charter. There are several lying idle here. Without the *Laurie,* Ace is running into traffic jams trying to book space. We should be able to operate an FS or another small freighter if we can get a good shipping manager. You probably know a few in Japan. He'll need papers, of course, and be experienced with contacts to get things done.

"One more thing. An apartment for customers who have long trips back and have to spend the night here. Couple of beds, hot shower, an amah to cook."

Otto laughed, "Don't forget me! I have a long trip back." Then he added, seriously, "Now, about your letter. After I received it I looked for a shipping manager. Did you ever know a Swede called Oley Olsson in Shanghai?"

I shook my head. "Well, I've seen him in action and he's good. Experienced in shipping and has worked all over Asia. He has Masters' papers and could easily manage our shipping. He was a prizefighter but decided he liked ships better. And get this: Oley's half Korean and speaks it fluently.

"My God! How old is he?"

"A bit older than we are: early thirties. You'll like him. And here's some more good news. Getz Brothers has offered us the Korea agency for their products–including Hiram Walker and National Distillers. That would give us exclusive distributorship for a whole range of whiskies and wines, including Canadian Club and the best bourbons like Jim Beam and Old Taylor. Our cost would be several dollars a case less than we've been paying Ace and we can probably work out a good financing arrangement as well. So, John," Otto leaned back with a satisfied smile, "Even with your ridiculously low list prices we'll finally be able to make a decent profit." He had been chafing at the low prices I insisted we keep on sales to our American military.

Otto continued that he had rented our Tradeship office at the Nikkatsu and had a contract for a Yokohama warehouse ready to sign if I liked it. By the time we finished I had decided to fly back to Tokyo with him.

Tradeship in Japan

From Haneda airport we went directly to the Nikkatsu Hotel where Otto took me to an office on the third floor. On the door, in large bold blue letters, the words Tradeship, Ltd. (Canada) proudly announced that we were in business. Otto stood back, observing my reaction.

"Not bad," I said. "It stands out. We'll do something like this in Pusan."

"I thought you'd like it. Come in."

The room was narrow, its blue walls bare except for a few photos. Otto's desk and two chairs were placed by a window crossing the back, and along one wall were several clerks' desks and chairs with filing cabinets squeezed between them. The telephone and telex were on a stand by the door.

I commented to Otto, "Very efficient."

Nishie, whom I had met earlier, introduced me to the clerk, and after we were seated a secretary brought us coffee.

Otto glanced at his watch. "Oley will be here in a minute. He's always punctual. After you've talked with him we're having lunch with our friends at Getz Brothers down the hall. They got me this office. If we can agree on terms we can probably sign a contract with them before you go back."

Oley

Oley needed no introduction when he came in. Although short, his tough, confident appearance and broken nose marked him to be a fighter and his swarthy color and black hair gave him a Eurasian look. He broke into a smile as he shook my hand. "Finally I meet you, John," he exclaimed.

Wincing at the pressure of his grip, I answered, "Glad you could come, Oley. I've been looking forward to this." Otto pulled over a chair for Oley and signaled for more coffee. When we started talking I sensed right away that we might have our man. Oley clearly had the experience and qualifications we needed. He had on his own initiative already applied for a visa to Korea. There was no family to complicate things since he was legally separated and had no children.

By lunchtime we had covered enough territory for me to be confident that Oley could handle our shipping, and we agreed on terms. He would move to Pusan with the title of Shipping Manager, Tradeship, Ltd. I wanted him there with me as soon as his visa was approved to take over some of my load. Meanwhile he could go to Yokohama to check out bonded warehouses.

Getz Brothers

Otto then took me down the hall to the Tokyo office of one of the largest American international trading companies. Started in San Francisco a hundred years earlier, Getz Brothers operated in countries all over the world and provided the overseas marketing push for many popular U.S. brands.

We were met by two impeccably dressed Americans. One, in his mid-forties, was responsible for the Getz operations in Japan and Okinawa. The other was his marketing manager. After a few moments of polite conversation they led us to the hotel's main dining room for lunch.

After an excellent meal we went directly to a conference table in their boardroom. The marketing manager took notes while I gave a briefing on the situation in Korea and our progress. I realized they were fully up to date on the Korean situation when they showed no surprise at my optimistic views.

This was reflected in the draft of our appointment as their Korea sub-agents which they had prepared. The terms were generous, covering everything I could have wanted. Essentially, we would have exclusive representation for their broad product line of whiskies and all other club supplies, and Getz would provide us with a line of credit up to one million dollars. We agreed to meet again the next morning.

An American lawyer Otto knew checked the document for us. His advice was to accept the offer after a few minor changes. "They have certainly made you an attractive proposal," he concluded with a big smile. "I would say that they want you very badly indeed."

The Three-Way Test

Back at the hotel I met Otto's attractive Russian wife, Val. Her parents, like Olga's, were "White Russian" refugees who had fled from the Bolsheviks. Val had heard that Olga was still in Shanghai, but could not be contacted.

After Val left Otto and I sat for dinner. The waiter, after bringing the menus, surprised me by placing three shot glasses of beer before each of us. Otto said, "Try them. See if you like any."

Well, I knew Otto had some reason for this weird request, so I tossed off all three jiggers. So did Otto. Then Otto asked, "Which is best?"

One struck me as too bitter. The other two tasted just fine, one slightly better. I said so. Then Otto announced his choice and we turned up our preferred glasses. On the bottom of each was a tiny label marked 3. The others were numbered 1 and 2. The waiter then produced three Japanese beer bottles with numbers marked on their labels. Number 1 was Sapporo, 2 Kirin, and our favorite, Number 3, Asahi.

"It looks like Asahi Beer is the winner," Otto said.

Amused, I replied, "OK. Now please tell me just what the hell you're doing."

Otto said seriously, "These three are the most popular Japanese beers. I know they're sold to some military clubs in Japan, but no big deal. All three breweries have contacted Nishie to see if Tradeship might be interested for Korea, and Getz doesn't handle them so there'd be no conflict." He paused, shaking his head. "But just look at those labels. Really crappy."

I agreed immediately. They looked like cheap imitations of foreign brands. "The labels would have to be changed, but the taste isn't so bad. What about price? Can we buy direct from manufacturers to eliminate any middlemen?"

"We haven't contacted any of them yet. Waiting for you. But Nishie said they were much cheaper than foreign beers."

"Well, what the hell. Let's check it out. I'll see if the clubs are buying any in Korea, and you could find out what the club buyers here say. Nishie can get info about prices, packing, and the usual. It'll take time, but you may just have something here. I'm getting a good feeling. If we could get this going, it might turn out to be very profitable."

The next morning we signed the Getz contract and Otto saw me off at the airport. We were exhilarated, laughing and joking like two young kids. We decided that I would remain in Pusan until Oley was settled and working. Then I would return to follow up the beer and other prospects.

"No Sweat"

Back in Pusan the shipping staff was working out well even without Cheung, who I had left with Pattison. By the time Oley arrived they had three Korean flag coasters in the 700-900 ton range waiting for his inspection. Oley gave them thorough surveys. Returning from sea trials he flunked two with his signature observation, "The fooker leaks–she's already half under." The third, registered as *Kyong In #3*, passed his grudging inspection.

We contracted her on long term charter and decked her funnel with our new Tradeship logo–an outright high jacking of Pattison's: a red T on a white diamond with a blue border. Inspired by its appearance, I ordered Tradeship flags made up for the ship and the office.

Oley quickly gained the respect of all who met him. Then, with a single incident, he established his authority among our staff and probably most of Pusan as well. This happened when a new hire, a tough and arrogant young dock laborer, complained loudly about his work load and even threatened his boss at a time when Small Kim was away.

Oley happened to come by and saw this. Without so much as a fare thee well he KO'd the rebel with one tap on the jaw, sending him flying into a pile of rusty bailing wires. Small Kim, upon learning this, broke into one of his rare smiles. From then on he and Oley worked together very well, and my latent concern about friction over authority dissipated.

Oley sailed with the ship on her first Tradeship voyage to Hong Kong to load a shipment from Ace. He had worked previously with our shipping agent there and things went smoothly. The round trip took two days less than usual, leading me to congratulate him on his selection of such a fast ship.

Oley grinned, "No sweat!"

From then on, "No sweat" became our standard response to any challenge.

Our Company Satyr

In his fluent Korean, Oley rented an apartment that suited his taste. This meant plenty of bed space and an obliging clean-up maid. Oley had a remarkable talent for fornicating. He was, in fact, a certifiable satyr.

I noticed Oley's talent after a series of young, and reasonably attractive, new girls joined the shipping department with Oley's endorsement. At first I paid no attention, assuming he knew what he was doing. Then, going over the accounts with my old friend Park, I noticed a big increase in shipping staff salaries. Park advised me that Oley took girls from his shipping department home regularly and excused many from being late to work. The staff was aware of this but afraid to blow the whistle.

I took a walk through the shipping area and noticed half a dozen new secretaries at their desks, all laboriously typing from an English language newspaper. Curious, I asked one what she was doing. She answered, "Mr. Olsson he want me learn so I practice."

"How much you practice?"

"Oh," she replied proudly. "I finish copy *taksan* page one day, sometime maybe ten, twenty page."

I thought of phoning Otto, but decided to talk with Oley first. He seemed at first genuinely surprised at my concern. But I showed him the monthly cost of having us subsidize his sex life and explained that the staff was aware of his activity. He shrugged, "They know I am training them."

"Oley," I responded in expiration. "I don't mind this screwing, but for God's sake, not our office girls. They're not working for Tradeship but still Otto and I are paying their salaries. Do you know how much we're paying?"

Oley shrugged and I showed him a statement of the girls' salaries. "Why should all this money come out of my pocket? And Otto–do you think he'll like it? Besides they're taking up space that we need. If you keep those girls it won't be here, and you'll have to pay them yourself."

At length he agreed that the girls should go. He objected strongly when I insisted that he refund their past salaries, but finally accepted monthly salary deductions when I told him I would keep the matter confidential.

Customer Service Pays Off

Our roster of customers grew to include most of the military units across the southern end of the Korean peninsula. As favorable word of mouth spread north, key personnel from support units in Seoul and even the divisions near the front made trips to Pusan to check us out for themselves. The result was usually new customers.

Much of our success could be attributed to the new apartment for our guests. We had fixed it up with the luxuries of a good hotel including comfortable beds with clean sheets, a full bath and shower, magazines, a radio, snacks and a well-stocked bar with fridge. Two amahs kept the place shipshape. On arrival visitors received a welcoming letter offering complimentary use of the bar and a fast laundry service.

To my surprise, laundry service won hands down in popularity. A typical comment from a happy customer was, "John, we can always find something to drink. But you're the only place gives us fast laundry. And free."

Our visitors - some literally right out of frozen bunkers on the front - were stunned to be thrown into this luxury. Nearly all became customers, and sales grew so fast that our ship was hard pressed to meet the new demand.

With Getz Brothers also supplying us, our ship loaded Class Six cargo in Yokohama as well as Hong Kong. At Pusan the liquor was stored in a bonded warehouse watched over by Small Kim's guards and customs officers on our payroll. Tradeship's customers now picked up their orders at any time they wished, rather than wait for deliveries on the open pier.

Most of them elected to spend at least one night enjoying the comforts of the new apartment. But for many, there was also another inducement: a large, boisterous dance hall improbably named the U.N. Officers Club.

PART TWO

The Business Matures

The U.N. Officers Club

Managed and staffed by Koreans, this was the only reasonably decent place in Pusan to drink and meet girls. Admittance was ostensibly restricted to military officers, but in fact it was a popular watering hole for ships' crews and some of us foreign businessmen.

I was taken there soon after arriving by an American businessman in Pusan who had acquired his live-in "moose" (which I learned was a G.I. corruption of the Japanese word *museme*, meaning girl) from among its thirty or forty hopefuls. These girls were generally in their late teens, reasonably attractive and able to communicate in G.I. English. Most wore American dresses given to them by appreciative customers. Nearly all hustled aggressively.

Oley became a regular customer, usually bringing in, and paying for, our military visitors. His language fluency and generous expense account made him a prized customer, so when he arrived with our customers they received fawning attention. Oley had no trouble "booking out" the best girls for them.

These usually included a young lady called Dynamite in appreciation of her explosive performance in the sack. She was their unchallenged leader and broke all records in a "suitability test" conducted by Otto, Oley and me. This required communication skills in English with a minimum of G.I. talk, relatively good looks and figure, and a genuine enthusiasm for sex. Before long our guesthouse was as familiar to these girls as their own Pusan dwellings, and the amahs earned well deserved extra compensation.

Suzi

It was at the U.N. Officers Club that I met Suzi. She interested me because she did not press me for drinks. In fact, she was quite reserved. Suzi was about seventeen, tall with a full figure, and unusually attractive–her face looked almost western, without the characteristic square jaw. Unlike the other girls, Suzi spoke correct English, which she had learned at a convent school in Seoul. She also had top marks and would have continued on to college had not the war destroyed her home and family. She was remarkably bright and popular with my office staff and friends. Before long Suzi became my "moose" and moved in.

My New Home

The idea of building a comfortable home had been germinating for months, especially during the nights when I shivered or sweltered in my rented firetrap. Now, with Tradeship organized, I set about doing this.

My first discovery was that foreigners were not permitted to own land. Even Small Kim and our local lawyer could not find a way to bypass this law. I had resigned myself to rent quarters when my secretary Park offered, "I am Korean and can own land. If you wish I will buy land for you."

Of course. Own it in a Korean citizen's name. But what would happen if the frail old man died? Park had anticipated this. He would will the property to a trusted relative who could hold it for me. When I proposed a commission Park indignantly refused.

The next step was to find a location. I wanted this to be far from the city's dirt and noise, overlooking the sea. The office staff joined in a search and began taking Park and me to prospective sites. A week later we found it.

The plot was about five miles south of Pusan on a hillside overlooking the main coastal highway. A hundred yards below was a rocky beach with a small pier. The only structures in sight were an American CID unit–which to my delight turned out to be commanded by my friend Steve–and a few fishing shacks. To the southeast were small islands, then clean blue ocean.

The property, just under an acre, included about 150 feet of frontage on the road. Once the sparsely wooded slope was leveled there would be plenty of room for a house and garden. No one else was interested and soon Park (and I) owned 40,000 square feet on a hillside in the *Song Do* District of Korea.

The Amazing Construction Project

The next stage was cutting into that hill to form a level base. There were few civilian earth moving companies available, but we found one. The manager, a Mr. Chung, was a hyperactive young man, jolly and chubby, wearing a faded green US military jacket. He agreed to complete the job in four months.

To level the land for my house, two retaining walls of stone and concrete were needed. One would stabilize the slope at the back of the property. The other, a monster, would tower 35 feet over the side of the road, eight feet thick at the base, tapering to three feet at the top. The higher ground at the back would be bulldozed and dumped behind this retaining wall for landfill.

For the final stage we selected a contractor. I had decided on a one–story, ranch-style house with a big living-dining room, three bedrooms with baths, a kitchen and pantry and generous servants' quarters with bath in back. The contractor made an acceptable proposal, which also included a fishpond. We then found a gardener with suitable references.

The Giant Log

Small Kim was delighted to add my house project to his responsibilities and took proprietary interest in every detail. There were no surprises until one day I thought I heard him say that the construction material would be one log. Knowing that he never joked, I questioned, "One log?"

"Yes," he said seriously.

"One log? To build the whole house?"

"Yes, I said that. The contractor recommends that you make the house out of *luan*," he explained patiently. "This is a big tree in the Philippine Islands. He says that you can save money because one log can be cut into enough pieces to make all the house frame. I have investigated. It is true."

One of my shipping friends confirmed that *luan* trees often grew to great size, like our sequoia redwoods. "Sometimes the wood is called Philippine mahogany," he added. Small Kim had already determined that by using heavy lift cranes such a log could be shipped as deck cargo.

By the end of spring the hill was cluttered with earthmovers, cement mixers and other heavy equipment, while a noisy generator supplied power. Workmen were everywhere–swarms of them, always industrious, always moving and carrying things. Foot by foot the retaining wall's building blocks were set into place and the giant stone face crept upward, towering over the road. As it rose, human conveyor belts of laborers moved loads of earth to fill in the newly created space behind. By July both walls were up and the landfill completed.

Small Kim's huge log arrived from the Philippines aboard a Korean tramp. It was moved to a side dock where the first cuts were made. Then the smaller sections, now manageable, were trucked to the road beneath my property and hoisted up over the retaining wall to feed a sawmill installed on the slope. Soon the frame of the house was standing near the back of my land. Plumbers and electricians joined the melee, abetted by the gardener and his crew tramping about the garden area. My home would soon be ready.

The Typhoon

It seemed too good to be true–and it was. Disaster struck with the year's first typhoon. Torrents of water flooded down the hill, overflowed the drainage ducts above the property and poured in. The pressure of tons of water, added to the new landfill, thrust relentlessly against the inside of the retaining wall. During the night the giant barrier gave way. *Song Do* Road, which had been designated a "critical artery" for military use, disappeared under an avalanche of mud and building blocks.

I learned of this at dawn when Small Kim picked me up in the office car. We raced through the storm to the site but were commanded to halt several hundred yards away by angry soldiers and police. All traffic along the southern coast of Korea–military as well as civilian–had halted.

A lot of things happened. Most serious was allocation of blame. Jolly Mr. Chung and several of his staff disappeared. Both Mr. Park and I were questioned as a formality, but quickly exonerated. Meanwhile the efficient Korean military cleared *Song Do* Road and even before the typhoon abated military traffic resumed. The hard-working crews even climbed onto my property to cart off some remaining parts of the wall that threatened to fall.

We could do nothing until Mr. Chung returned. Small Kim told me that he was still being interrogated and had already confessed to adulterating the cement in the wall with sand. To be released he would have to pay heavily.

Apparently he did. When he returned he was no longer the happy fellow that I hired. Dark circles outlined his eyes and I noticed a bandage on one finger. Small Kim spoke with him, then told me that he had claimed innocence but was not believed. His confession had been forced. Whether true or false, one thing was certain: the new wall he built was as strong as Hoover Dam. And apparently as impressive, too. Time and again people who flew or sailed into Pusan from the south said that the first landmark coming into sight from miles out was this massive grey barrier.

I Move into My Home Away from Home

Two months later the landfill was back in place and repairs completed. The final work on the house and garden was done by the end of summer and I, with a huge sigh of relief, moved into my *Song Do* hacienda. Less than two years had passed since I had come to Korea.

Inside, the spacious living room glowed with gentle warmth from the natural golden-hued *luan* walls. Piped water flowed into the kitchen and bathroom and the plumbing actually worked. The power line was connected, and if electricity failed, a back-up generator automatically kicked in. During winter, kerosene heaters and tightly fitting windows kept the interior warm.

Small Kim had arranged for a telephone line to be strung for hundreds of yards along *Song Do* Road and up to my roof. The long distance from the junction exacerbated the notoriously unreliable local phone service, but Steve solved this by having his technicians install a military phone line connected to his CID headquarters exchange down the slope.

A blanket of grass covered the garden and displays of flowers, shrubs and small trees lined the sides. With the aesthetic touch of a *feng shui* priest, the gardener had planted these in eye-pleasing patterns. Near the center was my pride and joy: a 20-foot-long blue tiled fishpond in the shape of the Korean peninsula, with a narrow footbridge spanning the center at the 38th parallel. A school of gray carp swam lethargically underneath, trailing long whiskers.

On the advice of Korean and US military friends I installed defenses against marauding Korean youths who occasionally fought with stolen guns in the neighboring hills. The most obvious was a strong chain fence topped with rolls of accordion wire that encircled the perimeter.

The Hound from Hell

The most formidable defense was Rastus. The name came to me from a ditty, which I learned in school. I acquired this big fierce animal from an American who left Korea. His advice: "Terrific watchdog. Hates Koreans–his mother killed one by going for her throat. Be careful not to let him loose around any."

Rastus was a ferocious mixture of Doberman, Rottweiler and the three-headed Cerberus from hell. If ever there were such a thing as a rabidly segregationist canine, it was he. Somewhere in his genes, or DNA, or wherever such murky instincts lurk, was a slavering hatred for anyone who was not white–particularly Korean men. Rastus prowled the garden and occasionally his Hound of the Baskervilles howl reverberated down *Song Do* Road causing pedestrians to glance anxiously up my retaining wall. Word about this devil dog spread rapidly.

The prospect of losing Suzi to Rastus' appetite concerned me until I arranged an introduction. I prepared this by bringing her inside the house while Rastus was away. To my amazement, when Suzi stepped out into the garden he turned into a docile pussy. His killer instinct apparently applied only to those who he perceived as intruders. Anyone already inside the property, regardless of race, creed, color or sex, was family to be protected.

So Suzi moved in. She was not alone, however. The comparatively spacious living quarters at the back were instantly filled with women. She introduced as assorted aunts–and with them came piles of personal belongings. This I reluctantly tolerated, but when they wanted to bring in *kimshi* pots I put my foot down.

Home, Sweet Home

The house warming party took place just after Thanksgiving. The weather was cold but not yet freezing, and my heaters had brought the interior to a comfortable warmth. I rounded up some fifty guests including my office staff, Col. Dow and his provost marshal team, Steve and his friends from the CID unit down the slope, some Pusan-based customers and our foreign business community.

The general reaction to the house was stunned surprise. Col. Dow, shaking his huge leonine head, summed it up. "By God, John," he exclaimed. "This is the only damned decent house in all of Korea!"

It was then that I realized my new home was indeed unique. There was simply no other modern house in all of the poor war-torn country.

Close Encounter of the Wrong Kind

After moving into my new home with Suzi and her entourage I was advised by military friends to keep a gun handy. The property was well outside of the town and there was always the possibility that a gang could break through the barbed wire fence and kill Rastus. Consequently I kept a carbine, given to me by an army sergeant, as protection. It was always loaded and under our bed. I practiced with a target in the garden and taught Suzi to shoot in case of trouble that Rastus couldn't handle if I were away. Suzi had become adept at using the gun when I left for a weekend trip to Tokyo.

In the hotel lobby I met a Korean girl who held a managerial position at another American company in Pusan. I remembered her immediately because of her striking body and exotic Eurasian features. I thought I saw invitation in her eyes then, but did not want to get involved since she worked for a potential competitor and word got around quickly in Pusan.

But Tokyo was different. We had dinner, then spent a long and turbulent night in my bed. Now I knew that Korean women were passionate, but this one carried passion to the stratosphere. She was utterly insatiable, but instead of doing the normal hollering and screaming, she just wept quietly as her body responded again and again.

She must have spent months of pent up sexual drive that night, and I could have easily died of heart failure. However, I didn't, then. My close encounter with death by heart failure took place a few nights later back home in Pusan.

When we went to bed I noticed that Suzi seemed to be acting strangely but didn't think anything of it. Then, sometime after midnight, I was awakened by the sound of crying off my side of the bed. I sensed that it was Suzi and opened an eye to see what was wrong. Then I froze. In the dim light I saw it was Suzi all right, standing right next to me–holding my carbine pointed directly at my crotch!

My mind raced desperately. In a second I realized that my playmate in Tokyo had spread news of our fun and games when she returned to Pusan, and Suzi had heard. I also knew that it was a toss-up between Korean and Russian women as to which were the most dangerous in the jealousy department–both had richly documented histories of stabbing and shooting unfaithful lovers. With my arms trapped under the blankets I had only two choices: to attempt to persuade Suzi to lower the deadly weapon, or to lie still and hope for the best. I chose to lie still, pretending to sleep. My heart pounded violently and I could taste fear in my mouth. Meanwhile Suzi remained standing there, sobbing, with that damned gun.

Then, with no prelude, my Guardian Angel did her magic. Suzi dropped the carbine, climbed in, and fiercely clung to me. I slipped my arms around her and spoke soothingly. Before long her trembling stopped and she drifted off to sleep.

Not me. I lay there for hours wondering what the hell to do. The idea of sending her away was unpalatable. Instead, I felt strangely protective.

Before dawn I slipped out, put the gun back under the bed, and returned for a few hours' sleep. Suzi stayed–and I was much, much more careful after that. She was deeply in love and I, for my part, grew very fond of her.

Near the end of 1953, when I had decided to leave, I wanted to make the break in a way that would least hurt her. The best possibility would be for her to marry a respectable foreigner, and the opportunity came when a friend asked for my permission. He was one of the Swedish doctors from a nearby hospital and would have given her a comfortable life back in Sweden. But Suzi refused, insisting she would come to America with me.

I knew that she wanted to finish her education and this gave me the idea of sending her to college in America. She agreed, saying that she would continue to see me there. So I looked for a good university that would accept her and helped her apply for student visa. With the help of Pete, who was still at our embassy, I was able to manage both. At year-end I sent Suzi to a good Midwestern college with financing arranged for tuition and living expenses. I was confident that she would be self-sufficient when she graduated–and I was right.

Suzi married a fellow Korean student and both became doctors. Before long, as naturalized Americans, they started a family. They must have been very happy because every Christmas, when I received a card from her and her husband, there seemed to be one more baby in the family picture.

PART THREE

Tradeship Goes Big Time

The Thunderbirds Want Asahi

As 1953 arrived, the cease-fire held along the 38th parallel. No major attack took place although nearly every night armed patrols probed deep into the two-mile-wide "exclusion zone" separating the two sides, sometimes clashing in deadly fire fights. These often brought down a barrage of artillery shells, followed by counter-battery shelling from the other side. Some of these artillery duels threatened to break the truce, but this did not happen. Still, troops were still being killed every month, mostly Chinese.

In Pusan, Tradeship had become an active participant in the local economy. Export shipments were increasing. Charlie Chan was issuing open policies for more companies. And our shipping department was so busy importing full loads of our Class Six and exporting cargoes for Pusan merchants that Oley jokingly complained he didn't have time to service his harem.

While local business continued to be important, our major thrust of course was Class Six sales. Business had expanded to the point where we were filling trial orders from the divisions, regiments and other large units in the north. We were finally reaching the big ones.

Our breakthrough came with the 45th infantry division–the distinguished Thunderbirds. Their special services officer, a cheerful red headed captain nicknamed Red, turned up to load an order for about 3,000 cases, mostly Canadian Club. This was our first division-size delivery, and although I thought we had prepared well there was still a logistics problem parking the fleet of deuce-and-a-half trucks, which had driven 230 miles south from beyond Uijongbu to take delivery. They cluttered the pier, impeding MSTS cargo movements until we arranged to spread them out in the town.

Red and three sergeants stayed that night in our guesthouse, while the Korean truck drivers had no trouble finding quarters in town. I passed word to Dynamite that this was a special occasion so she brought a troop of her best girls to enjoy the comforts of "The Tradeship House" with our visitors that night. The next morning Red's usual smile was positively ecstatic.

Before roaring off with his caravan, he assured me that if the quality of our supplies matched that of our service he would shift his prime supply source from the military-managed Japan Locker Fund to Tradeship. Then, in an afterthought, he asked whether we supplied beer. When I mentioned Japanese beer he looked startled.

"Jap beer? Here? Man, you know we just came over from Japan. Many of our guys got hooked on Jap beer when we were stationed there. They like it much better than that watered down pee the Locker Fund sends and they're always bitching about why I can't get them any." He thought a moment. "Send me a sample. If you can bring in decent Jap beer I'll give you my order and probably sign up several other divisions, too. Be sure to let me know and get that sample to me."

I replied, "Red, the beer is damn good. I've tasted it. But the labels on the bottles look crappy and we want to fix them up first."

"Labels? Who the hell drinks labels? Just get us that beer *hiyaku.*"

That did it. I called Otto to line up beer company reps to meet us urgently and prepared for another visit. My trip was short but fruitful. Nishie had arranged for us to visit the breweries of the two brands that we found acceptable during our taste test. At Sapporo we were met by a delegation including the manager. First came the introductions, conducted with ritual bowing between the manager and Otto, then me, then Nishie, then others until I thought of the limbo dance and almost burst out laughing.

After a tour, we were treated to a delicious sukiyaki lunch squatting around a low table in the boardroom. There was a lot of Japanese dialog with Nishie, and the occasional polite question to us which he translated. Finally they brought out samples of their products, explaining through Nishie their packing configurations, prices, deliveries and so on. We left with the feeling that we could work with these people, who were gracious and professional.

Hongo from the Congo

The Asahi brewery was next. We received the same ritual welcome and once again made a brewery tour. This one appeared newer and larger. We were spared the painful process of translation since their front man, Hongo, spoke fluent English. He was the perfect sales manager to interface with us–a short, bald, chubby bundle of good humor and jokes, relating easily with foreign *gaijins.* When Otto and I told him we referred to him privately as Hongo from the Congo he doubled over in wheezing laughter.

Hongo immediately agreed that their label could be changed and promised samples within two days. We could have any label designs we selected. When I told him the volume of business we anticipated, he hooked us solidly with his quotation. This was barely $5.00 per case of 24 quart bottles, each wrapped in its own protective straw shielding.

Otto and I left shaking our heads in wonder. Hongo's prices were so low that even with freight, insurance and a fat profit margin, our buyers could take delivery at prices barely half as much as they were paying for PX beer. They would get a terrific deal and we would have a once-in-a-lifetime opportunity.

We looked at each other, barely able to contain our excitement. "We've found a gold mine," I exclaimed. "Liquid yellow gold."

Otto, always chaffing at my insistence that our guys pay low prices, beamed, "Have we ever! This will be a really *umglaublich* business!"

"That sounds German. What the hell does it mean?"

"Liquid yellow gold!" Otto giggled at his wit.

The Asahi prospect was so important that I postponed my return trip to carry back Hondo's new label samples and some sample bottles. I would rush them from Pusan to Red so he could select the design he preferred.

That night there was a gentle knock on my door. The girl who slipped in was an angel, young and perfect. The next morning I realized that she must have been the top of the line, reserved for visiting royalty and beer salesmen.

Our First Asahi Beer Order

The samples which I had carried back reached Red at his division HQ four days later. He was so pleased that he phoned me his label choice, then sent the order I had been hoping for: the entire beer requisition for his 45th division plus those in other nearby units–over 25,000 men in all. With the heavy strong packing, the full shipment would weigh about 500 tons.

Moving so much beer from Pusan was out of the question, so Red stipulated delivery up north at Inchon where his division's facilities could handle it. This gave us a real challenge. The Inchon tides–second highest in the world–rose and fell about 30 feet. When the tide was out a tidal mud flat stretched out several miles from shore, cutting off all transport. Ships had to anchor far out at sea, discharging their cargoes into squadrons of barges to be towed ashore during the few hours of the flood tide.

When I gave the news to Oley he shook his head. "That's a bastard. A real bastard. Things always go wrong at that damn place. There'll be problems that add days of demurrage." After a moment, he added, "If we use our ship our schedule will be fooked up for months. Better a Jap charter."

Still, no sweat. Oley and I flew to Seoul and drove a borrowed Jeep west past Uijongbu to the old fishing port. The tide was out. Standing on Inchon's ancient stone seawall we looked out across a wasteland of stinking black mud. Scattered here and there on the surface were stranded small boats, but that was all. I shook my head, wondering how our First Marines could have ever fought their way ashore in this forbidding place.

We found a stevedore boss who had been recommended and I listened while he and Oley jabbered away in Korean. Oley seemed to use a lot of angry words and once I thought he was going to take a punch. Whatever his negotiating style was, it worked and we lined up some 30 barges with teams of laborers to offload the cargo when our shipment arrived. I estimated this would be in about six weeks, allowing time for Asahi to make up a special shipment with Red's labels, and delivery to Inchon.

With Oley's assurance that he would personally supervise the operation, I sent the order to Hongo. He didn't believe the quantity until I reconfirmed it. Otto then renegotiated even better payment terms.

Before leaving Inchon I checked whether we could arrange our own bonded warehouse there. This would greatly facilitate working with units around Seoul and the divisions protecting the front. With Oley's Korean language help, I learned that this could be done.

Dick Johnson: Star Sales Manager

I met Dick Johnson a few days after returning to Pusan when a tall, blond sergeant strolled into my office holding a handful of Class Six requisitions. He introduced himself then said, "I'm getting my discharge soon and want to go to work for you."

Surprised and amused, I asked, "Just like that?"

"Well, I figure you can use me. I'm a damned good salesman. I picked up some orders to show you."

I looked them over–requisitions from the Wolfhound Regiment, the 24th Signal Battalion, a M.A.S.H. outfit and a dozen or so other units stationed around Seoul, all made out to Tradeship, Ltd. I was impressed.

He had prepared well for this call. "Nice. Good work. How'd you get the idea of joining us?"

"I've talked to some of the club sergeants around Pusan who buy from you. You've got this place locked up. But there's nobody from your company up north and I think you can use someone like me there. I'm with a signal battalion near Seoul and meet a lot of people in my job. I can easily get to the buyers. Like these." He motioned to the orders. "I could even start now, in my spare time. After my discharge I can go to work full time. I already have a place lined up to stay in Seoul."

Better and better. And perfect timing. My experience with Red had convinced me that we needed a good sales and service presence in Seoul if we were serious about ongoing business with the big accounts there. I arranged for Dick to have dinner at my house with Oley and Small Kim.

We agreed afterwards that Dick would fit right in. My CID friends gave him a clean bill of health. I then sent Dick to Taego to meet Major Bill. He did so well there that I received a congratulatory call from the major, who also sent me an introductory letter for Dick if we hired him. Dick had an R&R to Tokyo coming up. Otto met him there and immediately approved. A few weeks later he was discharged and joined us as Sales Manager.

It didn't take long for me to discover that hiring him was one of the best moves I made in Korea. Although only 24, he had already been promoted to sergeant first class and was comfortable with authority and responsibility. He was also a hustler. With him on board to manage sales, Oley for shipping and Small Kim for everything else, I now had three stout legs to carry the heavy operating load that I had been shouldering by myself. It felt wonderful.

Down to (and Under) the Sea

Friends at the nearby CID unit had been trying for months to get me out on a fast air-sea rescue boat based near Pusan. It was nearly as big as the famous PT boats, and was used to transport underwater specialist units–called UDTs–to and from secret destinations up the coast. With my new free time, I went out one afternoon on a memorable fishing trip.

By the time we returned, two exciting events had taken place. First, I hooked a monster king mackerel that needed the muscle of a big Navy chief to pull aboard; and second, I made a shallow dive wearing a UDT face mask and flippers. The water was too cold for me to stay in more than two minutes, but this was enough to kindle a flame in my adventure circuit that–a few lives later–would explode unto a string of wild adventures beneath two oceans on the other side of the world.

I Visit the Big PX

I was listening to the AFRS one night when the radio played a medley from Guys and Dolls. Remembering the great time Ace and I had at our Guys and Dolls Mint Julep Gala in Hong Kong, I thought: why not go to New York and see the original on Broadway? And why not invite some friends, too?

Three weeks later I had a block of excellent seats for an evening show that Lila Tyng kindly arranged. I was delighted to receive acceptances from old college roommates Paul, Bud, Sandy, several D.U. Club friends with their wives. Jaye had married during the five years since we had romanced in New York, but my wild Hong Kong playmate, Nina, still gorgeous and now living in luxury in New York, would join me.

I traveled in comfort. After a short visit with Otto in Tokyo, I crossed the Pacific on the double-decker Boeing Stratocruiser, where I was spoiled with attention on the upper deck and slept comfortably in a full bed below.

Arriving in New York, I was met by a limo, which took me to my parents' home in Southampton. They had aged since leaving Shanghai, but were still enthusiastic with a full social life as members of the Southampton Meadow Club, Beach Club and Garden Club–of which Mother was president. Dad stayed busy maintaining their beautiful estate *Pao Hai* (Chinese for "Potter by the Sea"), assisted by their faithful retainer Dennis.

Hardly had I stepped from the car when I was assaulted by a tongue-licking, tail-wagging blanket of black fur clawing high onto my shoulders. Whining and yelping, my baby Cindy had somehow recognized me! For two days, in every moment I was not with Dad and Mom, I played with my baby Cindy.

It broke my heart to leave her. This visit to America also made me realize that I had been missing a whole lot by isolating myself from much of the events in the outside world. Now, with Tradeship established and those four strong legs of Otto, Oley, Dick and Small Kim in place, why should I stay longer? I decided that as soon as Olga was released, I would meet her and go to Europe together. I had enough saved from my accumulated sales commissions, and with Suzi set at school, there was no reason for me to stay.

Back in New York I joined my friends at the 46th Street Theatre. The production was outstanding with Vivian Blaine and the whole cast receiving rave reviews. In my mind I again thanked Lila Tyng for having made this event possible. At the close I was so fired up that I invited the group to the Stork Club, where during Patty's days as a leading debutante I was a *persona grata* and would routinely sign the bill and receive a gift from Sherman Billingsley.

But that was then and this was now. No gift arrived–only an astronomical bill including the cost of a drink which Nina had playfully poured on the bald head of a gentleman at the next table. To compound the slight, the waiter refused to accept my signature. In Korea I had become used to simply signing, and carried no money or checks. The impasse was solved by my friends, who lent me the cost of the bill.

Our Asahi Beer Causes Near Disaster

The day that our Asahi shipment came in Dick Johnson met Oley and me at Seoul's airport, and we reached Inchon harbor by mid-morning. An amazing spectacle was awaiting us: a line of barges stacked with wooden beer cases stretched from the Inchon sea wall clear out to our Japanese freighter in the distance.

At our feet, boards had been laid above the smelly black water to the nearest barges, and platoons of laborers bounced back and forth on them chanting in rhythm as they carried ashore the thousands of heavy beer cases. Our stevedore had organized well.

Red arrived with a train of boxcars. Aboard each car a military guard watched carefully as every case was tallied and brought aboard. The work went so fast that the final cases were loaded by dusk. Then Red rode with his cargo to a distribution point near Seoul, where consignees would pick up their allocations.

At my suggestion Oley stayed to start arrangements for a bonded warehouse. A few days later Small Kim joined us there, with the result that not long afterwards we were able to warehouse our customers' shipments at that port.

The reception for Red's shipment of Asahi beer promptly led to orders from other divisions for Inchon delivery. One happened to be on the front line when their consignment arrived–and was immediately consumed. Part of it went to an artillery battalion guarding a critical outpost facing an aggressive Chinese unit across the DMZ. Our gunners, used to the mild PX beer, were KO'ed by the high-powered Japanese beverage. I learned the results in a phone call from Major Bill.

"What the hell did you do to those gunners? The Chicoms started battery fire and our guys were so drunk they couldn't even level the bubbles on their guns!" Before I could reply he said, "The general is really pissed off. His aide told me he was thinking of shutting you down. He probably won't, but someone may call you to explain. So be ready to go and have a good answer."

The dreaded call never came, but plenty of worry did. I passed the word to all our buyers asking them to prevent any repetition.

PART FOUR

Wild Times in Land of Morning Calm

Poker

The facilities available to us civilians in Pusan offered little opportunity for higher-level cultural activities. Basically, apart from working, drinking and whoring there was little to do. So our thirst for culture led us to poker. At first we played low-stakes games with wild cards–deuces, one-eyed jacks, and anything else the dealer could think of. Times and locations were determined by availability.

Gradually our game matured. The casual players dropped out and more serious ones took over. Games were restricted to five-card draw and five and seven-card stud, nothing wild. We played table stakes, pot limit, with full settlement in cash or credible IOUs after each session. The changed mix of players brought real money to the table, and antes soared from one dollar to five or even ten. Raises climbed to hundreds of dollars and pots often held thousands.

The game continued to float until I moved into my new house. Then I became the permanent host. We started at seven every Friday evening and the last round was dealt at midnight. Players were restricted to our Pusan regulars, Korean National Airlines pilots Gene and Slim, U.N. officer Obie Mueting, and my old friend Big Louie, who was still here running his ship agency without being fired. Occasional outsiders, who had to be well recommended, were admitted. These were visiting business associates, U.S. military officers and senior U.N. civilians.

The most colorful overseas visitor was old friend Ace Smith, who was still supplying some of our military sales from Hong Kong. He flew up occasionally for the poker game, bringing excitement and humor to the usually serious business of trying to extract money from the other players. Undoubtedly the best player I ever met, Ace had sat with professionals in locations as diverse as Macao and Las Vegas. Always genial, he would smile as he raked in a pot full of chips, commenting cheerfully, "For some people the birds sing...for others it's lucky that cows don't fly", or "When a winner, go to dinner."

Like the others, I nearly always lost to Ace. Except for one hand sent from Heaven. In a seven-card stud game, with one card to go, he had four hearts showing and I had one ace up and two covered. The other five players had folded under a barrage of raises from us and the pot held over three thousand dollars. The last card was dealt down, and I didn't improve.

Ace didn't bother to look. Instead, he casually pushed out a thousand dollars, sat back and grinned at me–leered would be more accurate. Every shred of common sense told me: Get out! He made it. But some instinct...anyway, Ace ended with a busted flush and I took the fat pot, still shaking inside.

Later, after the game, as he handed me a check, Ace said, "John, I'd appreciate it if you don't talk about that hand. You know, I have a reputation to keep up." Ace died some years later and I suspect has by now cleaned out the players up there, genial as ever.

Another visitor left an indelible mark–literally as well as figuratively. He was a captain supervising a big shipment we were loading on a train in Pusan. He had just come in from a section of the front where fierce skirmishing was going on.

Handing me a mud-caked gun, he announced, "Hey, John, got a *presento* for you. From Mao Tse-dung. This a Chinese burp gun– just like Al Capone's." With the drum it sure looked like the tommy-guns in gangster movies.

He sat in our game that night as I passed his gun around to the other players. When one raised it to his waist, the captain said sharply, "Careful, it's loaded." He quickly took the gun and laid it on the floor. Not much later, a large and noisy black fly began distracting us from our game. After buzzing most of the players, it finally settled on the ceiling over the table.

I had been drinking with customers since early afternoon and that fly was really irritating me. There was no way to swat the bastard up there. So I did what seemed to be the only reasonable thing. I drew my S&W .38 from the holster I always wore, leaned back in my chair and blasted away at the insect. The noise startled several of the players, who jumped back. That–and six splintery holes dotting the ceiling around the fly– were the only immediate results of my effort.

It did, however, galvanize the captain into a second attack on the fly. Roaring with glee, he scooped up the burp gun from the floor, raised it to his shoulder and leaned into the trigger. The noise was deafening. We ducked, convulsed with laughter, as flying cartridges and chips of wood rained down on us. The room filled with choking acrid smoke. When the barrage finally stopped, we stared up through watering eyes at the ceiling–or what was left of it. That damned fly had moved a few feet, but was still there.

The next morning I summoned the contractor to repair the damage. As we looked at the gaping hole I noticed that it came within a few feet of the ridge beam. It was then that I realized we had been lucky that the stream of bullets had not chopped into that key support.

Over time, our game slowly deteriorated. Our self-imposed discipline eroded under the pressure of corrupting influences. There was more liquor freely available from breakage as our shipments increased. Players who had drunk, or lost, the most wanted to continue after midnight and the games straggled on until dawn. Dynamite's girls started to turn up and wandered about–often nearly naked–filling our glasses and providing relief to frustrated players in my two spare rooms.

Betting sometimes went completely crazy–one night I won Tom's little house in Tokyo, which turned out to be his only asset. I tore up his IOU and he dropped out for good. Fewer players showed up as businesses moved north to Seoul.

When I pulled out, what was left of the game went back to floating from house to house again.

I Become Pilot, Nearly Kill a Plane-Load of People

By the fall, 1953, most of my operational work had been delegated. This gave me plenty of opportunity to hop over to Tokyo for recreation. I usually left on Saturdays, flying the early morning "*Kimchi* Express" – an old Korean National Airlines C-46 that shuttled between Pusan and Tokyo. This twin-engine plane somewhat resembled the popular C-47, or DC-3, but was not so stable in flight and had a tendency to yaw.

One Saturday morning Gene, Slim and I went directly from my all-night poker game to the airport. The plane was packed, as usual, with Korean passengers and their bags, vegetables, chickens and other travel necessities including jars of *kimshi*. This morning its nauseating smell saturated the plane's cramped interior with a stronger kick than usual, even overwhelming the alcohol fumes which we exhaled.

Climbing the wobbly boarding ladder, co-pilot Slim shook his head. "Don't feel so good," he mumbled. He had tried to compensate for a run of bad cards by overdosing on straight scotches and Dynamite's girls. Spotting an empty seat, he flopped down and promptly fell asleep.

Gene motioned me toward the cockpit. "You can be my co-pilot." I thought nothing of this and settled into the right-hand seat next to him. He pushed and pulled levers, and presently one engine, then the other, exploded to life creating huge clouds of black smoke and heavy vibration. Before long, I was looking down on the checkerboard countryside as we headed toward Japan.

Gene yawned, then turned to me, "Ever fly a plane, John?" I started to make some wise rejoinder, then realized he was serious. "It's easy, no sweat," he reassured. He pointed out the compass. "See this dial? Just keep on an easterly vector, about 90 degrees like we're going now. And we want to maintain our altitude of about 5,000 feet." He showed me the altimeter. Then he called my attention to the twin steering wheels. "You steer with it, just like a car. Turn right to go right and left to go left. If you want to go up, pull the wheel back. If you want to go down, push it forward. It's easy, see?" Gene demonstrated, then I tried. Sure enough, the plane responded. I practiced until Gene was satisfied. Then he said, "OK, I'm going to knock off for a while. Wake me up when you see the Jap coast. Think you can handle it?"

"No sweat." I experimented with the wheel again, watching the instruments.

"Just remember, we're not far from the 38th parallel. Don't turn north unless you want to get us shot down by MIGs." He added, "And if you get sleepy be sure to wake me up. The passengers expect a live pilot flying their plane." Gene was soon asleep.

I concentrated on keeping the course, carefully watching the compass and altimeter as I practiced handling the wheel. This concentration was making my eyes feel heavy, but I was in complete control.

Something was wrong with the instruments. The altimeter said 9,000 feet and the compass was pointing north. With a shock I realized I had been asleep and the plane had changed course. My God, we were headed due north! We might be in North Korea! MIGs! Instinctively I swung the wheel to the right and jammed it forward. The plane responded with a diving spin to the right. In front of me the horizon flew past the windshield from right to left, faster and faster.

I was fighting to straighten it out when the gyrating plane and screaming passengers awakened Gene. He grabbed his wheel, struggling with it as he shouted to me, "Let go the wheel!" When he finally got us under control we had plummeted nearly a mile, to 4,000 feet. Gene glared at me, his face very pale, shaking his head. It was then that the realization really hit home.

I had nearly killed a whole plane-load of people! If my Guardian Angel had not been doing her job so well, I would be spread out among the other forty bodies, torn to pieces, somewhere down below.

It took us many drinks at Tokyo's most expensive hostess bar, the Gimbasha, to completely recover. In addition, to mollify Gene, I presented him with the featured club stripper for the full night, paid for in advance.

"Slicky-Slicky Boys" and the Pyramid of Pens

Small Kim continued to prove his value in just about every aspect of our work. As a detective and policeman, he repeatedly pulled Tradeship out of potential business problems. Now, unexpectedly, I provided him with the chance to apply his talents to me personally to recover a stolen gold Parker pen engraved with my name, that a girl had given me.

I was wearing it in the usual place, clipped to my shirt pocket, as I walked along Pusan's main street one afternoon. Out of the blue came a "slicky-slicky boy" wielding a simple but effective tool for robbing: several strands of horsehair folded in a loop with both ends grasped in one hand. These little thieves walk or run by someone wearing a pen like I was, and with an upward swish of the arm catch the clip of a pen in the hair and yank it loose from the shirt. Then, with the pen dangling from the hair, they take off.

Of course I knew about this trick, but simply did not notice the kid in time. I dashed after him but he vanished up an alley. Any further pursuit would be fruitless, since they quickly passed on such stolen items to others and are clean if caught. These "slicky-slicky boys" operated in groups of six or eight under the control of a *mamasan* who received and no doubt fenced the fruits of their thievery. No one that I knew had ever been able to recover his loss.

I was bitching about my stupidity when I returned to the office. Small Kim overhead me and quietly asked some questions, but I had nearly forgotten the incident when he returned later and asked me to accompany him. We walked to a nearby police station, which seemed unusually crowded as we entered. In fact, it was mobbed by old women and countless little urchins, many of them cowering and all of them clearly terrified.

A long table had been placed in the center and to my amazement I saw that it was covered with a tall pyramid of pens. There were thousands of them: Parker, Shaffer, Cross and brands I had never heard of in all shapes and colors. Several tough looking policemen stood there making occasional growling remarks at the women and kids, which set them cringing. Small Kim pointed to the loot and said, "Your pen is in here, John. You can take it." I thought I saw the trace of a smile on his face.

Somewhat bewildered, I began my search. Good God, I thought, where did they all come from? This must be the fruits of months of thievery. It took me over an hour, but there it was.

What would happen to the culprits? I started to ask, but I already know. The best pens would be confiscated and the mamas squeezed for bribes. Then they would all go back to business as usual.

The San Miguel Battlefield

The most popular beer across Asia was probably San Miguel, brewed in The Philippines and exported to countries all over the world. Toward the end of 1953 Tradeship was approached by their Japan sales representative. We were all familiar with the popular "San Mig" and often ordered it ourselves, so Otto and I had no hesitation in giving it a try.

The first shipments were well received and Tradeship's turnover jumped from hundreds of cases to several thousand each month. Although our profit did not approach that of Asahi, I felt we should handle San Miguel to avoid being known as a single beer marketer. Landed shipments were stored in our Pusan bonded warehouse with the other Class Six items pending delivery.

All went well until one afternoon when Dick and I were visiting the 3rd Infantry division up north. I received a call to rush back -- there were injuries in the warehouse and the laborers refused to work. I arrived the next day to find a situation beyond the control of even Small Kim. Our warehouse had turned into a battlefield. From half a block away I heard rifle shots, sometimes in short bursts like automatic fire.

"What the hell is going on?" I demanded.

"The bottles are exploding!" someone said.

"Broken glass flying everywhere! Don't go inside."

I quickly learned that the bottles in the last San Miguel shipment were exploding like hand grenades. They were packed, as usual, in cartons stacked about ten layers high. As each bottle shattered the beer soaked the cardboard which became soggy and collapsed, causing the stacks to settle into masses of cardboard sludge and broken glass on the concrete floor.

There were at least 20,000 bottles of beer here and they all seemed to be exploding together. The warehouse interior had turned into a fierce storm of glass shards whizzing through the air and cutting everything.

My first concern was the injured workers. Trapped inside when the exploding began, many were hit as they raced for the exit. I was hugely relieved to find that they had been immediately treated and no one was seriously hurt. With their safety assured, I attacked other questions. Fortunately, none of the other Class Six orders in the warehouse were stored close enough to be damaged. Our own cargo was protected in wooden cases. I was not surprised to learn that Small Kim had anticipated the arrival of customers coming to take delivery, and put them on hold.

That left the damaged cargo. I sent a report directly to Don Andres Soriano, founder and majority owner of San Miguel. Demonstrating his worldwide reputation for integrity, Don Andres replied promptly and personally. He apologized that the bottles were the first production run of a glass factory he had started. Unfortunately there had been a production error. A replacement shipment in strong bottles was being sent to us. To compensate for our losses and trouble he enclosed his personal check for US$50,000.

This was my first experience with Don Andres. As time passed, I learned that he was revered by thousands of employees in various Soriano enterprises all around the world, and highly respected by colleagues and competitors alike. Years later I met his planning officer at the Columbia Business School, but sadly never had the opportunity to meet this gentleman.

PART FIVE

Tradeship: The Champion

Suitors Come a-Knocking

I was still deciding the date to leave Korea when Val passed along a message that Olga had received U.N. documents for travel to most European countries and Macao. But not Hong Kong. What should she do? Communicating through Val, I decided she should get out of her refugee camp without delay and go to a good hotel in Macao, where I would send her money and a plane ticket. We could meet in Rome as soon as I could get there.

I was starting preparations to leave when Otto called me to Japan. There were developments that needed my presence with the American International Underwriters in Tokyo. I did not want any delay, but flew over anyway. Our first meeting was with Paul Aurell, senior AIU officer. I still respected his company as an aggressive competitor from my days in insurance in Shanghai. More recently, Paul and I had become friendly during my visits to Tokyo, and I suspected that he had our Korea insurance capabilities in mind. I was right. Over lunch at the Tokyo American Club, Paul–always direct–came right to the point. The AIU would like to discuss our appointment as their sub-agents for South Korea. The arrangement would be mutually exclusive.

This was no surprise. By this time Charlie Chan and two new assistants had locked up most of Korea's quality insurance business with our British principals. Paul had obviously considered this when planning for our meeting, because his starting offer was surprisingly generous.

I faced the classic tug of war between loyalty and common sense. On one hand, I could not bring myself to dump our British insurers, who had supported us from the start. On the other, I badly wanted to tie up AIU to prevent this powerhouse from going into competition with us on our own turf. We were exploring ways to break this apparent impasse when Paul said quietly, "I understand you have an appointment with the Japan Locker Fund after this."

Otto looked up in surprise. "You knew?"

"Well, I should, Otto. We handle all their insurance. In fact, I suggested they consider you for taking over their shipments to Korea."

I was stunned. The Locker Fund sent thousands of tons of Class Six goods and related supplies to Korea each month. I had long considered this huge business beyond our reach. If we could acquire it, our shipments–and profits–would increase enormously. The complexion of our discussion immediately changed. We parted company with an agreement in principal for Tradeship to maintain our present agency for existing business accounts, but for Charlie to set up and manage a separate Tradeship insurance department to book new business for AIU. Subject to his agreement, of course, and a satisfactory contract.

Otto and I reviewed our discussion with Paul all the way to Yokohama. By the time we reached the Locker Fund we had planned our approach. We were shown into a simple conference room where several army officers were expecting us. After preliminaries, their senior officer, a colonel, explained the reason for this invitation.

Their organization was set up to provide overseas U.S. forces with non-essential commodities including Class Six goods. The responsibility of purchasing and delivering these products was strictly theirs. They did not have special access to military transport like the M.S.T.S., and operated under many of the same constraints as commercial companies.

The Locker Fund had been experiencing heavy losses from theft and pilferage, and breakage, on shipments to Korea. Despite their best attempts they had not been able to reduce these losses, but hoped that an organization more familiar with Korea could do so. They decided to put the transport of their Class Six up for tenders. Would Tradeship be interested in bidding?

I knew immediately that they needed a complete secure superintendence service. We were the only organization that could provide this, with our network of ground transport and bonded warehouses and the tight security, but I was not sure that they appreciated this. After obtaining basic data like monthly tonnage, we excused ourselves to prepare Tradeship's offer.

The colonel, obviously puzzled, consulted with his staff. Then he cautioned, "You recognize that this is a big commitment. Over a million dollars every month. Don't you have to run this through a board, or a management committee for approval?"

Otto and I grinned at each other. Then Otto replied as seriously as he could, "Colonel, we *are* the management committee. We will need five minutes to run some numbers by and then will give you Tradeship's firm offer."

As we worked at a table at the far end of the room, I chuckled, "You sounded pretty serious there, Otto. Lots of *gravitas*."

We did not want competition and recognized the importance of derailing any tendering before it got started. To do this we decided to force a quick acceptance by making a compelling "shut out" offer with an early deadline.

When we rejoined the officers, Otto presented a summation:

"US$3.25 per case of twelve fifths in standard cardboard or wood cases from warehouse Yokohama to bonded warehouse Pusan with a US$0.75 per case surcharge to bonded warehouse Inchon. Offer firm for one week from today. Contract for one year with Tradeship's option to renew for a second year. Any dispute to be settled by arbitration. Tradeship to provide all requested documents and U.S. bank guarantee."

The next day our Tokyo lawyer fleshed this out in legalese. Otto had it typed on Tradeship stationery and delivered by messenger. Early the following week, after a few final discussions, our terms were accepted. I returned several times with Oley to set up the operation.

Five weeks later we loaded Tradeship's second chartered Korean ship, complete with our insignia on its funnel, with 900 tons of Locker Fund cargo for Inchon. The project was successful. Paul, carrying the insurance, was delighted at our loss ratio of less than 1% and I learned later that Tradeship's contract was renewed for several years.

Tying up Loose Ends: The First Marines

During my stay I had acquired assets to be disposed of. First was my house and furnishings. The value had diminished by half, as businesses moved to Seoul, but I was still able to find a buyer. He was a pleasant Swede representing the Scandinavian shipping company Holme Ringer. Nils had visited my home several times and wanted to keep my furniture, fittings and especially Rastus. He would also retain my household help. I arranged for Nils to meet Park and we worked out an ownership transfer satisfactory to everyone. Before leaving, I slipped Park an envelope with a letter expressing my gratitude and a US$ payment large enough to support him and his family for several years. I also arranged for Small Kim to oversee his continuing supply of PAS.

Other odds and ends took care of themselves. I transferred my two S&W .38 revolvers to Oley and Dick, the carbine to Small Kim and the Chinese burp gun to Colonel Dow. Finally, I assured myself that Suzi was secure at her college in America and her family was back at their old home in Seoul.

After a series of emotional good-by parties in December, I flew to Seoul to do a final errand. During the past months I had been with most of our infantry divisions: the 45th, 3rd and 25th along the western half of the front and the 7th somewhere near the middle. But our First Marines, who I wanted to visit most of all, had always been elusive. I was determined to catch them before leaving.

My chance finally came just before Christmas. I set off from Seoul early in the morning in a borrowed 3rd Division Jeep, picking a really great day for traveling. The whole country was in deep freeze under the worse Siberian winter of recent times, with temperatures running 20 and even 30 degrees below freezing. Snowdrifts were piled high everywhere by hurricane force winds. Worst of all, the Jeep's windows were iced over and pelted by sleet, making it necessary to poke a head out to see anything.

The Jeep was winterized. In Korea this had a special meaning. Not only did the vehicle have chains on the tires and a tightly buttoned down canvas top, but it also had central heating–literally. In the center of the back seat, fixed to the frame, a small gas furnace roared ferociously as it threw off torrents of evil smelling high-octane fumes. The interior stank of seared metal. I realized that one accident and I could be toast.

Following directions, I drove very, very carefully north to Uijangbu then east toward Chunchon with the Jeep slipping all over the deserted icy road–cow trail would be more accurate. Then, just as I began to feel confident, it slid into a ditch. Gently, thank God. I tried to back out but it would not respond.

There was no AAA handy to pull me out, or any other living creature in sight, or even a way to communicate for help. I began to seriously doubt my wisdom in making this insane journey. It could easily end with me being found right there hours or days later, frozen solid after the furnace ran out of gas.

My journey ended right there all right, but not in that Jeep. By incredible good fortune a patrolling MP wagon came by. The crew somehow recognized the Jeep as U.S. military before it was buried under snow, and stopped to investigate. The magic name of Colonel Dow took care of the rest and I got a welcome ride back to Seoul. This time, my Guardian Angel had *really* been working overtime.

3. Goodbye, Asia – Hello, Europe

On December 29 I flew south to Hong Kong en route to Italy, where I had arranged to meet Olga. As the plane gained altitude over the coast

I looked back at the massive grey retaining wall I had erected over *Song Do.* My feeling of sadness over leaving so many friends behind presently gave way to satisfaction. Satisfaction over having improved the lives of hundreds of men and women that I had brought into Tradeship's businesses, set up in their own businesses, or helped in other ways.

I was mildly dissatisfied to be leaving without seeing some pending projects through to completion. But before long, thoughts of unfinished ventures faded away with the final view of my retaining wall. As I exited my first nine lives, I was already moving toward new lives in the future.

I knew they would be rewarding and exciting. But not even in my wildest imagination could I have foreseen such events as winning the big one at Monte Carlo, wrestling with a giant conger eel deep under the Mediterranean as it ripped a 60-pound grouper off my spear, drinking with Errol Flynn and Ava Gardner, getting to know Prince Juan Carlos, future King of Spain, leading the first big SCUBA-equipped treasure salvage expedition off Spain (covered by a four-man team from *Life* Magazine), salvaging 23 cadavers from the deep wreckage of a trawler lost in an Atlantic storm, or receiving a consignment of the *Atocha's* treasure from the world-famous treasurer hunter Mel Fisher, in appreciation for starting him on the path to that wreck.

Acknowledgments

Joanie, my wife for a half century, and first proofreader since this book's inception, was always eager to encourage me with exclamations like, "I love this–don't change a word!"

During the years leading to this book's publication, several friends gave me serious help through suggestions, corrections and–most onerous of all–proofreading.

The paragon without whose guidance and counsel this book could–literally–never have been written, is former editor of *Sports Illustrated* Les Woodcock, who for month after month over two years encouraged, bullied, corrected, proofread and held my hand.

The other indispensable angel, my "little sister," publisher Patricia Chapman, constantly inspired me, and as this work approached the stretch, guided me through the various stages of getting the book published.

The author flanked by Rick Herrick & Les Woodcock; alongside is L.C. Schraeder.

Former *Life* Magazine editor Ralph Graves (who calls me "Admiral Buto" after an evil, hairless character in one of his books), applied his editorial genius to several of my lives and concluded with the tongue-in-cheek comment on the back cover.

Good buddy and fellow author Rick Herrick stood with me again and again, motivating me with lashings of good humor and professorial wisdom to spur me on.

My daughter-in-law Deborah Potter spent half a week retrieving a chapter which my computer had stolen and hidden.

My Girl-Friday angel L.C. Schraeder, cheerfully responded to emergency calls to rein in that computer's wayward habits.

From the halls of academe: Harvard professors Robert Hillier and James Munn guided me into the exciting world of creative writing; St. George's School's Bill Douglas kindly brought me up to date on school events; and David Hayes, archivist at the U. of Colorado, routinely kept us "Boulder boys" informed of the activities of fellow graduates.

Ernie Richards, producer of the indispensable news magazine *Plus Ultra;* and Val Martin, dean of Florida Classics Library and publisher of my *The Treasure Diver's Guide*, both gave me valuable marketing suggestions.

The dedicated and friendly folks at the Tisbury Printer worked miracles to ensure that this book was of high quality: Janet Holladay designed the book and was a joy to work with; president Chris Decker offered powerful suggestions and proofreading corrections; Kevin Cain, Don Groover and Lindsay Medeiros did the many things needed to produce a book.

Others contributed importantly: Dad and Mother; Sandy Cunningham, Bud Lane and Henry Bittner, all introduced in these pages; Bob Lamb, marine engineer, helped me with descriptions of ships' engines; and finally, to the many who have sadly left us: wherever you are, my heartfelt thanks!

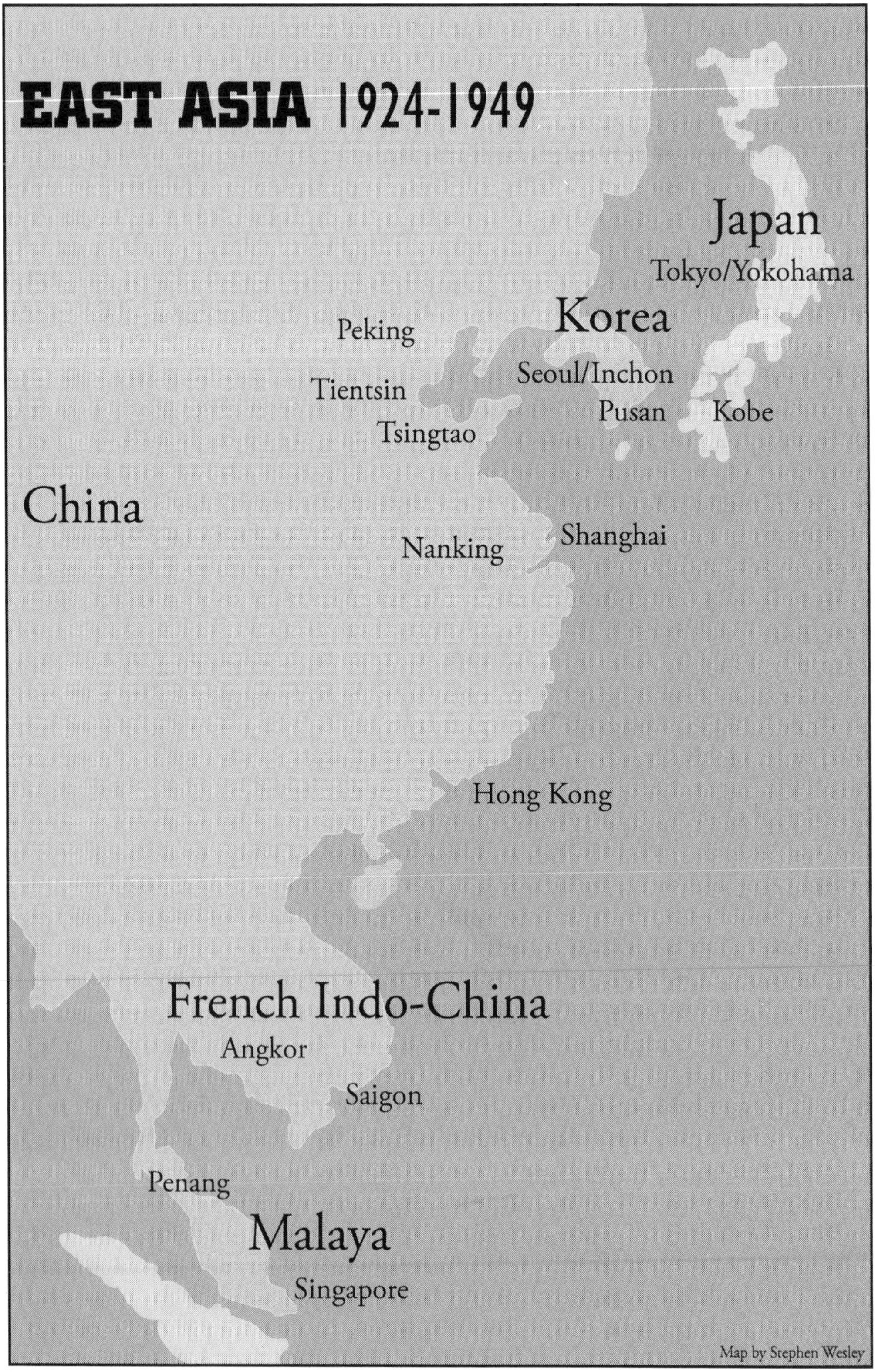

EAST ASIA 1924-1949

Japan
Tokyo/Yokohama
Korea
Peking
Seoul/Inchon
Tientsin
Pusan
Kobe
Tsingtao
China
Shanghai
Nanking
Hong Kong
French Indo-China
Angkor
Saigon
Penang
Malaya
Singapore

Map by Stephen Wesley